Studies in the Psychosocial

Series Editors
Stephen Frosh, Department of Psychosocial Studies, Birkbeck, University of London, London, UK
Peter Redman, Faculty of Arts and Social Sciences, The Open University, Milton Keynes, UK
Wendy Hollway, Faculty of Arts and Social Sciences, The Open University, Milton Keynes, UK

Studies in the Psychosocial seeks to investigate the ways in which psychic and social processes demand to be understood as always implicated in each other, as mutually constitutive, co-produced, or abstracted levels of a single dialectical process. As such it can be understood as an interdisciplinary field in search of transdisciplinary objects of knowledge. Studies in the Psychosocial is also distinguished by its emphasis on affect, the irrational and unconscious processes, often, but not necessarily, understood psychoanalytically. Studies in the Psychosocial aims to foster the development of this field by publishing high quality and innovative monographs and edited collections. The series welcomes submissions from a range of theoretical perspectives and disciplinary orientations, including sociology, social and critical psychology, political science, postcolonial studies, feminist studies, queer studies, management and organization studies, cultural and media studies and psychoanalysis. However, in keeping with the inter- or transdisciplinary character of psychosocial analysis, books in the series will generally pass beyond their points of origin to generate concepts, understandings and forms of investigation that are distinctively psychosocial in character.

Series Peer Review Policy:

Proposals for books in this series are single-blind peer reviewed by experts in the field as well as by the Series Editors. All manuscripts will be reviewed and approved by the Series Editors before they are accepted for publication.

More information about this series at
https://link.springer.com/bookseries/14464

Joanna Kellond

Donald Winnicott and the Politics of Care

palgrave
macmillan

Joanna Kellond
School of Humanities and Social Science
University of Brighton
Brighton, UK

ISSN 2662-2629   ISSN 2662-2637 (electronic)
Studies in the Psychosocial
ISBN 978-3-030-91436-3   ISBN 978-3-030-91437-0 (eBook)
https://doi.org/10.1007/978-3-030-91437-0

© The Editor(s) (if applicable) and The Author(s), under exclusive license to Springer Nature Switzerland AG 2022

This work is subject to copyright. All rights are solely and exclusively licensed by the Publisher, whether the whole or part of the material is concerned, specifically the rights of translation, reprinting, reuse of illustrations, recitation, broadcasting, reproduction on microfilms or in any other physical way, and transmission or information storage and retrieval, electronic adaptation, computer software, or by similar or dissimilar methodology now known or hereafter developed.

The use of general descriptive names, registered names, trademarks, service marks, etc. in this publication does not imply, even in the absence of a specific statement, that such names are exempt from the relevant protective laws and regulations and therefore free for general use.

The publisher, the authors and the editors are safe to assume that the advice and information in this book are believed to be true and accurate at the date of publication. Neither the publisher nor the authors or the editors give a warranty, expressed or implied, with respect to the material contained herein or for any errors or omissions that may have been made. The publisher remains neutral with regard to jurisdictional claims in published maps and institutional affiliations.

Cover credit: Sutthipong Kongtrakool/GettyImages

This Palgrave Macmillan imprint is published by the registered company Springer Nature Switzerland AG

The registered company address is: Gewerbestrasse 11, 6330 Cham, Switzerland

Acknowledgements

This book was made possible by the support of many people, including family members, friends and colleagues who, over the years, have become very familiar with my persistent interest in Winnicott and the relevance of his ideas for thinking about culture and society. The book would not have been possible without the inspiration, support and guidance of Vicky Lebeau, who piqued my interest in Winnicott many years ago and set me on a course that culminated in my Ph.D. on Winnicott at Sussex University, which was funded by the AHRC. This book is very different to that Ph.D., but my doctorate prepared the ground for me to develop my interests in the direction of this text. I'm grateful to Caroline Bainbridge for providing the link that allowed me to make some important connections in the early stages of my research.

I'm also grateful to many colleagues for their engagement with and feedback on my ideas in a range of contexts. Vicky Margree, Zoe Sutherland, Katja Čičigoj, Bob Brecher and Ian Sinclair were inspiring interlocutors in exploring the politics of care and reproduction. Becca Searle, Mark Devenney, Clare Woodford, German Primera and Tim Huzar have also provided considerable support and engagement over the years and added significantly to my understanding of social history, political philosophy and critical theory. I'm grateful to Stephen Frosh for extensive editorial advice on the proposal which helped me to give form to the project and to the reviewers whose thoughtful and generous comments helped my clarify my aims. Many others have engaged with my work in earlier iterations, including Lynne Layton, Murray Schwartz and Candida Yates, and I'm extremely grateful for their feedback.

I am also extremely grateful to my family, in particular my mum Jan (who took over the domestic labour necessary to the task of social reproduction in the final stages of writing, so I could get this finished, creating our very own 'care fix'), my dad Kelvin and my step mum Liz, as well as to Heather, Steve and Alice. You have all been there when I needed a chat, some love, or a bit of motivation to get it done! Thank you for everything. I'd also like to thank Benji and Bubbles for reminding me, always, what makes life worth living.

I also thank some of my other friends for their unwavering support. Kim Elcock, Eleanor Bennett, Chantal Irtelli, Rebecca Fisher, Lucia Cordani, Charlie Brown and Katie Blackwell. You have made me laugh, given me love and helped me forget the world for a while.

The outline of the argument developed in this book was first published in Kellond, J. 2019. "Present-day Troubles": Winnicott, Counter-culture and Critical Theory Today. *Psychoanalysis, Culture & Society*, 24(3), pp. 323–343. Revised sections of that article appear in the Chapters 1, 3, 4, 6 and 7.

Some of the material in Chapter 3 was previously published in Kellond, J., 2019. Modernity, Alienation, and the Mirror in the Work of Lacan and Winnicott. *American Imago*, 76(1), pp. 15–38.

My thanks to the journal editors for permission to reproduce here.

Contents

1	**Introduction: Winnicott and the Politics of Care**	1
	Winnicott Now	5
	Winnicott and the Politics of Care	8
	Theories, Methodologies, Outline	18
	References	24
2	**Healthy Life: Care, *Cura* and Flourishing**	31
	"Healthy Life"	35
	The Capacity for Concern	49
	Flourishing and Society	53
	References	57
3	**Oedipus and Capitalism: Denying Dependence, Effacing Care**	63
	Capitalism, the Family and the Privatisation of Dependence	66
	Subjectivity, Separation and the Denial of Dependence	73
	Ways Out: Towards a New Symbolic	84
	References	93

4	**Caring States: Maternal Care, Holding and Social Provision**	99
	Maternal Thinking and the Longing for Care	100
	Holding and Society	108
	Maternal Attitudes and Caring States	121
	References	127
5	**Care, Power, Justice**	133
	Capacities, Care and Justice	136
	Subjectivity and Power	145
	Justice, Capacities and the Organisation of Care	157
	References	161
6	**Attacks on Holding**	165
	Changing Structures of Care	167
	Traumatogenic Environments and Careless Subjects	172
	Caring Relationships in an Uncaring World	180
	References	188
7	**The Politics of Holding**	193
	Holding and Growth	195
	The Radical Politics of Holding-Care	201
	A Psychosocial Argument	206
	References	222
References		227
Index		251

1

Introduction: Winnicott and the Politics of Care

> I believe cure at its roots means care. About 1700 it started to degenerate into a name for medical treatment, as in water-cure. Another century gave it the added implication of successful outcome; the patient is restored to health, the disease is destroyed, the evil spirit is exorcised. (D. W. Winnicott 1986a, 113)

> What, we now ask, would happen if we were to begin instead to put care at the very centre of life? (The Care Collective 2020, 5)

In a talk delivered in Hatfield in October 1970, the British paediatrician and psychoanalyst Donald Woods Winnicott explores the relationship between the words "cure" and "care." Winnicott points out—to an audience of doctors and nurses—that the etymological root of "cure" can be found in "care." The *Oxford English Dictionary* explains that "cure" derives originally from the Latin word, "cura," meaning care, tracing its etymology through the French "cure," which again translates as "care," dating from the eleventh century. Over time, the two words have parted ways, and Winnicott describes the shift in meaning of "cure"—"the passage from care to remedy"—in terms of an impoverishment. Something has been lost in the movement from one meaning to another, he suggests; the meaning degenerates. "Cure, in the sense of remedy, successful eradication of disease and its cause, tends today to overlay cure as care," he writes (113). The imperative of successful outcome effaces the healing potential of relationship and practice. In the talk, Winnicott sets out to complicate the meaning of cure for medicine, foregrounding the importance of a concept of care to medical work. "Applied science" and the "specific remedy" have become the focus of knowledge and treatment in the field of medicine, but these can be taken for granted, whereas the relational aspects of the healing process have been, and often continue to be, elided. "What is significant," he writes, "is the interpersonal relationship in all its rich and complex human colours" (113, 115).

Winnicott's discussion of care and cure points towards a dichotomy with considerable history, and one in which care has long been the inferior partner. Describing a range of "medico-social distinctions in care," Judith Phillips notes that "cure" is aligned with the highly valued world of the hospital and the male doctor, possessing an authority derived from its knowledge base of rational, bio-medical hard science (2007, 126–27). "Care," on the other hand, is associated with the home, with emotion, intuition and the low status female nurse. Care lacks the authority of cure, and it is tied to the soft and sometimes disputed science of the therapeutic tradition (126–7). Winnicott, however, refuses to accept an economy of value that erases care or replaces it with the vicissitudes of medical cure. Instead, he reiterates care's vital importance and links it to his understanding of psychoanalysis, which he sees as more than "a matter of interpreting the repressed unconscious," but a practice that involves "the provision of a setting for trust, in which such work can take place" (114–5). Once again, Winnicott emphasises the effect of the relationships in which specific interventions occur and he draws attention to the weightiness of aspects of existence that have long been debased and femininised. Care-cure, he writes, is an "extension of the concept of holding," which is a central feature of "the facilitating environment enabling personal growth" (119). "It starts," he insists, "with the baby in the womb, then with the baby in arms, and enrichment comes from the growth process in the infant, which the mother makes possible because of her knowing just what it is like to be this one particular baby that she has given birth to." Care-cure is a description of "the family function, and this leads on to the whole build-up of democracy as a political extension of family facilitation, with the mature individuals eventually taking part according to their age and capacity in politics and in the maintenance and rebuilding of the political structure" (119). Care is, for Winnicott, vital for the development of subjectivity and for the relational capacities necessary for political deliberation and change. If a relationship of care is as essential as cure for medical practice, Winnicott here also foregrounds the *curative* potential of care for society. "In terms of society's sickness," he writes, "care-cure may be of more importance than remedy-cure, and all the diagnosis and prevention that goes with what is usually called a scientific approach" (120). Winnicott seems to suggest that a society that doesn't care, or cannot recognise the importance of care, is ill-equipped to deal with the problems that blight it. In fact, the devaluing of care may well be central to the shape and form of those problems.

The ideas that Winnicott expresses in this talk are central to the aims of this project, which uses his thinking to explore the historical, political and ontological significance of care; its relationship with human life, psychic change and social transformation. Care was an abiding and important theme in Winnicott's work, and one that distinguishes him from other psychoanalysts. Jan Abram's indispensable guide to *The Language of Winnicott* does not contain a chapter on care, but references to the concept run through and connect all of the entries in the text, including "environment," "dependence" and "primary maternal preoccupation," providing a kind of unobtrusive support that might easily be taken for granted and go unacknowledged, a common-sense, good-enough idea (2007). Wendy Hollway notes that "psychoanalytic literatures, with the important exception of Winnicott, hardly use the word care" (2006b, 16). Many of the concepts that Winnicott formulated represent attempts to unpack and give form to some of the vicissitudes, aspects and practices of care—specifically during the earliest stages of life, but with broader clinical and social implications—which had hitherto been insufficiently acknowledged in both psychoanalytic thinking and established socio-cultural discourses. Winnicott's work represents the first sustained psychoanalytic account of early care and its vital importance. He foregrounds care as the condition of possibility for subjectivity, even for what he understands to constitute "life," and his work proposes that existing, feeling real, feeling alive and having a sense that life is worth living are all states of being made possible by experiences of care, which take the form of both physical and psychic holding practices. Though care is an implicit aspect of much psychoanalytic thinking and praxis, it is Winnicott who primarily acknowledges the importance of care—specifically, but not only, the work of care performed by primary caregivers and psychoanalysts—and its imbrication with and implications for understanding and analysing the structures and relations of collective life.

Winnicott's discussion of care-cure touches on many of the themes that are central to this book. Firstly, by tracing the origins of care-cure to the Latin, Winnicott links his own perspective to a tradition of thinking about care, and its central place in human life and flourishing, with a long philosophical genealogy, one that reaches back at least to Ancient Greece. Winnicott's interest in care evokes the myth of "Cura" and the "Care of Souls" tradition, it ties his thinking to Romanticism, to Existentialism and to Phenomenology, philosophical approaches concerned with meaning, freedom and experience in human life (Reich 2004). Winnicott's articulation also demonstrates an awareness of care's imbrication in historical process and change. He describes a shift in values, which he locates in modernity (he says 1700), in which care's status falls and the scientific method and rationalism are in ascendence. His comments therefore evoke the privatisation and feminisation of care that takes place in modernity and in the transition to capitalism. Additionally, Winnicott identifies care as important for curing society of its ills, of its "sickness" as he calls it, and here he touches on debates about the place of care in social life, its role in conceptualising ethical and social responsibility towards others. These issues pertain to debates about politics and social welfare policy dating from the mid-twentieth century, in which Winnicott himself was involved, and they characterise more recent discussions in (often feminist) social theory and political philosophy about the politics surrounding the provision and distribution of care, and the relationship between care and questions of justice and power.

Winnicott's work informs an assessment of the justness of the current organisation of care and welfare, and it conjures something like a politics of holding, a form of "care for all" capable of curing society of its sickness, or at least contributing to that task.

Winnicott Now

Like many other scholars, I find Winnicott's ideas of immense interest and value for understanding the contemporary world. Winnicott has had a significant influence in a range of fields, including in the work of feminist theorists including Nancy Chodorow, Jessica Benjamin, Jane Flax and Wendy Hollway; he features in the social theory of Anthony Giddens, the media theory of Roger Silverstone and the political philosophy of Martha Nussbaum (Chodorow 1978, 1989; Benjamin 1977, 1978, 1990, 1995, 1998; Flax 1991; Hollway 2006b; Giddens 1991; Silverstone 1994, 2007; Nussbaum 2001, 2004). In the field of critical theory, Winnicott's thinking informs the work of Axel Honneth (Honneth 1996, 1999). In the French context, Winnicott has influenced the thinking of Deleuze and Guattari, as well as Luce Irigaray, and he inhabits the work of philosopher Bernard Stiegler (Abou-Rihan 2008; Whitford 1991; Stiegler 2013). In recent years, Winnicott has been gaining ever-wider recognition, as the recent publication of his *Collected Works* demonstrates (D. W. Winnicott 2017). He has become more prominent in critical political theory, notably in the work of Fred Alford, Gal Gerson and Bonnie Honig, though the recent essay collections, *Winnicott and Political Theory* and *Transitional Subjects: Critical Theory and Object Relations*, point up the breadth of interest within the field (Alford 2002; Gerson 2004a, b, 2005a, b, 2017; Honig 2012, 2017; Bowker and Buzby 2017a; Allen and O'Connor 2019). As Maggie Nelson puts it in her memoir, *The Argonauts,* you can find Winnicott everywhere right now, "from mommy blogs to Alison Bechdel's graphic novel *Are You My Mother?* to reams of critical theory" (2016, 23). One possible title Nelson suggests for her book, in an alternate universe, is *Why Winnicott Now?*

In recent years, Hiʻilei Julia Kawehipuaakahaopulani Hobart and Tamara Kneese note, "care has re-entered the zeitgeist" (2020). Though interest in care has a long history, in recent years the corrosive effects of neoliberal capitalism have precipitated a resurgence of interest in the conditions of possibility for the reproduction of 'life.' Winnicott's preoccupations resonate today, in the era of the 'care crisis,' a moment when both the time and capacity to care for others have become scarce, and 'self-care' serves to (re)produce a profitable and productive body (Hochschild 2001; Booth and Wolfe-Robinson 2021; Lorey 2015, 95). We are living in a time characterised by 'care deficits' and inadequate 'care fixes,' where privatisation, financialisaton, global care chains, the gig economy and personal responsibilisation underwrite and create increasingly precarious existences (Hochschild 2003; The Care Collective 2020; Dowling 2021; Butler 2009). This is a situation, the authors of the *Care Manifesto* state, in which "carelessness reigns," a fact that is, however, often concealed behind a patina of "*talk* of care" (2020, 1–2). Particularly in the wake of the COVID-19 pandemic, the importance of care work—and its unequal distribution along lines of gender, class and 'race'—has become difficult to ignore (Chang 2020). Infrastructures that were not previously viewed as providing forms of care, including school systems and supermarkets, have come to be perceived as such. Additionally, many people have been compelled to adopt new forms of caring, from mutual aid to self-isolation. Rhetorically at least, governments responded, and major care packages, including the furlough scheme in the UK, which covered a large percentage of workers' wages in order to prevent widespread redundancies, were rolled out "in the name of care for the nation" (The Care Collective 2020, 2). However, many of these interventions, like the cut to stamp duty in the UK, benefitted the rich, and the forms of support on offer have not been sufficient to counteract the "decades of organised neglect" suffered by caring infrastructures (2). Though journalists have begun heralding a "new variant of capitalism" emerging out of the pandemic, characterised by increased state intervention and spending, if growth remains its aim, it is likely to continue to prioritise the economy at the expense of the well-being of citizens (L. Elliott 2021).

1 Introduction: Winnicott and the Politics of Care

What interests me primarily in this project is to think about what Winnicott's ideas can contribute for understanding the ontological, historical and political significance of care at this particular juncture, a time when care is both increasingly apparent and elusive. Probably more than any other psychoanalyst, Winnicott provides a "theory of the caring subject" (Hollway 2006b, 131). This includes an account of the vital role of care in the development of subjectivity, specifically a "healthy" form of subjectivity, which, for him, involves the capacity for freedom of thought as well as care for others (Widlöcher 2012). For Winnicott, subjectivity develops through experiences of holding and handling in infancy, through object-relating to object-use, into a form of creative living characterised by a range of capacities, including the capacity for spontaneity, for concern and for autonomy. Winnicott writes that:

> The life of a healthy individual is characterised by fears, conflicting feelings, doubts, frustrations, as much as by the positive features. The main thing is that the man or woman feels he or she *is living his or her own life*, taking responsibility for action or inaction, and able to take credit for success and blame for failure. In one language it can be said that the individual has emerged from dependence to independence, or to autonomy. (1986b, 27)

Winnicott has a normative understanding of what constitutes a healthy form of subjectivity, which is not a subjectivity devoid of difficulty or conflict, but characterised by agency and, as Nussbaum puts it, mature interdependence (2004, 223). He considers this to be the product of an experience of "good enough" care in the context of early relationships, or, failing that, psychoanalytic psychotherapy. However, though he foregrounds the centrality of dependence in these contexts, he also insists on the significance of social environments of care in shaping capacities. His thinking provides an account of what is necessary to reproduce aliveness and make life feel like it is worth living, and this has important implications for understanding, and transforming, the relationship between care and society. Winnicott does not offer an account of what has happened to care-cure in the modern period, but his work speaks to and informs scholarship that has charted the historical and global privatisation and coercion of care, as well as reproduction more broadly, and the effacement of care and dependence from dominant conceptions of knowledge and subjectivity, a practice that continues to shape contemporary life. This, I suggest, is what makes Winnicott's work so useful, not to mention vital, to critical reflection on the politics of care today.

Winnicott and the Politics of Care

The resurgence of interest in care in recent years is part of a longer history. In the last fifty years, the politics of care and social reproduction have received significant attention from feminist scholars working across a range of fields, including economics, political philosophy and sociology (Folbre 1994; Tronto 1993; Vogel 2013). Synthesising a rich literature on the topic, Nancy Fraser defines social reproduction as the "activities of provisioning, care-giving and interaction that produce and maintain social bonds" on which "the capitalist economy relies" though "it accords them no monetised value and treats them as if they were free" (2016, 101). Fraser's definition captures the idea at the heart of social reproduction theory, that the failure to recognise the value of care and social reproduction, or to provide recompense for them in the form of time and money, is central to capitalist accumulation. Interest in care and social reproduction grew out of second wave feminism, specifically feminists' concern with the domestic work, or labour, that was allotted to women, and with understanding the apparent naturalness of this arrangement, domestic labour's widespread invisibility and its inherent devaluation (Stoller 2018). The subject of women's household work was first raised by late nineteenth- and early twentieth-century feminists, but it re-emerged as a political concern in post-war Europe and the USA, notably in Simone de Beauvoir's, *The Second Sex*, first published in 1949 and then later in Betty Friedan's *The Feminine Mystique* of 1963 (Friedan 2010; Beauvoir 2011). These texts informed socialist-feminist analyses of domestic labour in the 1960s. In 1972, Selma James and Mariarosa Dalla Costa published *The Power of Women and the Subversion of the Community*, which sparked an international domestic labour debate and over a decade of attempts to theorise women's household work within a Marxist framework, as well as informing the international campaign for Wages for Housework, which sought to draw attention to the unpaid work of care and domestic labour on which capitalism depends (Dalla Costa and James 1975; Barrett 2014; Stoller 2018). Ultimately, feminists in the 1970s advocated for care to become a more equitably shared responsibility. Stoller writes that "a world in which care for the elderly and for children was shared more equally—both between men and women and between state and the private family—was viewed as one in which everyone would thrive" (2018, 107).

Michèle Barrett highlights the influence on feminist theory of the publication of the famous essay, "Ideology and Ideological State Apparatuses," by the French Marxist philosopher, Louis Althusser, in 1969 (2014, 267). Althusser's essay was concerned in part with the "reproduction of the conditions of production," namely the ways in which the institutions of society, including the school and the family, reproduced and maintained the conditions necessary for capitalist production to take place (1969). Althusser had emphasised the role of ideological state apparatuses in reproducing social class, but feminists extended this analysis, linking women's role in biological reproduction, the provision of care and in domestic labour, in order to develop a "unitary theory" of the relationship between women's oppression and capitalism, in terms of their role in the reproduction of labour power (Vogel 2013). Stoller highlights that, in the second wave debates, the drudgery of domestic labour was often contrasted with a sense of the social value of relationships of care, especially the care of dependents, which highlights the sense, still prevalent in contemporary discussions, that care cannot be reduced simply to a means of reproducing the conditions of capitalist production (2018). As Emma Dowling insists, care is "more than the necessary labour of reproducing a healthy workforce" (2021, 45). It has emotional and affective dimensions, and it involves an ethical consideration of why and how we care for ourselves and others. Care has radical potential as well as the ability to contribute ideologically to the reproduction of the status quo.

Inspired by the New Left and counter-cultural radicalism, from the late 1960s, feminists turned to psychoanalysis in order to explore the psychic co-ordinates of the gendered division of labour that was, and remains, central to capitalist accumulation (Mitchell 1974; Rubin 1975). Juliet Mitchell's work with psychoanalysis, set out in *Woman's Estate* but coming to fruition in her crucial intervention of 1974, *Psychoanalysis and Feminism*, uses an Althusserian-Lacanian Freud as a supplement to Marxist theory in order to explain how the forms of identification presupposed by the Oedipus complex (re)produce the gendered division of labour (Mitchell 2015, 1974). Mitchell's work represents an invaluable attempt to understand the psychic dimensions of social reproduction, specifically how those identified as women are conscripted into reproductive work through the mechanism of gendered identification. Influenced by a structuralist psychoanalysis, however, her early work offered a somewhat ahistorical view of sexual difference, extending beyond the frame of capitalist modernity (Mitchell 1974, 412). The exclusive association of women with caring and reproduction, and their (never complete) separation from the sphere of production, is a historical phenomenon, linked to the growth of capitalism (Mies 2014; Federici 2014). The process of primitive accumulation, begun in the fifteenth century, depended on dual processes: global colonisation and the coercion of labour (both productive and reproductive) through enslavement, and the coercion of labour in Europe (both productive and reproductive) through the enclosure of common land, the mechanism of the family wage and the ideology of separate spheres, a process that involved the privatisation of caring and the feminisation of the qualities associated with it (Mies 2014). Mitchell does, however, draw attention to the significance of the devaluation of the work of care and reproduction. A few years after *Psychoanalysis and Feminism*, she writes that "from its inception until today, many feminists have argued not [...] for the end of the family but for, in whatever kin or communal form it occurs, an equality of reproduction with production; producing people should be as important as producing things" (1978, 200). Elizabeth Wilson questions, however, how this position can be reconciled with a Freudian/Lacanian view of sexual difference that seems to reify the existing gendered division of labour in capitalist societies (1980, 199).

Winnicott's work has not been absent from these debates. Though some feminists, including Mitchell, critique the emphasis that object relations theorists like Winnicott place on maternal care for shoring up the gendered division of labour and ensuring the reproduction of the workforce, others have argued that Winnicott's work draws attention to the work of care that capitalism exploits and devalues (Mitchell 1974; Doane and Hodges 1993; Chodorow 1978; Benjamin 1990). Dorothy Dinnerstein, for instance, "like Winnicott," emphasises the impact of early relations of care on the development of subjectivity, stressing that the repression of maternal dependence is a necessary part of the development of masculine rationality and estrangement from nature, which is counterposed to women's retention of relatedness (Flax 1991, 160; Dinnerstein 1999). Using Winnicott's thinking, Nancy Chodorow grounds her understanding of gender norms and the division of labour in the specific organisation of social relations in capitalist modernity (Barrett 2014; Doane and Hodges 1993). In Chodorow's work, Winnicott's unique preoccupation with the maternal role makes visible the work of reproduction missing from traditional Marxist accounts of political economy, and provides theoretical resources for theorising the role of caring practices in the reproduction of gendered subjectivities in the context of contemporary capitalism. She uses Winnicott to formulate a psychosocial account capable of attending to the pre-oedipal aspects of development that were largely absent in the Freudian/Lacanian account of Mitchell. Chodorow highlights that "women as mothers are pivotal actors in the sphere of social reproduction" (1978, 11). She employs Winnicott's ideas of holding and projective identification to question the biological basis of the tendency for women to care for children, whilst also focusing on how unconsciously gendered forms of maternal care contribute to reproducing the gendered division of labour and capitalist social relations, causing differences in the psychic and emotional capacities developed by those identified as men and women (23, 29). Mothers' identification with daughters, Chodorow theorises, leads girls to develop the relational and caring capacities associated with caregiving, whilst the absence of identification between mothers and their sons encourages the formation of a defensive form of autonomy (92–110). Chodorow emphasises the role of care in reproducing workers and the need for different arrangements of care if this situation is to be overcome.

Chodorow's ideas concerning the gendered ways in which subjectivities are shaped within capitalism have influenced a range of feminist work that emphasises and often celebrates the relational difference characteristic of women's social and psychic position (Gilligan 1990; Flax 1985; Ruddick 1995; Keller 1995). Carol Gilligan's *In a Different Voice*, first published in 1982, proposes that the gendered experiences of children, which are related to the gendered division of labour, lead to differences in the moral reasoning of men and women (1990). Whilst men tend to respond to ethical dilemmas using ideas of rules and justice, women, Gilligan claims, often attend more to the particulars of circumstance and person, eschewing rules in favour of tailored responses. Gilligan argues that women's ethics are thus founded in practices of care, which are shaped by their experiences, which, in turn, are influenced by the division of labour. For Gilligan, the ethic of care is "a psychological logic of relationships, which contrasts with the formal logic of fairness that informs the justice approach" (73). Gilligan, as well as others influenced by Chodorow including Jane Flax, Evelyn Fox Keller and Sara Ruddick, sought to revalue the qualities of care and relation devalued and effaced by the masculine psychic economy. This work prompted criticism on the grounds of essentialism, for its failure to think intersectionally about the interrelation of gender with class, 'race' and sexuality, and it also aroused concern about the political implications of focusing on care for women (DiQuinzio 1993; Doane and Hodges 1993). However, it also gained considerable attention because it highlighted the gendered character of previous theories, which had overlooked the importance of care practices and the relational principles associated with them.

Informed by the work of Chodorow and Keller, as well as Dinnerstein's influential account of the social significance of women's mothering, Jessica Benjamin uses Winnicott to develop a theory of the relationship between oedipal identification and the devaluation of the care and reproduction on which capitalism depends (1990). Benjamin charts the psychosocial (oedipal) processes that make possible the disavowal of early caring relationships and their role in psychic development, and lead to the splitting of ideas of relatedness from autonomy and their association with specific genders, foregrounding the place of Winnicott's work in understanding and theorising the relationship between care and autonomy that is in excess of the appropriation of caring practice to serve the ends of capitalism. Concurrently, she insists on the radical quality of the demand that society overcome the devaluation of those tasks and attributes deemed feminine and associated with women, care and social reproduction in particular. "Though maternal care is still regarded as vital for small children," she writes, "its values are nearly irrelevant for life outside the nursery" (208). There is a need, she insists, to recognise the value of and apply the principles of care in a range of contexts outside the feminised domestic sphere.

Fiona Williams identifies a "second wave" of care theory, coming to fruition in the 1990s, which emphasises the political significance of an ethic of care (2001). In 1990, Bernice Fisher and Joan Tronto proposed an influential definition of care: "on the most general level, we suggest that caring be viewed as a species activity that includes everything that we do to maintain, continue, and repair our 'world' so that we can live in it as well as possible. That world includes our bodies, our selves, and our environment, all of which we seek to interweave in a complex, life-sustaining web" (cited in Tronto 1993, 103). Tronto was instrumental in moving debates about care into the political field, challenging the gendered dichotomy between a public conception of justice and a private idea of care (1993, 2002, 2013). She argues that the gendered separation of the spheres of production and reproduction means that public life and political decision-making are too often blind to care perspectives, which are associated with the private sphere and parochial, personal concerns. Tronto insists that more attention needs to be paid to care, in order to reimagine ideas of subjectivity beyond the rational autonomous subject and make human need central to political decision making, which would radically shift the values at the centre of political life and challenge the hegemony of the profit motive central to capitalism.

Tronto and another influential theorist of the politics of care, Selma Sevenhuijsen, conceptualise care as a practice (Tronto 1993; Sevenhuijsen 1998). Sevenhuijsen writes that "the core idea of the ethic of care in my view is that care is a practice, and that it is crucial for developing a moral attitude – and thus also a moral vocabulary – of care by engaging in the practice of care. By doing so care can in fact grow into a disposition, a part of our everyday thinking and doing" (cited in Hollway 2006b, 9). Here, Sevenhuijsen demonstrates an appreciation of the fact that the capacity to care is something that has to be learnt and practised, however, as Hollway suggests, this "leaves it unclear if, how and when, such a process takes place" (10). Both Tronto and Sevenhuijsen are critical of a model of care that is based on a paradigm of motherhood, arguing that it invisibilises the pervasive role that care plays in all human relationships. Drawing on the work of Winnicott, Chodorow and Benjamin, as well as other psychoanalytic theorists, Hollway problematises this view for failing to provide an account of how the capacity to care develops (11). For Hollway, this oversight leads to a misunderstanding of the relationship between care and politics. Hollway writes that "with the exception of psychoanalysis, most of the influential contributions to debates about care lack a psychology, notably a full, critically based theorisation of the self, and its relational development, on which the capacity to care is founded" (16). Whilst Hollway accepts the necessity of recent critiques of developmentalism, she holds that to abandon the baby of development along with developmentalism is misguided, because the capacity to care is not a natural given and the process through which it does, or does not, develop needs to be set out (14). She stresses the importance of early relations in the development of the capacity to care, foregrounding the primary caregiver/mother-baby relation in this process.

Hollway emphasises intersubjective relations and their role in creating caring subjects, however, she doesn't explore the relationship between this and the distribution of care, or the relationship between the means necessary to reproduce psychic life and anti-capitalist politics. As the foregoing discussion has outlined, the gendered division of labour that persists in contemporary societies, albeit in an ever-evolving form, skews the development of capacities in gendered ways, which must also be understood in relation to other axes of inequality, including class and 'race.' Capitalism requires "life" to be reproduced for it to function, but it does not provide the conditions necessary for the reproduction of healthy or caring forms of subjectivity. Whilst there is no guarantee that specific external factors and caring infrastructures will ensure the development of specific capacities, including the capacities for caring and autonomy that are fostered through intersubjective relations, it would also be wrong to suggest that some ways of organising these infrastructures are not likely to be better than others and more conducive to the development of certain capacities. Given the crisis that is capitalism, how might we theorise the conditions necessary for the development of healthy, caring (relationally) autonomous subjectivity, and what is the relationship between the provision of those conditions and the processes of taming and eroding capitalism (Wright 2015)? Amy Buzby and Matthew Bowker suggest that Winnicott's thinking contains a "rudimentary political theory of the subject" that centres on "psychic needs" and "the premise that healthy, developed subjectivities, subjective capacities, and intersubjective norms are defensible political ideals" (2017b, 2). I wholeheartedly agree with this assessment, and I set out to demonstrate that there is an important relationship between the conditions needed for such subjectivities to have the best chance of coming into existence and the equitable redistribution of care and, more broadly, the recognition of the work of social reproduction, that feminists have long advocated for.

Emma Dowling suggests that the idea that contemporary society is experiencing a "care crisis" might imply that the situation was better in the past, though the status quo has never in fact been up to standard (2021, 8). The struggle at the heart of the politics of care is not for a return to a better past, but a struggle for a better future. This does not mean that contemporary scholars do not turn to the past for inspiration, however. In recent years, the idea of "the commons," rooted in a conception of the collective access to land characteristic of pre-capitalist social relations, has gained traction in the work of various thinkers (Linebaugh 2014; De Angelis 2017; Federici 2019). What the commons signifies, in the context of late capitalism, is a form of collective access to the means to reproduce (to hold?) life that has been eroded by capitalism. Capitalism has privatised the means of reproduction, historically locating them within the family. Though the twentieth century saw the development of caring infrastructures to support the reproduction of life, the current social formation precipitates their erosion. In this context, the commons offer a vision of how social life might be organised so as to ensure that everyone has access to the means to life. It is my contention that Winnicott's work can contribute to the project of imagining and fighting for access to 'the means to life,' which I understand (following him) to be both material and psychic, or in other words, psychosocial.

As Arne De Boever suggests, "it may very well be that care is turning into the key issue of the twenty-first century" (2013, 4). De Boever notes a "political turn" in the humanities and social sciences prompted by "the post-9/11 era of crises—political, economic, and now social; not to mention the climate crisis and the food crisis" (2). His references are mainly French-theoretical, and he describes a "vitalist turn" in the work of intellectuals working in the Foucauldian tradition, notably Giorgio Agamben (bare life), Eric Santner (creaturely life) and Judith Butler (precarious life) (Agamben 1998; Santner 2006; Butler 2004). Locating this tendency in relation to contemporary politics, De Boever suggests that "at times of emergencies, crises, and exceptions, care rises to the surface not simply as an ethical concern about how one is supposed to go on living, but also as a political one" (2). Given the history of thinking about both the ethics and politics of care in feminist theory and beyond, De Boever more accurately describes a turn in critical political theory towards questions that have long been central to feminist thinking. De Boever also notes that much of the work on "biopolitics," or the production of life, that has come out of the Foucauldian tradition has been largely concerned with the critique of governmentality and political interventions into the lives of citizens (5). Given this critical focus, how, he asks, is it possible to defend infrastructures against budget cuts and privatisation drives, or to formulate ideas of the kind of care we might want, without giving up on politics (5)? De Boever warns against the tendency, common to certain critical political philosophies, to equate the state itself with totalitarianism, a stance Foucault himself warned against (39). To do so risks aligning oneself with forces of thought—neoliberal theory dating from the 1930s to the 1950s—that were explicitly anti-statist. It also makes answering vital questions impossible: What would a good state look like? How would it care for citizens in non-controlling ways? How could the state itself be used to erode capitalism and increase equality? How might we distinguish between inadequate/intrusive/controlling forms of care and care that might be "good enough"?

Pursuing a similar line of thought from a slightly different perspective, Bowker and Buzby reiterate the limits of the critique of the subject that has dominated much late modern, poststructural and postmodern philosophy, including the work of Friedrich Nietzsche, Theodor Adorno, Jacques Lacan, Georges Bataille, Michel Foucault, Jacques Derrida and Jean-Francois Lyotard (2017b). As Nietzsche illustrates in *The Genealogy of Morals*, "no such agent exists; there is no "being" behind the doing, acting, becoming; the "doer" has simply been added to the deed by the imagination—the doing is everything" (cited in Bowker and Buzby 2017b, 2). The critique of the subject has been a necessary philosophical project, given the inherent relationship between specific modes of thought and relationship—identity thinking, narcissism, detachment—and the extractive and exploitative politics of modern capitalism. The subject that dominates in modernity, the masculine subject of philosophical reflection that believes that it depends only on itself for its existence and for certainty, certainly requires critique and deconstruction, but this strategy has ultimately stalled, producing a perpetual repetition of "the advocacy of subjective disruption and recognition of the profound interdependence, vulnerability, contingency, and precariousness of the subject's capacity to maintain contact with herself" (6). As Lacan would have it, the subject is split, a state that undermines any pretensions to mastery. However, Bowker and Buzby argue that poststructural perspectives get stuck at this point, lacking the theoretical resources necessary for developing an alternative conception of the subject.

Bowker and Buzby propose that Winnicott's understanding of subjectivity offers a corrective to "the ills of subjectivity decried over the past century-and-a-half" (6, see also Martel 2019). This is "a subjectivity grounded in the relinquishment of aggression, illusions of omnipotence, symbolic violence, and subjective control over others which is, itself, rooted in the healthy indulgence of the same in the emerging subject" (6). From my own perspective, Winnicott offers a positive account of what constitutes a healthy subjectivity and a theory of the psychic consequences that can follow from early experiences of loss, deprivation and impingement. As I hope to show, the theory of subjectivity that Winnicott offers is not simply an alternative to the masculine philosophical subject and his heir, the liberal individual, conceptions that have dominated in modernity. Winnicott's theorisation of subjectivity is an account of how the self is formed through the practices of care that are disavowed, devalued, privatised and under-recompensed as an integral part of modern capitalism. Concurrently, Winnicott's normative view of subjective development is difficult to realise under the current conditions of capitalism. Achieving it may necessitate a confrontation, at the level of policy, with capitalism's exploitation of care.

Theories, Methodologies, Outline

My approach draws on a range of disciplinary areas and theoretical perspectives including psychoanalysis, feminist theory, Marxian theory, sociology, philosophy and political theory. Broadly, this project attempts to draw together these different influences in order to create a social philosophy, perhaps more accurately a *psycho*social philosophy in the Critical Theory tradition. Describing the approach of the critical theorists commonly associated with the Institute of Social Research in Frankfurt during the late 1920s and 1930s (Max Horkheimer, Theodor Adorno, Herbert Marcuse, Leo Lowenthal and Friedrich Pollock primarily), David Held writes that:

> They placed history at the centre of their approach to philosophy and society. Yet the issues they addressed went beyond a focus on the past and embraced future possibilities. Following Marx, they were preoccupied, especially in their early work, with the forces which moved (and might be guided to move) society towards rational institutions – institutions which would ensure a true, free and just life. But they were aware of the many obstacles to radical change and sought to analyse and expose these. They were thus concerned both with interpretation and transformation. (2004, 15)

Always with an eye on the past, the early critical theorists sought to understand how the conditions that dominate in society are formed, how they might be changed, and what impedes change. Given their concern with understanding what limits and facilitates human freedom, their research necessarily drew on a range of theoretical resources, including psychoanalysis, philosophy and sociology, in order to address "questions concerning the conditions that make possible the reproduction and transformation of society" (16).

Whilst my own project draws on a similar range of theoretical orientations in order to produce a transdisciplinary account, the specific theories that I draw on are different to those of the Frankfurt School. Horkheimer, Adorno and Marcuse famously engaged with the work of Freud and Marx, and, whilst these thinkers remain influential in my account, their perspectives are supplemented by feminist approaches to understanding both the psychic and the social. Jessica Benjamin makes a case for supplementing the Freudian account of development with a relational, intersubjective perspective informed by Winnicott's work that pays due attention to the significance of the early care relationship in shaping subjectivity. Marxian and socialist-feminist perspectives attentive to questions of care, domestic and affective labour and social reproduction inform my approach (Mies 2014; Federici 2014; N. Fraser 2013; Barrett 2014; Barrett and McIntosh 2015; Bhattacharya 2017; Vogel 2013). Attempting, in the tradition of Critical Theory, to synthesise these theoretical perspectives, I employ and develop a theoretical understanding of the development of subjectivity that is inherently psychosocial in its approach.

In taking this approach, I follow Hollway and affirm "a commitment to understand subjectivity and agency in a way that transcends individual-social dualism and draws on psychoanalysis for that purpose" (Hollway 2006a, 468). Hollway unpacks the inherently psychosocial character of subjectivity:

> We are *psycho*-social because we are products of a unique life history of anxiety- and desire-provoking life events and the manner in which they have been transformed in internal reality. We are psycho-*social* because such defensive activities affect and are affected by material conditions and discourses (systems of meaning which pre-exist any given individual), because unconscious defences are intersubjective processes (i.e. they affect and are affected by others with whom we are in communication), and because of the real events in the external, social world which are discursively, desirously and defensively appropriated. (2006a, 468)

Hollway's description here resonates with Diane Reay's definition, which characterises psychosocial study as "about inquiry into the mutual constitution of the individual and the social relations within which they are enmeshed" (2015, 10). The idea that subjectivity cannot be understood in isolation from the social relations in which it develops is a fundamental element of the approach pursued in this book, which sets out to explore how subjectivities and social relations are mutually constituted, and could be reconstituted, in late capitalism, and against the background of what was always a global capitalist modernity (Mignolo 2011).

Hollway argues that getting at the psychosocial character of subjectivity "requires…a life-historical, developmental account of selves, albeit formed in the process of their practical engagement with the social, material and discursive worlds" (2006a, 468). This is a perspective, she suggests, that is missing from poststructural constructivist perspectives, including Foucauldian discourse analysis, which though taking account of "the central importance of relational dynamics in the constitution of selves" emphasise "how subjects are positioned, or take up positions, in dialogue with others" without any account of "intersubjective, unconscious processes" or "a concept of unconscious conflict" (466). In contrast to this kind of approach, Hollway advocates a theory of subjective development focused on how selves are formed in primary relationships of care, and she identifies British object relations theory as highly useful in this context (467–8). These theories, she contends, are both useful and sound; useful because "they have been tested and theoretically refined through professional practice," and sound because "they are inserted in a history of openness to complex, socially based evidence, informed by sophisticated ontology and epistemology" (467). Hollway also gives a helpful account of the status of these discourses and the psychosocial understanding of subjectivity she derives from them, one that also informs my own position on their relationship to claims to truth. Both are historically situated and thus provisional accounts of developmental processes (480). They do not uncover psychic processes that are "just there" to be found, but rather they offer theoretical constructions that are useful for understanding the psychosocial character of subjectivity. They offer better ways to account for the "unruly evidence" that clinicians and theorists encountered through their experience with child and adult patients than the discursive constructions that existed prior to their creation, which were unable to account for certain aspects of behaviour and experience (471). Hollway is careful to note that this does not commit her to an idea of progress—future theoretical constructions can also entail "new blindnesses" (469).

All theoretical constructions have blind spots. The focus on the mother-child dyad in British object relations theory makes certain assumptions about the structure of early relationships, and the distribution of caring labour along lines of gender. However, whilst Winnicott refers to mothers and maternal care almost exclusively, he did not insist that early care need be performed by the person who gestates a child, or by a woman. Though this often remains the case, it is by far not the only way in which early care is organised and experienced. In consequence, in what follows I use the terms 'mother' and 'primary caregiver' interchangeably and somewhat fluidly. Any reference to one should be understood to also extend to and include the other. Additionally, the dyadic focus of object relations theory risks deemphasising the significance of other relationship sin the formation of selves. As Sally Swartz has highlighted, it is critical to keep in mind that, "in writing about mother/baby units in the first months of life, Winnicott's argument assumes a single caregiver 'preoccupied' with the baby as a primary task, and this is not easily translated into situations in which multiple caregivers for babies are economically a necessity" (2019, 27). This is an issue that this book will return to, using it to consider the historical specificity of Winnicott's theory, as well as the extent to which the principles of psychic development he theorised might translate into less dyadic contexts. Finally, whilst employing a model of subjectivity founded in early relationships, this project will also remain attentive to how the capacities of subjects can be reformed, for better or worse, in other relationships and forms of experience that replicate or evoke aspects and experiences of early relations.

Hopefully the foregoing discussion demonstrates that the methods employed in this project will extend beyond applying Winnicottian ideas in a range of contexts. It is a major contention if this project that Winnicott's ideas are implicated in historical processes and intellectual debates, and that understanding the interrelation of his thought with these contexts is central to establishing the full significance of his contribution. My methods are rooted in the Humanities and include historical, conceptual and textual analysis. My methodology is speculative and contains both descriptive and normative aspects. In this way, I hope to produce a critical theory that is ultimately a useful construction. In his essay on "Traditional and Critical Theory," Horkheimer defines a critical theory as one that seeks to bring about human "emancipation from slavery," acting as a "liberating…influence," and working "to create a world which satisfies the needs and powers" of human beings (Horkheimer 2002, 246). A critical theory aims for "the idea of a reasonable organisation of society that will meet the needs of the whole community," and "a certain concern is…required if these tendencies are to be perceived and expressed" (213). Critical Theory employs a useful construction of psychosocial subjectivity in order to identify what is wrong with society, and it offers a response, a way to meet a need that is unmet, much like a caregiver or an analyst. In many ways, Critical Theory approaches a practice of care, one that, hopefully, offers a useful construction that might contribute to curing society of its sickness.

Chapter 2, "Healthy Life: Care, Cura and Flourishing," provides an account of the centrality of care in Winnicott's conception of flourishing. Locating Winnicott's perspective, and psychoanalysis more broadly, in relation to philosophical understandings of flourishing originating in ancient Greece, the chapter draws attention to the relationship between the experience of being cared for and the development of specific capacities, including the capacity to care, in Winnicott's account. The chapter also considers the implications of Winnicott's perception of the interrelation of care and capacities for understanding the relationship between flourishing and society.

Chapter 3, "Oedipus and Capitalism: Denying Dependence, Effacing Care," locates Winnicott's theory of subjective development within the historical context of modernity. It explores the relationship between the development of capitalism, the family form and the denial of dependence, and considers the role of the Oedipus complex in mediating the effacement of care in the period. Additionally, the chapter considers the place of Winnicott's ideas within alternative conceptions of subjectivity drawn from psychoanalytic feminism, focusing specifically on his place in Jessica Benjamin's theories and their political implications.

Chapter 4, "Caring States: Maternal Care, Holding and Social Provision," positions Winnicott's thinking in relation to, and as part of, a growing interest in and recognition of the relationship between care and subjectivity taking shape in modernity. Considering the connection between a burgeoning preoccupation with the mother/child relationship and the ethics and politics of social provision, the chapter explores how Winnicott's clinical work with mothers and children shaped public policy both during and after the Second World War. The chapter also examines the affinities between Winnicott's mid-century influence and contemporary work in feminist political philosophy on the relationship between vulnerability, infancy and ethical and social responsibility.

Chapter 5, "Care, Power, Justice," considers what theories of intersubjective development influenced by Winnicott's ideas contribute to debates about care, power and justice. After summarising recent debates, which have often eschewed the model of the caregiver-child dyad, the chapter explores how a relational understanding of subjectivity focused on the development of subjective capacities enriches an account of the relationship between subjectivity and power. Additionally, the chapter analyses how an intersubjective account of development relates to and supplements the feminist conceptions of social justice found in the work of Iris Marion Young, Martha Nussbaum and Nancy Fraser.

Chapter 6, "Attacks on Holding," develops an account of contemporary capitalism as a sustained attack on "holding" in collective and individual life. After discussing the ways in which state provision of welfare has been eroded in recent decades, the chapter provides a psychosocial analysis of the relationship between neoliberal thinking and practice, structures of care and subjective capacities. Engaging with the work of Anthony Giddens and Bernard Stiegler, it theorises the effects on subjectivity of changes in the character of welfare provision. It also explores the effects of care chains on the development of capacities, foregrounding the multidimensional implications of failures of holding in contemporary society.

Chapter 7, "The Politics of Holding," advances a theory of the significance of holding for a radical politics of care. It employs Steven Groarke's account of holding to theorise the character of institutions capable of holding citizens. The chapter reads holding in relation to recent work on the politics of care in order to assess its significance for an anti-capitalist politics of care, before going on to provide a detailed exploration of the psychosocial significance of policy proposals such as Universal Basic Income, conceptualised as a form of "holding-care." The chapter explores the potential psychosocial implications of social forms of holding that might facilitate a shift in the structure of caring relations, making possible the development of subjective capacities, such as the capacity for concern, that might contribute to social change.

References

Abou-Rihan, Fadi. 2008. *Deleuze and Guatarri: A Psychoanalytic Itinerary*. London and New York: Continuum.

Abram, Jan. 2007. *The Language of Winnicott a Dictionary of Winnicott's Use of Words*. London: Karnac.

Agamben, Giorgio. 1998. *Homo Sacer*. Meridian. Stanford, CA: Stanford University Press.

Alford, C. Fred. 2002. *Levinas, the Frankfurt School and Psychoanalysis*. London: Continuum.

Allen, Amy and Brian O'Connor, eds. 2019. *Transitional Subjects: Critical Theory and Object Relations*. New York; Chichester: Columbia University Press.

Althusser, Louis. 1969. *Lenin and Philosophy and Other Essays*. London: Verso.

Barrett, Michèle. 2014. *Women's Oppression Today: The Marxist/Feminist Encounter*. London and New York: Verso.

Barrett, Michèle, and Mary McIntosh. 2015. *The Anti-Social Family*. Brooklyn, NY: Verso.

Beauvoir, Simone de. 2011. *The Second Sex*. Translated by Constance Borde and Sheila Malovany-Chevallier. New York: Vintage Books.

Benjamin, Jessica. 1977. 'The End of Internalization: Adorno's Social Psychology'. *Telos* 32: 42–64. https://doi.org/10.3817/0677032042.

———. 1978. 'Authority and the Family Revisited: Or, a World without Fathers?' *New German Critique*, no. 13: 35–57.
———. 1990. *The Bonds of Love: Psychoanalysis, Feminism and the Problem of Domination*. London: Virago.
———. 1995. *Like Subjects, Love Objects: Essays on Recognition and Sexual Difference*. New Haven and London: Yale University Press.
———. 1998. *Shadow of the Other: Intersubjectivity and Gender in Psychoanalysis*. New York: Routledge.
Bhattacharya, Tithi, ed. 2017. *Social Reproduction Theory: Remapping Class, Recentering Oppression*. London: Pluto Press.
Booth, Robert, and Maya Wolfe-Robinson. 2021. 'Homecare Services Crisis in England at Worst Point yet, Say Operators'. *The Guardian*, 12 December 2021, sec. Society. https://www.theguardian.com/society/2021/dec/12/homecare-services-crisis-uk-at-worst-point-yet-say-operators.
Bowker, Matthew H., and Amy Buzby, eds. 2017a. *D.W. Winnicott and Political Theory: Recentering the Subject*. First edition. New York: Palgrave Macmillan.
———. 2017b. 'Introduction'. In *D.W. Winnicott and Political Theory: Recentering the Subject*, edited by Matthew H. Bowker and Amy Buzby, First edition, 1–34. New York: Palgrave Macmillan.
Butler, Judith. 2004. *Precarious Life: The Powers of Mourning and Violence*. London and New York: Verso.
———. 2009. *Frames of War: When Is Life Grievable?* London and New York: Verso.
Chang, Clio. 2020. 'Once Social Isolation Is Over, We Can't Return to a World That Doesn't Value Care'. Vice. 2020. https://www.vice.com/en/article/jge39g/taking-care-of-each-other-is-essential-work.
Chodorow, Nancy. 1978. *The Reproduction of Mothering: Psychoanalysis and the Sociology of Gender*. Berkeley, CA: University of California Press.
———. 1989. *Feminism and Psychoanalytic Theory*. New Haven and London: Yale University Press.
Dalla Costa, Mariarosa, and Selma James. 1975. *The Power of Women and the Subversion of the Community*. Bristol: Falling Wall Press.
De Angelis, Massimo. 2017. *Omnia Sunt Communia: On the Commons and the Transformation to Postcapitalism*. London: Zed Books.
De Boever, Arne. 2013. *Narrative Care: Biopolitics and the Novel*. London and New York: Bloomsbury Academic.
Dinnerstein, Dorothy. 1999. *The Mermaid and the Minotaur: Sexual Arrangements and Human Malaise*. New York: Other Press.

DiQuinzio, Patrice. 1993. 'Exclusion and Essentialism in Feminist Theory: The Problem of Mothering'. *Hypatia* 8 (3): 1–20.

Doane, Janice, and Devon Hodges. 1993. *From Klein to Kristeva: Psychoanalytic Feminism and the Search for the 'Good Enough' Mother*. Ann Arbor: University of Michigan Press.

Dowling, Emma. 2021. *The Care Crisis: What Caused It and How Can We End It?* London and New York: Verso.

Elliott, Larry. 2021. 'During the Pandemic, a New Variant of Capitalism Has Emerged'. *The Guardian*, 30 July. https://www.theguardian.com/commentisfree/2021/jul/30/pandemic-new-variant-of-capitalism-spending-covid-state.

Federici, Silvia. 2014. *Caliban and the Witch: Women, the Body and Primitive Accumulation*. New York: Autonomedia.

———. 2019. *Re-Enchanting the World: Feminism and the Politics of the Commons*. Oakland, CA: PM Press.

Flax, Jane. 1985. 'Mother-Daughter Relationships: Psychodynamics, Politics, and Philosophy'. In *The Future of Difference*, edited by Hester Eisenstein and Alice Jardine, 20–40. New Brunswick, NJ: Rutgers University Press.

———. 1991. *Thinking Fragments: Psychoanalysis, Feminism, and Postmodernism in the Contemporary West*. Berkeley, CA: University of California Press.

Folbre, Nancy. 1994. *Who Pays for the Kids? Gender and the Structures of Constraint*. London and New York: Routledge.

Fraser, Nancy. 2013. *Fortunes of Feminism: From Women's Liberation to Identity Politics to Anti-Capitalism*. Brooklyn, NY: Verso Books.

———. 2016. 'Contradictions of Capital and Care'. *New Left Review*, no. 100 (August): 99–117.

Friedan, Betty. 2010. *The Feminine Mystique*. London: Penguin.

Gerson, Gal. 2004a. 'Object Relations Psychoanalysis as Political Theory'. *Political Psychology* 25 (5): 769–94. https://doi.org/10.1111/j.1467-9221.2004.00397.

———. 2004b. 'Winnicott, Participation and Gender'. *Feminism & Psychology* 14 (4): 561–81. https://doi.org/10.1177/0959353504046872.

———. 2005a. 'Liberalism, Sociability, and Object Relations Theory'. *The European Legacy* 10 (5): 421–37. https://doi.org/10.1080/10848770500173623.

———. 2005b. 'Individuality, Deliberation and Welfare in Donald Winnicott'. *History of the Human Sciences* 18 (1): 107–26.

———. 2017. 'Winnicott and the History of Welfare State Thought in Britain'. In *D.W. Winnicott and Political Theory: Recentering the Subject*,

edited by Matthew H. Bowker and Amy Buzby, 311–32. New York: Palgrave Macmillan.
Giddens, Anthony. 1991. *Modernity and Self-Identity: Self and Society in the Late Modern Age*. Stanford: Stanford University Press.
Gilligan, Carol. 1990. *In a Different Voice: Psychological Theory and Women's Development*. Cambridge, MA: Harvard University Press.
Held, David. 2004. *Introduction to Critical Theory: Horkheimer to Habermas*. Cambridge: Polity Press.
Hobart, Hiʻilei Julia Kawehipuaakahaopulani, and Tamara Kneese. 2020. 'Radical Care: Survival Strategies for Uncertain Times'. *Social Text* 38 (1 [142]): 1–16. https://doi.org/10.1215/01642472-7971067.
Hochschild, Arlie Russell. 2001. *The Time Bind: When Work Becomes Home and Home Becomes Work*. New York: Owl Books Holt.
———. 2003. *The Commercialization of Intimate Life: Notes from Home and Work*. Berkeley, CA: University of California Press.
Hollway, Wendy. 2006a. 'Paradox in the Pursuit of a Critical Theorization of the Development of Self in Family Relationships'. *Theory & Psychology* 16 (4): 465–82. https://doi.org/10.1177/0959354306066201.
———. 2006b. *The Capacity to Care: Gender and Ethical Subjectivity*. London and New York: Routledge.
Honig, Bonnie. 2012. 'The Politics of Public Things: Neoliberalism and the Routine of Privatization'. *No Foundations* 10, 59–76.
———. 2017. *Public Things: Democracy in Disrepair*. New York: Fordham University Press.
Honneth, Axel. 1996. *The Struggle for Recognition: The Moral Grammar of Social Conflicts*. Translated by Joel Anderson. Cambridge, MA: MIT Press.
———. 1999. 'Postmodern Identity and Object-Relations Theory: On the Seeming Obsolescence of Psychoanalysis'. *Philosophical Explorations* 2 (3): 225–42. https://doi.org/10.1080/10001999098538708.
Horkheimer, Max. 2002. 'Authority and the Family'. In *Critical Theory: Selected Essays*, translated by Matthew J. O'Connell, 47–128. New York: Continuum.
Keller, Evelyn Fox. 1995. *Reflections on Gender and Science*. New Haven, MA: Yale University Press.
Linebaugh, Peter. 2014. *Stop, Thief! The Commons, Enclosures and Resistance*. Oakland, CA: PM.
Lorey, Isabell. 2015. *State of Insecurity: Government of the Precarious*. Translated by Aileen Derieg. London and New York: Verso.

Martel, James. 2019. '"True-Enough Self": Winnicott, Object Relations Theory and the Bases of Identity'. In *Transitional Subjects: Critical Theory and Object Relations*, edited by Amy Allen and Brian O'Connor, 159–83. New York; Chichester: Columbia University Press.

Mies, Maria. 2014. *Patriarchy and Accumulation on a World Scale: Women in the International Division of Labour*. London: Zed Books.

Mignolo, Walter. 2011. *The Darker Side of Western Modernity: Global Futures, Decolonial Options*. Durham, NC: Duke University Press.

Mitchell, Juliet. 1974. *Psychoanalysis and Feminism: A Radical Reassessment of Freudian Psychoanalysis*. London: Allen Lane.

———. 1978. 'Erosion of the Family'. *New Society*, 2 July.

———. 2015. *Woman's Estate*. London: Verso.

Nelson, Maggie. 2016. *The Argonauts*. Minneapolis, MN: Graywolf Press.

Nussbaum, Martha C. 2001. *Upheavals of Thought: The Intelligence of Emotions*. Cambridge and New York: Cambridge University Press.

———. 2004. *Hiding from Humanity: Disgust, Shame, and the Law*. Princeton, NJ: Princeton University Press.

Phillips, Judith. 2007. *Care*. Cambridge and Malden, MA: Polity.

Reay, Diane. 2015. 'Habitus and the Psychosocial: Bourdieu with Feelings'. *Cambridge Journal of Education* 45 (1): 9–23. https://doi.org/10.1080/0305764X.2014.990420.

Reich, Warren Thomas. 2004. 'Care'. In *Encyclopedia of Bioethics*, edited by Stephen Garrard Post, 348–59. New York: Macmillan Reference USA.

Rubin, Gayle. 1975. 'The Traffic in Women: Notes on the "Political Economy" of Sex'. In *Toward an Anthropology of Women*, edited by Rayna R. Reiter, 157–210. London and New York: Monthly Review Press.

Ruddick, Sara. 1995. *Maternal Thinking: Toward a Politics of Peace*. Boston, MA: Beacon Press.

Santner, Eric L. 2006. *On Creaturely Life: Rilke, Benjamin, Sebald*. Chicago: University of Chicago Press.

Sevenhuijsen, Selma. 1998. *Citizenship and the Ethics of Care: Feminist Considerations on Justice, Morality, and Politics*. London and New York: Routledge.

Silverstone, Roger. 1994. *Television and Everyday Life*. London and New York: Routledge.

———. 2007. *Media and Morality: On the Rise of the Mediapolis*. Cambridge and Malden, MA: Polity Press.

Stiegler, Bernard. 2013. *What Makes Life Worth Living: On Pharmacology*. Translated by Daniel Ross. Cambridge and Malden, MA: Polity.
Stoller, Sarah. 2018. 'Forging a Politics of Care: Theorizing Household Work in the British Women's Liberation Movement'. *History Workshop Journal* 85 (April): 95–119. https://doi.org/10.1093/hwj/dbx063.
Swartz, Sally. 2019. *Ruthless Winnicott: The Role of Ruthlessness in Psychoanalysis and Political Protest*. London and New York: Routledge.
The Care Collective. 2020. *The Care Manifesto: The Politics of Interdependence*. London and New York: Verso Books.
Tronto, Joan C. 1993. *Moral Boundaries: A Political Argument for an Ethic of Care*. New York: Routledge.
———. 2002. 'The "Nanny" Question in Feminism'. *Hypatia* 17 (2): 34–51.
———. 2013. *Caring Democracy: Markets, Equality, and Justice*. New York: New York University Press.
Vogel, Lise. 2013. *Marxism and the Oppression of Women: Toward a Unitary Theory*. Leiden: Brill.
Whitford, Margaret. 1991. *Luce Irigaray: Philosophy in the Feminine*. London and New York: Routledge.
Widlöcher, Daniel. 2012. 'Winnicott and the Acquisition of Freedom of Thought'. In *Donald Winnicott Today*, edited by Jan Abram. The New Library of Psychoanalysis. London and New York: Routledge.
Williams, Fiona. 2001. 'In and beyond New Labour: Towards a New Political Ethics of Care'. *Critical Social Policy*, no. 4: 467–93.
Wilson, Elizabeth. 1980. *Only Halfway to Paradise: Women in Postwar Britain, 1945–1968*. London and New York: Tavistock Publications.
Winnicott, D. W. 1986a. 'Cure'. In *Home Is Where We Start From: Essays by a Psychoanalyst*, 112–20. Harmondsworth: Penguin.
———. 1986b. 'The Concept of a Healthy Individual'. In *Home Is Where We Start From: Essays by a Psychoanalyst*, 21–38. Harmondsworth: Penguin.
———. 2017. *The Collected Works of D.W. Winnicott*. Edited by Lesley Caldwell and Helen Taylor Robinson. Oxford and New York: Oxford University Press.
Wright, Erik Olin. 2015. 'Why Class Matters'. *Jacobin*, 23 December. https://www.jacobinmag.com/2015/12/socialism-marxism-democracy-inequality-erik-olin-wright/.

2

Healthy Life: Care, *Cura* and Flourishing

Life does not simply appear into the world. It must be reproduced and sustained. (Threadcraft 2016, 153)

What is life about? You may cure your patient and not know what it is that makes him or her go on living. (D. W. Winnicott 1991d, 100)

Winnicott's interest in care, and its central role in shaping subjective and relational experience, is part of a long history of thinking that reaches back to Greco-Roman myth. The story of 'Care,' *Cura* in the Latin, found in a second-century Latin collection of myths edited by Hyginus, emphasises the fundamental significance of care to being human. In a classic discussion of the history of the concept, Warren Thomas Reich provides a useful summary of the myth worth quoting at length:

> As Care (Cura) was crossing a river, she thoughtfully picked up some mud and began to fashion a human being. While she was pondering what she had done, Jupiter came along. (Jupiter was the founder of Olympian society, a society of the major gods and goddesses who inhabited Mount Olympus after most of the gods had already appeared.) Care asked him

to give the spirit of life to the human being, and Jupiter readily granted this. Care wanted to name the human after herself, but Jupiter insisted that his name should be given to the human instead. While Care and Jupiter were arguing, Terra arose and said that the human being should be named after her, since she had given her own body. (Terra, or Earth, the original life force of the earth, guided Jupiter's rise to power.) Finally, all three disputants accepted Saturn as judge. (Known for his devotion to fairness and equality, Saturn was the son of Terra and the father of Jupiter.) Saturn decided that Jupiter, who gave spirit to the human, would take back its soul after death; and since Terra had offered her body to the human, she should receive it back after death. But, said Saturn, "Since Care first fashioned the human being, let her have and hold it as long as it lives." Finally, Jupiter said, "Let it be called homo (Latin for human being), since it seems to be made from humus (Latin for earth)." (2004, 350)[1]

The myth proposes that the human is created by care, and that there is an inherent relationship between care and human life. Care isn't the material that the human is made from as such, but it is key to the form the human takes. Reich suggests that the myth understands care as a form of "uplifting, attentive solicitude" that is "key to the process of becoming truly human" (350). Using the myth, Reich makes a value judgement in which the "truly human" is defined in relation to the value and practice of care. Care involves a particular way of relating to and regarding others, one alert to their needs and circumstances. However, Reich notes that the myth also points towards care's other sense, its association with worry and concern: "the lifelong care of the human that would be undertaken by Cura entails both an earthly, bodily element that is pulled down to the ground (worry) and a spirit-element that strives towards the divine" (350). The task of Care is to balance these opposing elements, to "*hold* the human together in wholeness while cherishing it" (350, emphasis added).

---

[1] Incidentally, recent translators, Smith and Trazaskoma, offer a different reading, translating "cura" as "worry." On their reading, the myth is a playful take on human foibles. In short, the human life is characterised by worry and then death (Apollodorus and Hyginus 2007, 166–67). Smith and Trazaskoma do not note the dual meaning of care, as both solicitude and worry, unlike Reich.

Concurrently, the myth says something about the roots of power, as well as agency and the capacity to care. Reich writes that "modern psychology teaches us that those who are cared for from birth (which is the image conveyed in this myth) develop the nurturing power to care for others" (2004, 350). That the mythical first human described in the story is not named after the most *powerful* gods and goddesses suggests that the cared-for human is not dominated by them, that "truly solicitous care protects humans from oppressive and manipulative power" (350). There is a sense, in this ancient myth, that care is important for the development of specific subjective capacities, including the ability to feel for others a form of concern that is one of the term's meanings, and for subjective agency and autonomy, capacities necessary for resisting forms of domination and oppression that raise the threat of subjection and compliance. The myth conveys the idea that these are things that it is good for humans to be. The development of the capacities to care for others and to resist domination are inherently connected and constitute a particular way of being and relating. However, the myth suggests that the growth of these capacities is inseparable from an experience of solicitous care on the part of an other.

The myth of Cura places care—as practice, experience and capacity—at the centre of what it means to live a good life. Using the myth and tracing its legacy in philosophy, Reich makes a normative claim about what makes life worth living. This is a tendency common to subsequent work in the tradition that Reich describes (2004, 350–57). In the *cura animarum*, or Care of Souls tradition, originating in Ancient Greek philosophy, the task of the philosopher is to develop in the pupil-student the capacity to care in the right way and about the right things. Socrates saw himself as the physician or healer of the soul, a word with many translations, but with close links to the idea of the personality and a literal translation of the Greek, *psyche* (McNeill 1977, vii; Lear 1991, 4). The philosopher, on this account, is a kind of mind doctor, cultivating the development of the spiritual and intellectual aspects of the personality necessary for the good life. In the romantic poetry of Goethe's *Faust*, who wants to be without care in life, the capacity to express concern for the world is pivotal to the protagonist's moral salvation (Goethe 2009; Reich 2004, 352). For the existentialist Søren Kierkegaard, care is an essential aspect of human authenticity, describing an interested and personal way of relating to the world that takes its distance from detached objectivity (Kierkegaard 2001). In Martin Heidegger's phenomenological account of being, *Dasein* is *Sorge*: human being *is* care. The sense of being connected to what one can and cannot do in the world saves us from inauthentic being and anxiety, calling us back to ourselves (Flynn 1980). In the field of psychology, Rollo May draws on Heidegger to foreground that the capacity to feel that something matters is basic to human existence, and the possibilities of willing and wishing, and he demonstrates care's importance through reference to the centrality of maternal care in keeping a newborn alive (2007, 289). For Erik Erikson, the capacity to care, understood in terms of cultivating strength in the next generation, is constitutive of an important stage in development and the achievement of adult maturity (Erikson and Erikson 1998).

The tradition that Reich explores understands care, conceived as a specific attitude towards the world, as an essential part of what it means to be human and to live a good life. In ways that resonate with Reich's discussion, Winnicott's work, and the object relations tradition that he is part of, makes care central to the good life, or human flourishing. Winnicott provides an account of solicitous care, and its role in emotional development, understanding the good life in terms very similar to those described by the myth of Cura. He offers a sustained account of the relationship between early care and the development of both an authentic or personal sense of self and the capacity for concern. For Winnicott, good life, or perhaps better "healthy life," as the next section will explore, is characterised by the capacity to resist compliance, to feel alive and authentic and to feel concern for the other. In his account, what makes life worth living is an experience of care that fosters in the one who receives it the capacities for aliveness and care. The rest of the chapter unpacks Winnicott's account of the relationship between care and human flourishing. Echoing the myth of Cura, Winnicott makes care central to what it means to live a fully human life.

"Healthy Life"

Socrates was the first to pose the question: "how should one live?" The question has a moral aspect, linked to the idea of what it is good to do, but it also communicates something new, namely an interest in what gives life meaning, what makes it worth living (Honderich 2005, 519). The investigation established by Socrates into what it means to live a good or happy life is taken up, most famously, by Aristotle in the *Nicomachean Ethics* (2000). For Aristotle, *eudaimonia* links the moral aspects of living well (having and living in accordance with the virtues) with the idea of a flourishing, or successful, life. MacIntyre describes *eudaimonia* as "the state of being well and doing well in being well" (2011, 174). The term can be variously rendered, as happiness or human good, but is often translated as "human flourishing." To "flourish" shares an etymological root with "flower" in the French "florir" (Darwall 2002, 76). When applied to plants, the term means to "grow vigorously to the point of putting out leaves or flowers," especially when facilitated by a suitable environment. More broadly, something flourishes "when it thrives or prospers as a healthy plant does coming to full flower" (76). *Eudaimonia* and flourishing, then, are linked to human well-being and welfare, to the question of what it means, and what is needed, for humans to live well and thrive.

Jonathan Lear suggests that psychoanalysis is also concerned with answering Socrates' question: "in what way should one live?" (1998, 4). Peter Lomas writes that, though it is rare for a patient to arrive at the therapist's office with it on their lips, the experience of distress will bring up questions about how to act and think and, in time, attention will shift to the question of living (1999). But, Lomas asks, how does a therapist know what constitutes a good life? Is the aim of psychotherapy to help the patient towards health, or to make them a better person (4)? From Winnicott's perspective, the difference between these outcomes may be negligible. Lesley Caldwell describes Winnicott as "the pre-eminent psychoanalyst of health and of what it means to be a healthy individual" (2013, xvi). Winnicott's understanding of health was inherently linked to moral development, as will be discussed in detail below. His interest in health sets him apart from Freud, who often resisted the language of health and well-being, worried that psychoanalysis would eventually be reduced to psychotherapy, remembered as no more than a treatment listed in psychiatric textbooks (Frosh 1999, 263). In a famous early rubric, he suggests the discipline aims to transform "hysterical misery into common unhappiness" (Freud 1895, 305). There is no cure for the human condition, which does not mean that psychoanalysis is uninterested in making people better, or perhaps in making better people. Adam Phillips, however, points out some of the tensions that surround the idea. "To know" he writes, "what a cure is—what recovery looks like—the doctor must already know what a life is supposed to look like" (1994, xiv). Having a conception of cure involves a positive idea of what makes a life good or a good life. Elizabeth Roudinesco argues that psychoanalysis aims not to cure but to change, describing the "cure" the discipline offers as "the existential transformation of the subject" (2003, 34–35). As Roudinesco puts it, even if psychoanalysis may not be able to end suffering, it offers the opportunity "at least to become conscious of its origins and so to take it on," a comment that links the Freudian enterprise to the examined life that Socrates endorsed (15). Tying the value of psychoanalysis to the potential for revelation, Roudinesco evokes what Philip Rieff famously termed an "analytic attitude," which aims to allow the analysand to know and come to terms with the truth of their being (1966). In his essay on Jensen's *Gradiva*, Freud defines the nature of the psychoanalytic cure in precisely these terms, describing the "analytic method of psychotherapy" as involving "the making conscious of what is repressed and the coinciding of explanation with cure" (1907, 89).

Freud emphasised the difficulties that surround obtaining self-knowledge, but he also explored how blocks in understanding can be resolved through specific forms of experience (Lomas 1999, 3). The context of the transference is essential to the process: "the process of cure is accomplished in a relapse into love" (Freud 1907, 89). The analyst takes on a role analogous to the Platonic philosopher, the "midwife" whose "duty is to help us be who we are" (Scruton cited in Lomas 1999, 3). Freud's resistance to the association of psychoanalysis with medicine can also be understood as a comment on the different kinds of healing that bodies and minds require. Whilst the body can be treated with "applied science" and the "specific remedy," treating psychic suffering depends on relationship, on a form of experience that repeats and gradually challenges ways of unthought knowing and being that cause misery and distress (D. W. Winnicott 1986, 113). For Freud, the transference, wherein "the patient unconsciously ma[kes] the doctor play the role of loved or feared parental figures," can be used by the patient in the service of resistance, but "in the hands of the physician it becomes the most powerful therapeutic instrument and it plays a part scarcely to be overestimated in the dynamics of the process of cure" (Laplanche and Pontalis 1988, 458; Freud 1923, 247). More recently, Julia Kristeva has suggested that "the process of transference and countertransference involved in the psychoanalytic cure is an example of the economy of care" (Zournazi and Kristeva 2002, 65–66). On this analysis, relieving distress and bringing about psychic change are rooted in "careful" ways of relating.

Freud did not engage with Aristotle's approach to human flourishing, which Lear describes as "a psychologically informed account of how to build good character" (2001, 5). Though Elisabeth Young-Bruehl suggests that Freud began his career as an Aristotelian, she reserves the status of the "truly Aristotelian" for thinkers in the object relations tradition, including Winnicott and Bowlby (2011, 180, 191). The claim at the centre of object relations approaches is that humans "are born for and into relationships, without which they cannot live, they fail to thrive" (191). Stephen Mitchell and Jay Greenberg capture much of what is at stake in object relations perspectives: humans "cannot be said to exist meaningfully apart from others. Human nature is completely realised only in relationship, interaction, participation with others" (1983, 401). "By himself," the individual "cannot create a fully human life" (402). Object relations theorists emphasise the role of the environment in bringing about human flourishing, understood in terms of "the moral and emotional growth of the self, the character" (Waddell 2002, 3). Harry Guntrip describes the task of psychoanalysis in analogous terms: "Freud said that at best we can only help the patient to exchange his neurotic suffering for ordinary human unhappiness. That, I believe, is too pessimistic a view, and the patient has glimpses of feeling the possibility of experiencing himself and life in a much more real and stable way" (1973, 279). Through the relationship with the therapist, the patient develops a way of functioning characterised by "insight, integration, individuation and personal relationship" (356). Guntrip describes this is a process of "regrowing" the self, which demonstrates the extent to which object relations theories emphasise the relational character of flourishing: the self comes into being through relationships that allow it to thrive, and this thriving consists of the capacity to relate to others in specific ways (317).

Recent work in the field of neo-Aristotelianism and virtue ethics links the concerns of that tradition with object relations theory, and with Winnicott's work in particular (Nussbaum 1994; MacIntyre 2006; Harcourt 2015). Edward Harcourt suggests that the Greek ethicists and analysts working in this tradition are engaged in the same project, namely the task of answering Socrates' question (2015, 603). Certainly, Winnicott's ideas have an affinity with the questions that preoccupied the Ancient Greek philosophers. Abram underlines that in the last ten years of his life, Winnicott's "primary questions…are associated with a philosophical inquiry" (2012, 95). During that period, he "asks fundamental questions related to what it is that makes life worth living, and what it is that gives the human being a sense of feeling real" (95). Additionally, Nussbaum foregrounds the theoretical contribution Winnicott's focus on early development makes to the field, underscoring that the ancient philosophers lack a detailed theoretical account of child development of the kind object relations theories provide (1994, 491). Similarly, MacIntyre criticises Aristotle for formulating an account of ethics from the perspective of the independent man. "In most moral philosophy," he writes, "the starting point is one that already presupposes the existence of mature independent practical reasoners whose social relationships are the relationships of the adult world. Childhood, if noticed at all, is a topic that receives only brief and incidental attention" and this failure is "apt to obscure some features of rational agency" (2006, 81, 8). MacIntyre emphasises that the intellectual powers that the Greek ethicists consider so central to human flourishing do not exist as such, but have to develop in the context of relationships. Others—parents, caregivers, teachers and the wider social environment—are all central to their development. Human flourishing, which MacIntyre conceptualises along neo-Aristotelian lines in terms of the capacity for practical reasoning, is fundamentally dependent on the help and care we receive from others.

For MacIntyre, object relations theory, specifically Winnicott's work, provides an important supplement to established understandings of flourishing because it contributes to an account of the formation of the capacity for practical reason in childhood (2006, 85, 89). What early care, or a later experience of analytic care, has the potential to provide is "a situation in which the child's unqualified trust in such adults releases the creative physical and mental powers expressed in play, resulting in a sense of self sufficient for an increasing degree of independence in practical reasoning" (85). What care makes those who receive it able to do, on this Aristotelean account, is to "put in question the relationship between my present set of desires and motives and my good" (86). It enables me to reflect on what I want and assess whether a particular course of action will contribute to "my flourishing *qua* human being" (86). Harcourt also emphasises the significance of what takes place in early relationships of care for future capacities, with a focus on deliberation, evaluation and planning (2015, 614). The integration of mind that relationships make possible "subserves practical rationality" (615). Winnicott writes that "in [a healthy mature person] the id becomes gathered into the service of the ego, and the ego masters the id, in contrast to pathological states in which 'the id remains relatively or totally "external" to the ego'" (1990e, 40). In a later text he adds that "it is the self that must precede the self's use of instinct; the rider must ride the horse, not be run away with" (1991f, 99).

It is certainly true that Winnicott sees the capacity for purposive action, for the concentration, absorption and attention characteristic of play, as an important element of healthy life. However, one of the most unique aspects of his work is his attention to what "makes a baby begin to be, to feel that life is real, to find life worth living" (98). Thinkers like MacIntyre and Harcourt turn to psychoanalysis for an account of flourishing framed in terms of rational agency or practical reason. However, Winnicott also emphasises flourishing as a form of moral and emotional development characterised by the capacities to resist compliance and feel concern, which is co-extensive with mature subjectivity. As Eric Rayner notes, British object relations theory took inspiration from philosophical

Romanticism and the underlying belief that "the ultimate foundation for all things is the urge to self-expression…essential knowledge must be emotional and intuitive, there must be depth of feeling if reality is to be understood" (1991, 6). Whilst practical reason is an important aspect of development, object relations perspectives shift the focus slightly, towards emotional development and the capacity to care—about and for the self, for others and the world—making this central to their conception of human flourishing.

Abram highlights that "Winnicott's propensity is always to look for health, as opposed to pathology" (2007, 26). This tendency is likely the product of his initial training and extensive work as a paediatrician, though his interest in psychoanalysis and clinical experience running free clinics at Paddington Green Hospital from 1923 soon led him to appreciate the emotional sources of many of the physical symptoms he encountered in his patients (D. W. Winnicott 1958b). However, Winnicott's interest in health ultimately has less to do with a medical conception than with a developed account of human flourishing, with what makes life worth living. In the posthumously published *Human Nature*, Winnicott writes that "it is really much easier, and more usual, for a doctor to write about illness. Through the study of illness, we come to the study of much that is important about health. But the doctor's assumption that health is a relative absence of disease is not good enough. The word health has its own meaning in a positive way, so that absence of disease is no more than the starting point for *healthy life*" (D. W. Winnicott 1988, 1, emphasis added). Noting that there is no "simple statement" for defining psychic ill-health, Winnicott nonetheless writes that it is "always a disorder of emotional development, even when caused quite obviously by adverse environmental factors" (16). It can take neurotic or psychotic forms, depending on the age at which difficulties first arise; whether the child "is able to be a whole person among whole persons," and thus capable of experiencing the "powerful instinctual experiences based on love between persons" (neurosis), or whether the difficulties started at an earlier date, before the age of around two, when the child was not yet a whole person able to relate to other whole persons (psychosis) (16).

Winnicott "takes as his own province the relatively unexplored area of psychotic and borderline-psychotic phenomena" (Greenberg and Mitchell 1983, 208). He was "gradually lured into the treatment of the more psychotic type of adult patient" around the time of the Second World War (D. W. Winnicott 1988, 2). It was this kind of work that led him to reflect seriously on the question of "healthy life" (1). In the seminal work, *Playing and Reality*, he poses the fundamental question that dates back to ancient philosophy:

> What is life about? You may cure your patient and not know what it is that makes him or her go on living. It is of first importance for us to acknowledge openly that absence of psychoneurotic illness may be health, but it is not life. Psychotic patients who are all the time hovering between living and not living force us to look at this problem, one that really belongs *not to psychoneurotics but to all human beings*. (D. W. Winnicott 1991f, 100)

Winnicott is saying here that, whilst the absence of disease is important, it is not a good-enough end point. What is needed, in fact, is a positive conception of healthy life, of human flourishing or well-being, and psychotic forms of disturbance reveal something important about what might constitute it, what makes life worth living and what underpins the sense of aliveness and the capacity to feel real that are, for the psychotic, regularly in doubt.

Scholars have long foregrounded the significant contribution that Winnicott's ideas about aliveness and care have made to psychoanalytic theory. Thomas Ogden writes that "Winnicott's effort to conceptualise in analytic terms the experience of being alive" represents "a major advance in the psychoanalytic conception of the subject" (1992, 619). Winnicott's contribution rests on his detailed iteration of the fundamental importance of care for the development of mind. Bernard Stiegler suggests that the earliest experience of care that the child receives, the mother's holding, is a pharmakon, something with the capacity to kill or cure (2013, 4). Early care has a life and death significance for the physical future of the child, but the life and death that Winnicott and Stiegler refer to is also psychic. Care has the capacity to enable the development of the *psyche* or to act as a deathly presence. "Human infants," Winnicott writes, "cannot start to *be* except under certain conditions" (1990e, 43, emphasis in the original). Care is the condition of possibility for the infant to start to be, to live, as a *psyche*, a psycho-somatic entity. Stiegler writes that "a mother, according to Donald Winnicott, by taking care of her infant, even before the child is old enough to speak, teaches it that life is worth living. She instils in the child the feeling that life is worth living" (2013, 1). A mother or caregiver who is not able to do this, perhaps she is ill or suffering under adverse environmental conditions, will not function as a "source of vitality for the child," precipitating a state of inner deadness (A. Green 2005, 142). Ogden notes that "Winnicott was the first to place the psychological state of the mother on an equal footing with that of the infant in the constitution of the mother-infant" (1992, 620). As Green highlights, though Winnicott's concepts have led to a shift in attention from the internal object to the role of the external object, he is "much more interested in the interplay of the external and the internal," with "the area of the *intermediate*, and the failure to create it" (2005, 68). Ogden observes that "the creation of the subject" takes place "in the space between the infant and mother," but, at least initially, there is a paradox in that this space has not yet come to exist, because at the beginning "the mother is part of the child" (1992, 620–21). Good-enough care makes the development of potential space possible. "There is something that holds," writes Stiegler, "*between* the mother and her child" (2013, 1). Or not. Aliveness is, for Winnicott, key to what makes life worth living, what constitutes healthy life, wellbeing, or *eudaimonia*, and it is made possible by care. Without the provision of an "environmental minimum," the infant will not come to exist at all (D. W. Winnicott 1991e, 151). However, it may not be enough to say that the infant requires care/society/others in order to thrive. Winnicott's intervention makes it clear that the form this care takes is vitally important. An infant who is "hungry, cold and wet" requires specific actions to be performed to meet their needs (1958d, 160). Whilst it is the case that the potential for life is "only realised in relationship," the idea of relationship, unless supplemented with a theory of good-enough care, does not go far enough (Greenberg and Mitchell 1983, 401).

Care refers to "the qualities and changes in the mother that meet the specific and developing needs of the infant towards whom she orientates" (1990e, 42). Of course, the infant's need for care, and the fact that care is generally received, do not ensure that the conditions of possibility for "living" will be met. As Abram observes, Winnicott's awareness of dependence developed concurrently with an appreciation of the vital role played by the *character* of the care the infant received, "Winnicott's realisation that 'there's no such thing as a baby' meant that he never again conceptualised without recognising the infant's dependency on the object; he always insisted that because of the baby's dependent state, the m/other's attitude would colour her baby's internal world and impact on his emotional development" (2007, 6). The mother, or other primary caregiver's, capacity, during the first weeks of life, to enter into a state of "heightened sensitivity" that Winnicott names "primary maternal preoccupation"—to develop, temporarily, an attitude of close identification with, and adaptation to, the infant's needs—is fundamental if "the infant's own line of life" is not to be disturbed (1958e, 302–3). Around the time of birth, "processes in the mother (and in the father) bring about, in health, a special state in which the parent is orientated to the infant, and is thus in a position to meet the infant's dependence" (1990e, 55). The mother "through identification of herself with her infant knows what the infant feels like" which makes possible a "live adaptation to the infant's needs" (54). In general, mothers who are not "distorted by ill-health or by present-day environmental stress do tend to know accurately enough what their infants need," and are able to provide it. This, he insists, is "the essence of maternal care" (54). The "good enough" mother "serves as interpreter of the infant's experience" (Ogden 1992, 620). She is able to "feel herself into her infant's place and so meet her infant's needs" (1958e, 304).

Winnicott has been criticised for seeming to insist that the mother of the newborn renounce her own subjectivity—at least temporarily—if her care is to be good enough. Madelon Sprengnether argues that Winnicott's thinking "emphasises the mother's presence and influence at the same time that it desubjectivises her, substituting stereotypes of 'good' mother and 'bad' mother for the complexity of a fully developed adult personality" (1990, 186). However, as Hollway notes, the mother/primary caregiver "has a relatively developed self and is wholly responsible for the intersubjective field for her new baby" (2006, 67). The ability to accurately identify and meet the infant's needs depends on the caregiver's own independent subjectivity, and her capacity to differentiate between her own needs and those of the child (52). The infant's coming to feel alive depends on the caregiver's capacity to be concerned with, and make sense of, the child's experience. It depends on the caregiver's capacity to, and for, care, formed through her own experiences as child and now primary caregiver.

This is not to suggest that caring is ever easy or without conflict. Winnicott writes that "the mother...hates the baby from the word go," and he offers a long and well-known list of reasons why this would be the case (1958c, 201). For instance, the baby "is ruthless, he treats her like scum, an unpaid servant, a slave." Additionally, "he is suspicious, refuses her good food, and makes her doubt herself, but eats well with his aunt." The infant "is an interference with her private life, a challenge to preoccupation," "the baby at first must dominate, he must be protected from coincidences, life must unfold at the baby's rate and all this needs his mother's continuous and detailed study. For instance, she must not be anxious when holding him, etc." (201). Therefore, though Winnicott thinks that the mother/caregiver must be able to become preoccupied with the child in order for healthy development to occur, it is not the case that the mother merges with the child, in the sense of becoming desubjectivised and unable able to differentiate between her own needs and those of the child. Whilst the mother in this state is not quite the same self that she was before she had children, her subjectivity is changed but not obliterated by the experience of becoming a parent. In fact, the child's development is dependent on the mother being a subject in her own right, one capable of providing care which means not over-identifying or merging. As Winnicott's description of maternal hate shows, care always involves a tension between self-assertion and recognition of the other, and this process constantly breaks down, however not irredeemably. Additionally, from the mother's perspective, the conflict inherent in the dyadic relationship is acutely apparent. As Hollway describes it, "struggling to meet the ruthless demands of an infant (and of course, sometimes failing) is inescapable" (2006, 67). In the earliest period of life, the child's "narcissistic demands place terrible strain on mothers, as, in this relationship, they are getting no consideration whatsoever" (68). Certainly, then, the caregiver's subjectivity is an essential part of the child's development, whilst experiencing the conflict between her own needs and wants and those of the child is a fundamental part of maternal subjectivity.

At the earliest stage of life, Winnicott insists, "the main thing is the physical holding" (1990e, 54). It includes "the whole routine of care" and is "not the same for any two infants." It is also attuned to the "day-to-day changes belonging to the infant's growth and development, both physical and psychological" (49). Holding of this kind is a "form of love" that makes it possible for the infant to become a person, "to have an inside and an outside" and for observers to "postulate a personal or inner psychic reality for the infant" (49, 44, 45). This capacity develops in "a three-dimensional space relationship with time gradually added" in which "experiences that are inherent to existence" and "belong to infant psychology" are managed "in a complex psychological field, determined by the awareness and empathy of the mother" (44). Adam Phillips identifies in Winnicott a growing awareness of the need for an adult to "hold together the threads of [the child's] experience," offering continuity and support that are at once both physical and psychic (2007, 66). The infant's self cannot come into being without the help of an other capable of identifying, imagining, feeling and attuning in a way that fosters the infant's own development. On the basis of good-enough care, the infant is able to "to have a personal existence" and to "build up what might be called *a continuity of being*" that forms the basis of aliveness and life (D. W. Winnicott 1990e, 54, emphasis in the original).

Michael Eigen describes Winnicott's work as "a kind of biography of the sense of aliveness as it unfolds in infancy and throughout a lifetime" (2005, xxi). The capacity for aliveness is, for Winnicott, an innate potential, inherently linked to aggression and creativity. "Synonymous with activity and motility," aggression is the energy of development, evident in the foetus's kicking or the young infant's chewing and grasping (Abram 2007, 15; D. W. Winnicott 1958a, 206; A. Phillips 2007, 105). This is an aggression linked to appetite or "some other form of instinctual love" (Winnicott cited in Abram 2007, 20). The infant "does not yet appreciate the fact that what he destroys when excited is the same as that which he values in quiet intervals between excitements" (D. W. Winnicott 1958a, 206). The infant's appetitive love of the mother includes an imaginative attack, with no concern for its results, a ruthless relation (A. Phillips 2007, 107). Primary creativity, which Abram describes as an "innate drive towards health," depends on the mother's capacity to survive the child's ruthless love (2007, 115–16). Creativity, Phillips notes, is "bound up with a capacity for ruthlessness" (A. Phillips 2007, 113).

Winnicott considers creativity to be foundational to health, and he locates its origins in what he terms the "theoretical first feed," in reality a "build-up of memories of events" rather than a "single happening" (D. W. Winnicott 1988, 100). At this first feed "the baby is ready to create, and the mother makes it possible for the baby to have the illusion that the breast, and what the breast means, has been created by impulse out of need" (101). This process, which Winnicott describes as "complex," needs to be done "in such a way that the baby creates the object" (1990b, 62). Winnicott writes that "by reason of an aliveness in the infant and through the development of instinct tension the infant comes to expect something; and then there is a reaching out which can soon take the form of an impulsive movement of the hand or the movement of the mouth towards a presumed object. I think it is not out of place to say that the infant is ready to be creative" (1988, 102). "The pattern is thus: the baby develops a vague expectation that has origin in an unformulated need. The adaptive mother presents an object or a manipulation that meets the baby's needs, and so the baby begins to need just that which the mother presents. In this way *the baby comes to feel confident in being able to create objects and to create the actual world*" (1990b, 62, emphasis added). In this formulation, the infant's confidence in their own creative capacity depends on an experience of care. The mother who is able to care adequately can sense their child's needs and respond in a way that allows the infant an illusion of omnipotence, and a sense that it is possible to create what they need. This is a madness of a special kind that is "conceded to babies" (1991a, 71). The baby's sense of what it needs is "unformulated," but the mother's ability to identify with the child and to attune her response makes it possible for the baby to "feel confident" about its own capability to create both objects and "the actual world." On Winnicott's model, creativity is not borne out of frustration, as it is for Freud, but out of the experience of the attentive meeting of need that facilitates trust and hope. This is a complex moment, both illusory and elusive, that is crucially if not brutally determinative: on the success or failure of these experiences depend the possibilities of a life, the futures and non-futures of living and not living. These futures pivot around a specific competence, namely the ability to imagine a world in which ones needs will be met.

The developing capacity for a creative relation with the world, rooted in a potential based on bodily needs and the "impulse to grow," is the basis for a meaningful life (Abram 2007, 7). Winnicott writes that "it is creative apperception more than anything else that makes the individual feel that life is worth living" (1991a, 65). This capacity depends on a specific form of experience and communication between the caregiver and the child: "the communication to the baby is: 'Come at the world creatively, create the world; it is only what you create that has meaning for you.' Next comes: 'the world is in your control'" (1987, 101). On the basis of this experience of omnipotence, which is grounded in responsive care and the recognition of need, develops the capacity to distinguish between the me and the not-me. Winnicott describes the sequence thus:

> When I look I am seen, so I exist.
> I can now afford to look and see.
> I now look creatively and what I apperceive I also perceive.
> In fact I take care not to see what is not there to be seen (unless I am tired). (1991c, 114)

When the infants' needs are not met, their "creative capacity begins to atrophy" (112). "The world and its details" are recognised, "but only as something to be fitted in with or demanding adaptation" (1991a, 65). "If the maternal care is not good enough," Winnicott writes, "the infant does not really come into existence, since there is no continuity of being; instead the personality becomes built on the basis of reactions to environmental impingement" (1990b, 54). The development of the true self depends on the mother meeting the infant's spontaneous gesture and omnipotence and making sense of it (1990a, 145). The mother who "fails to meet the infant's gesture," instead substituting "her own gesture which is to be given sense by the compliance of the infant," sets in motion the development of a false self, the origin of which "belongs to the mother's inability to sense her infant's needs" (145). Winnicott insists that "it is an essential part of my theory that the True Self does not become a living reality except as a result of the mother's repeated success in meeting the infant's spontaneous gesture or sensory hallucination" (145). The sense that life is meaningful and worth living depends on an experience of responsive care.

Phillips notes that, though the idea of the true self is an "essentialist theory," it constitutes an essence that cannot be formulated "except in the most rudimentary terms" (2007, 127). Winnicott writes that: "at the earliest stage the True Self is the theoretical position from which come the spontaneous gesture and the personal idea. The spontaneous gesture is the True Self in action. Only the True Self can be creative and only the True Self can feel real. Whereas a True Self feels real, the existence of a False Self results in a feeling unreal or a sense of futility" (1990a, 148). The true self, rooted in the "aliveness of the body tissues and the working of body-functions," "does no more than collect together the details of the experience of aliveness" (148). The infant's self is a potential that depends for its realisation on a good-enough holding environment, on the recognition by the mother of its gestures. As Phillips puts it, "Winnicott assumes that everyone 'has' a self that, like a plant, depends for its realisation on a nurturing environment" (A. Phillips 2007, 128). The capacities for aliveness, creativity and spontaneity depend precariously on the experience of a specific form of care, a curing pharmakon that has the capacity to make life worth living. MacIntyre highlights that flourishing depends on a form of "responsive recognition" (2006, 90). An unresponsive attitude fosters compliance and hinders the process of finding external reality and the self, making it difficult to distinguish between fantasy and reality, a capacity necessary for later development and learning. Whilst useful, this conception doesn't quite capture the emotional and experiential dimensions of Winnicott's account, which grounds good life in a deeply romantic idea of creative spontaneity and subjective connection with the world.

The Capacity for Concern

The experience of responsive care in early life is the precondition for coming to feel real and alive, and for developing a sense that life is worth living. However, for object relations theorists like Winnicott, human flourishing is not only the product of social relationships but includes the development of particular capacities for relating to others; it includes a specific form of socialisation. "A sign of health in the mind," Winnicott writes, "is the ability of one individual to enter imaginatively and yet accurately into the thoughts and feelings and hopes and fears of another person; also to allow the other person to do the same to us" (1991c, 117). This is a capacity, rooted in early experiences of dependence and care, that is not guaranteed to develop. Phillips highlights that Winnicott "tends throughout his work to write of capacities rather than positions or stages. The emphasis on capacity in his work allows for individual differences. 'Capacity,' with its implication of stored possibility, and its combination of the receptive and the generative, blurs the boundary between activity and passivity" (2007, 58). This captures the fact that capacities are potentials that are realised in individual ways through intersubjective experiences. Drawing on Klein's account of the depressive position, Winnicott theorises the capacity to recognise the other as a separate being with their own thoughts and feelings, and to feel concern for them, as a developmental achievement inherently linked to the experience of good-enough care.

Rustin argues that Klein's theory offers "a view of human beings [that] assumes them to be moral in their fundamental nature" and locates their constitution "as social beings in a primary and continuing interdependency with others" (1991, 19–20). Klein's paranoid-schizoid and depressive positions are at least in part stages of development that can be defined in terms of the moral capacities typical to them (1975). The paranoid-schizoid mode of experience is characterised by omnipotence. This is the dominant mode in young babies, "with the consequence that outside objects—the mother or primary caregiver in particular—are ruthlessly used as an extension of the baby's narcissism" (Hollway 2006, 53). The position is characterised by relating to part-objects, seen as wholly either bad or good. The capacity to relate to whole objects which have both good and bad aspects is characteristic of the depressive position. For Klein, the movement from the paranoid-schizoid position to the depressive position involves the child coming to realise that the object of their ruthlessly destructive attacks is the same person who "is responsible for the total infant-care situation" (Winnicott 1990b, 22). What is seen here is "the beginnings of concern—concern at the results of the instinctual moments that belong to the developing love of the mother" (22). The movement from the paranoid-schizoid to the depressive position is a fundamental process in psychic development, ushering in the capacity to feel concern and guilt for the effects of one's actions. Here acceptance of "the demands of reality," and the overcoming of illusory omnipotence, is fundamentally linked to the growing ability to recognise and care about others.

Winnicott follows Klein in emphasising the relationship between psychic, emotional and moral development, but, characteristically, he supplements her account by emphasising the significance of what the mother or primary caregiver does in the relationship with the child. There is a need for her to "hold the infant-care situation over a period of time" which enables the infant to "go through complex experiences" (23). Hollway underlines that the ability to move from a state of ruthlessness or pre-ruth (literally a state without concern) to one of concern "is core to the development of ethical subjectivity," and the development of this capacity depends on the caregiver's survival of the child's ruthless attacks (2006, 53). The infant's use of the mother "tests her to the point of destruction" in fantasy, but her survival facilitates the child's sense that she is a separate subject, modifying omnipotence (53). This is a process that Winnicott describes in detail in one of his most crucial papers, "The Use of an Object" (1991g). In "the early stages of emotional growth," he writes, the child's capacity to recognise others as outside of their omnipotence depends on the caregiver's ability to survive the child's ruthless attempts at destruction. Doing so initiates a different form of relation: "the subject says to the object: 'I destroyed you,' and the object is there to receive the communication. From now on the subject says: 'Hullo object!' 'I destroyed you.' 'I love you.' 'You have value for me because of your survival of my destruction of you.' 'While I am loving you I am all the time destroying you in (unconscious) fantasy.' Here fantasy begins for the individual. The subject can now *use* the object that has survived" (90). The caregiver's capacity to survive destruction facilitates the child's awareness of the external world, forming one half of the conditions necessary for concern to develop. Winnicott writes that:

> The favourable circumstances necessary at this stage are these: that the mother should continue to be alive and available, available physically and available in the sense of not being preoccupied with something else. The object-mother has to be found to survive the instinct-driven episodes, which have now acquired the full force of fantasies of oral sadism and other results of fusion. Also, the environment-mother has a special function, which is to continue to be herself, to be empathic towards her infant, to be there to receive the spontaneous gesture, and to be pleased. (1990d, 77)

The infant's capacity to bear the complex ambivalences and anxieties in their attitude to the object-mother and the environment-mother is encouraged "by the fact that the baby has a contribution to make to the environment-mother. There is a growing confidence that there will be opportunity for contributing-in," which allows the child "to hold the anxiety" (77). The environment-mother's "reliable presence" provides opportunities for the child to make reparation and enables the infant to "become more and more bold in the experience of id-drives" (77). Her presence has "a specific value for the infant," allowing "freedom of expression" (77). At the same time, confidence in the opportunity for reparation creates a "benign circle" (77). Rather than feeling guilt about the effects of their ruthlessness, the experience is modified and takes on the character of concern. "The infant is now becoming able to be concerned," which involves taking "responsibility for his own instinctual impulses and the functions that belong to them" (77). This ability is fundamental to work and play and it is made possible by "the opportunity to contribute" (77).

Alford describes the morality of the depressive position, which Winnicott frames as the capacity for concern, as "caritas," or love (1989, 8). Hollway suggests an alternative definition: "the expression of care and the capacity that underpins it" (2006, 48). Concern, as Winnicott puts it, "refers to the fact that the individual cares, or minds, and both feels and accepts responsibility" (1990d, 73). This capacity is not simply a case of making sacrifices to make up for phantasised aggression, rather it is based on an ability to identify deeply with others and to "feel connected with their fates" (Alford 1989, 8). The failure to develop this capacity is linked to the early experiences one has, or has not, had. Towards the end of *Playing and Reality*, Winnicott recounts a consultation with a woman patient of forty who suffered the "impoverishment of her life because of her inability to 'stand in other persons' shoes,'" she "lived in a world that was all the time distorted for her by her own inability to feel concerned with what the other person was feeling" (1991b, 131). This was a way of thinking which made her friends "sensible of something lacking, however intangible, in her personality" (132). In the place of an imaginative engagement with others, the patient employed projective mechanisms; she "was actually forcing *stuff* into someone else" (134). In order to foster the patient's capacity for relating, Winnicott found the need for "phases of regression to dependence in the transference, these giving experience of the full effect of adaptation to need that is in fact based on the analyst's (mother's) ability to identify with the patient (her baby)," in the process "enabling the patient to live and to relate" (137). From this state of dependence, the patient could then be disillusioned, undergoing "the painful process whereby the object becomes separated off and is placed outside the omnipotent control," ultimately gaining a capacity to identify, an ability to "begin to stand imaginatively in the analyst's shoes." The ability to differentiate oneself from the other and identify their thoughts and feelings, as distinct from one's own projections, depends on a prior experience of receptivity, an act of understanding, on the part of the other. As Winnicott puts it elsewhere, the mother makes possible the "growth process in the infant…because of her knowing just what it is like to be this one particular baby she has given birth to" (1986, 119). Hollway discusses how the caregiver's own capacity to care, to identify the needs of the child without projecting their own needs and subjectivity onto them, is an essential prerequisite for the child to develop their own capacity for concern (2006, 52). The capacity to care is an intersubjective and intergenerational achievement premised on the capacities of others, the environment of care.

From an object relations perspective, the achievement of the capacity for care/concern is an inherent, if always incomplete, part of the development of mature subjectivity. As Rustin puts it, the "capacity for moral feeling...in its more or less benign forms, is seen as a defining attribute shared by human beings, rather than an unavoidable external constraint upon them" (1991, 20). The capacity to feel for others and take responsibility for one's own destructiveness is part of achieving mature interdependence. Winnicott writes that: "maturity of the human being is a term that implies not only personal growth but also socialisation" (1990c, 83). The self must come into being, and the sense that life is worth living is rooted in early development, but "healthy life" is also characterised by the capacity to feel concern for oneself and for others. This capacity is closely related to practical reasoning because, if one cannot care about the world, one cannot deliberate, evaluate and plan what it would be best to do. Care and concern underpin the capacity for practical reason. In ways similar to the tradition Reich discusses, Winnicott and object relations theories make care constitutive of human being and flourishing. Winnicott in particular provides a detailed account of the forms of interaction through which flourishing is made possible.

Flourishing and Society

Reich describes care as a kind of "glue" that holds individuals and collectives together (2004, 350). Similarly, Winnicott foregrounds the significance of care for individual and collective life. Not only does solicitous care make the development of subjectivity possible, it shapes the form subjectivity takes and facilitates the capacity to care for others. Winnicott also underlines the social significance of the capacity to care. "Let us say that in health," he writes, "which is almost synonymous with maturity, the adult is [also] able to identify with society without too great a sacrifice of personal spontaneity" and can "take some responsibility for the maintenance or for the modification of society as it is found" (1990c, 83). Winnicott here links healthy subjectivity to the capacity to care not only about ourselves and other people, but also to care about society more broadly, and to seek to change it when we find its form wanting. He also evokes the intergenerational character of the capacity for concern/care: "we get left with certain social conditions, and this is a legacy we have to accept, and, if necessary, alter; it is this that we eventually hand down to those who come after us" (83). Our early experiences shape our capacities and our relationship with society. Our capacity for concern is shaped by the care environment, and, if developed, can play a role in shaping the social environments in which living takes place.

Many scholars note that object relations theories take a positive view of the relationship between flourishing and socialisation that extends into a positive assessment of the potential for society to contribute to human flourishing (Michael Rustin 1991, 2001; Nussbaum 2004; Harcourt 2015). If for Freud, society prohibits, like a father, for Winnicott, the process of socialisation is enabling, and society, by implication, also has the capacity to nurture or impede development, like a mother (A. Phillips 2007, 7). Winnicott's way of thinking about the relationship between flourishing and society, which will be further unpacked in subsequent chapters, also resembles Aristotle's view, which emphasises the interrelation of *eudaimonia* and the social environment in which selves take shape and act. As Tronto puts it, echoing Aristotle, "a good polis [is] no guarantee that citizens [will] be ethical, but…it was almost impossible that good men could exist in a bad polis" (1993, 7). Similarly, Winnicott writes that "full maturity for the individual is not possible in an immature or ill social setting" (1990c, 84). The maternal environment can serve as a starting point for thinking about the inherent sociality of life, however that relationship remains implicated in and affected by the web of social relations that surround it. Juliet Mitchell describes Winnicott's as a "quintessentially 'psychosocial' approach," evoking the ways in which his thinking foregrounds an inherent link between the development of subjectivity, or "healthy life," and the interlinked environments of care and society (2009, 46). The fact that we grow within, not out of, relationships, which object relations perspectives emphasise, has implications for how we understand social life. The central role of care in fostering healthy life and development draws attention to the need for both dyadic and institutional forms of holding and support. The capacity for concern can be brought to bear on society, to facilitate change, but society itself, and the forms of support it does or does not provide, can ameliorate or hamper the development and expression of a caring attitude. When society inhibits this capacity, the possibility that positive changes will take place is placed in question, because citizens may be rendered incapable of caring for themselves and for the world.

As well as conveying an understanding of the centrality of care in and for human life, the myth of Cura offers what Judith Shklar describes as a "subversive genealogy" (1972). In place of the independent, autonomous subject, the myth provides an account of subjectivity that is grounded in relation, providing a way to rethink the place of care in human society and underscoring its role as a kind of "glue" holding individuals and collectives. The myth prompts reflection on what a society would look like that placed care at its centre. What kinds of change and reorganisation could foster the development of the capacity to care which both the myth of Cura and Winnicott consider central to human flourishing? Subsequent chapters will return to this question, but such imagining also provokes reflection on why and how a care perspective has come to stand for the subversive and countercultural. If care is so vital and central to life and flourishing, why isn't this more widely recognised and centralised in social and political life?

Winnicott's way of thinking has often been linked to the romantic sensibilities emblematised by Rousseau, who esteemed care and linked it to flourishing, whilst concurrently connecting the effacement of natural virtue with reason (Rudnytsky 1991, 111). Critics characterise Rousseau as "the originator of a specific socio-philosophical way of reasoning in which an idea of human flourishing provides the measure against which societal processes can be judged as distortions, or…as pathologies" (Varga and Gallagher 2012, 244; Honneth 2007). Rousseau addresses human flourishing and the relationship between mother and child at several points in his work. In his *Discourse on Inequality*, for instance, he constructs a vision of the "noble savage" as an ideal of human nature and flourishing (1984). The construction rests on a problematic idea of non-European peoples as somehow outside of time and society, but it holds some interest because of the emphasis Rousseau places on compassion as the "natural virtue" characteristic of man in a state of nature, of animals and of the mother–child relationship. He suggests that compassion is the basis for the most important social virtues, including kindness, generosity, mercy and humaneness, however, these virtues are impeded by socialisation in modern society, where people have become concerned with the opinions of others and *amour de soi* has degenerated into *amour propre*, into narcissism rather than identification with the other. He writes that:

> In fact, pity becomes all the more intense as the perceiving animal identifies itself more intimately with the suffering animal. Now it is clear that this identification must have been infinitely closer in the state of nature than in the state of reason. It is reason which breeds pride and reflection which fortifies it; reason which turns man inward into himself. (155–6)

Modern man and society, Rousseau claims, is alienated by an excessive esteem for reason, which covers over and inhibits flourishing, understood to involve the capacity for compassion, or concern. Rousseau doesn't discuss the role of care specifically in this process, but in *Emile* he does propose—again not unproblematically—that maternal care has the capacity to "bring everyone back to his first duties," evoking a link between care and morality (1979, 46).

For Marx, human flourishing is linked to "institutional practices and specific patterns of intersubjective interaction that allow the genuine realisation of human potential," understood in terms of a meaningful form of labour distinct from the alienation of modern capitalist work practices (Varga and Gallagher 2012, 246). On his analysis, capitalist society fosters institutional practices and patterns of interaction that prevent this potential, which involves a creative relationship between self and world, from growing and being realised. Marx didn't offer any sustained reflection on reproduction and care in his thinking, but an important part of the institutional practices that oil the wheels of capitalist production is the family form that accompanies its development. This is a family form characterised by oedipal structures of identification, forms of intersubjective interaction that take their name from and reach back towards another myth, *Oedipus Rex*. The forms of knowledge and subjectivity that Oedipus inaugurates are very different to those of Cura. Here autonomy is privileged over heteronomy and reason over relation. The next chapter will unpack the relationship between Oedipus, reason, capitalism and the effacement of care that renders Winnicott's work part of a subversive genealogy. It will explore why Cura, and her central place in healthy life, has long been relegated to the shadows of philosophy and society.

References

Abram, Jan. 2007. *The Language of Winnicott a Dictionary of Winnicott's Use of Words*. London: Karnac.
———. 2012. 'The Evolution of Winnicott's Theoretical Matrix: A Brief Outline'. In *Donald Winnicott Today*, edited by Jan Abram, 73–112. The New Library of Psychoanalysis. London; New York: Routledge.
Alford, C. Fred. 1989. *Melanie Klein and Critical Social Theory: An Account of Politics, Art, and Reason Based on Her Psychoanalytic Theory*. New Haven: Yale University Press.
Aristotle. 2000. *Nicomachean Ethics*. Edited and translated by Roger Crisp. Cambridge; New York: Cambridge University Press.
Apollodorus, and C. Julius Hyginus. 2007. *Apollodorus' Library and Hyginus' Fabulae: Two Handbooks of Greek Mythology*. Translated by R. Scott Smith and Stephen Trzaskoma. Indianapolis, IN: Hackett Publishing.
Caldwell, Lesley. 2013. 'Foreword'. In *Little Madnesses: Winnicott, Transitional Phenomena and Cultural Experience*, edited by Annette Kuhn, xv–xx. London; New York: I.B. Tauris.
Darwall, Stephen L. 2002. *Welfare and Rational Care*. Princeton, NJ: Princeton University Press.
Eigen, Michael. 2005. *Psychic Deadness*. Repr. London: Karnac.
Erikson, Erik Homburger, and Joan Mowat Erikson. 1998. *The Life Cycle Completed*. Extended version. New York: W.W. Norton.
Flynn, Thomas. 1980. 'Angst and Care in the Early Heidegger: The Ontic/Ontologic Aporia'. *International Studies in Philosophy* 12 (1): 61–76.
Freud, Sigmund. 1895. 'The Psychotherapy of Hysteria'. In *SE 2*, 253–305.
———. 1907. 'Delusions and Dreams in Jensen's "Gradiva"'. In *SE 9*, 7–95.
———. 1923. 'Two Encyclopaedia Articles'. In *SE 18*, 235.
Frosh, Stephen. 1999. *The Politics of Psychoanalysis: An Introduction to Freudian and Post-Freudian Theory*. Basingstoke: Macmillan.

Goethe, Johann Wolfgang von. 2009. *Faust: The Second Part of the Tragedy*. Edited and translated by David Constantine. London: Penguin.
Green, André. 2005. *On Private Madness*. London: Hogarth.
Greenberg, Jay, and Stephen A. Mitchell. 1983. *Object Relations in Psychoanalytic Theory*. Cambridge, MA: Harvard University Press.
Guntrip, Henry James Samuel. 1973. *Psychoanalytic Theory, Therapy, and the Self*. New York: Basic Books.
Harcourt, Edward. 2015. 'The Place of Psychoanalysis in the History of Ethics'. *Journal of Moral Philosophy* 12 (5): 598–618. https://doi.org/10.1163/174 55243-4681030.
Hollway, Wendy. 2006. *The Capacity to Care: Gender and Ethical Subjectivity*. London; New York: Routledge.
Honderich, Ted, ed. 2005. *The Oxford Companion to Philosophy*. Oxford; New York: Oxford University Press.
Honneth, Axel. 2007. *Disrespect: The Normative Foundations of Critical Theory*. Cambridge: Polity Press.
Kierkegaard, Søren. 2001. *Johannes Climacus: Or: A Life of Doubt*. Translated by T. H. Croxall. London: Serpent's Tail.
Klein, Melanie. 1975. 'A Contribution to the Psychogenesis of Manic Depressive States'. In *Love, Guilt and Reparation*, 262–89. London: Virago.
Laplanche, Jean, and J. B. Pontalis. 1988. *The Language of Psychoanalysis*. Translated by Donald Nicholson-Smith. London: Karnac.
Lear, Jonathan. 1991. *Love and Its Place in Nature*. New York: Noonday Press.
———. 1998. *Open Minded: Working out the Logic of the Soul*. Cambridge, MA; London: Harvard University Press.
———. 2001. *Happiness, Death, and the Remainder of Life*. Cambridge, MA: Harvard University Press.
Lomas, Peter. 1999. *Doing Good?: Psychotherapy Out of Its Depth*. Cambridge; New York: Oxford University Press.
MacIntyre, Alasdair C. 2006. *Dependent Rational Animals: Why Human Beings Need the Virtues*. Chicago: Open Court.
———. 2011. *After Virtue: A Study in Moral Theory*. London: Bloomsbury.
May, Rollo. 2007. *Love and Will*. New York: W.W. Norton.
McNeill, John Thomas. 1977. *A History of the Cure of Souls*. New York: Harper and Row.
Mitchell, Juliet. 2009. 'Using Winnicott'. In *Emotion: New Psychosocial Perspectives*, edited by Shelley Day-Sclater, David W. Jones, Heather Price, and Candida Yates, 46–56. New York; Basingstoke: Palgrave Macmillan.

Nussbaum, Martha C. 1994. *The Therapy of Desire: Theory and Practice in Hellenistic Ethics*. Princeton, NJ: Princeton University Press.

———. 2004. *Hiding from Humanity: Disgust, Shame, and the Law*. Princeton, NJ: Princeton University Press.

Ogden, Thomas. 1992. 'The Dialectically Constituted/Decentred Subject of Psychoanalysis: II. The Contributions of Klein and Winnicott.' *The International Journal of Psychoanalysis* 73 (4): 613–26.

Phillips, Adam. 1994. *On Kissing, Tickling, and Being Bored: Psychoanalytic Essays on the Unexamined Life*. Harvard University Press.

———. 2007. *Winnicott*. London: Penguin.

Phillips, Judith. 2007. *Care*. Cambridge; Malden, MA: Polity.

Rayner, Eric. 1991. *The Independent Mind in British Psychoanalysis*. New Jersey, NY: J. Aronson.

Reich, Warren Thomas. 2004. 'Care'. In *Encyclopedia of Bioethics*, edited by Stephen Garrard Post, 348–59. New York: Macmillan Reference USA.

Rieff, Philip. 1966. *The Triumph of the Therapeutic: Uses of Faith After Freud*. London: Chatto and Windus.

Roudinesco, Elisabeth. 2003. *Why Psychoanalysis?* Translated by Rachel Bowlby. New York; Chichester: Columbia University Press.

Rousseau, Jean-Jacques. 1979. *Emile: Or, On Education*. Edited and translated by Allan Bloom. New York: Basic Books.

———. 1984. *A Discourse on Inequality*. Translated by Maurice Cranston. London: Penguin.

Rudnytsky, Peter L. 1991. *The Psychoanalytic Vocation: Rank, Winnicott, and the Legacy of Freud*. New Haven, CT: Yale University Press.

Rustin, Michael. 1991. *The Good Society and the Inner World: Psychoanalysis, Politics, and Culture*. London; New York: Verso.

———. 2001. *Reason and Unreason: Psychoanalysis, Science, and Politics*. London; New York: Continuum.

Shklar, Judith N. 1972. 'Subversive Genealogies'. *Daedalus* 101 (1): 129–54.

Sprengnether, Madelon. 1990. *The Spectral Mother: Freud, Feminism, and Psychoanalysis*. Ithaca: Cornell University Press.

Stiegler, Bernard. 2013. *What Makes Life Worth Living: On Pharmacology*. Translated by Daniel Ross. Cambridge; Malden, MA: Polity.

Threadcraft, Shatema. 2016. *Intimate Justice: The Black Female Body and the Body Politic*. New York: Oxford University Press.

Tronto, Joan C. 1993. *Moral Boundaries: A Political Argument for an Ethic of Care*. New York: Routledge.

Varga, Somogy, and Shaun Gallagher. 2012. 'Critical Social Philosophy, Honneth and the Role of Primary Intersubjectivity'. *European Journal of Social Theory* 15 (2): 243–60. https://doi.org/10.1177/1368431011423606.

Waddell, Margot. 2002. *Inside Lives: Psychoanalysis and the Growth of the Personality*. London: Karnac.

Winnicott, Donald W. 1958a. 'Aggression in Relation to Emotional Development'. In *Collected Papers: Through Paediatrics to Psycho-Analysis*, 204–18. London: Tavistock.

———. 1958b. *Collected Papers: Through Paediatrics to Psycho-Analysis*. London: Tavistock.

———. 1958c. 'Hate in the Countertransference'. In *Collected Papers: Through Paediatrics to Psycho-Analysis*, 194–203. London: Tavistock.

———. 1958d. 'Paediatrics and Psychiatry'. In *Collected Papers: Through Paediatrics to Psycho-Analysis*, 157–73. London: Tavistock.

———. 1958e. 'Primary Maternal Preoccupation'. In *Collected Papers: Through Paediatrics to Psycho-Analysis*, 300–305. London: Tavistock.

———. 1986. 'Cure'. In *Home Is Where We Start From: Essays by a Psychoanalyst*, 112–20. Harmondsworth: Penguin.

———. 1987. 'Communication between Infant and Mother, and Mother and Infant, Compared and Contrasted'. In *Babies and Their Mothers*, 89–103. Reading, MA: Addison-Wesley.

———. 1988. *Human Nature*. New York: Routledge.

———. 1990a. 'Ego Distortion in Terms of True and False Self'. In *The Maturational Processes and the Facilitating Environment*, 140–52. London: Karnac and the Institute of Psycho-Analysis.

———. 1990b. 'Ego Integration in Child Development'. In *The Maturational Processes and the Facilitating Environment*, 56–63. London: Karnac and the Institute of Psycho-Analysis.

———. 1990c. 'From Dependence Towards Independence in the Development of the Individual'. In *The Maturational Processes and the Facilitating Environment*, 83–92. London: Karnac and the Institute of Psycho-Analysis.

———. 1990d. 'The Development of the Capacity for Concern'. In *The Maturational Processes and the Facilitating Environment*, 73–82. London: Karnac and the Institute of Psycho-Analysis.

———. 1990e. 'The Theory of the Parent-Infant Relationship'. In *The Maturational Processes and the Facilitating Environment: Studies in the Theory of Emotional Development*, 37–55. London: Karnac and the Institute of Psycho-Analysis.

———. 1991a. 'Creativity and Its Origins'. In *Playing and Reality*, 65–85. London: Routledge.

———. 1991b. 'Interrelating Apart from Instrinctual Drive and in Terms of Cross-Identifications'. In *Playing and Reality*, 119–37. London: Routledge.

———. 1991c. 'Mirror-Role of Mother and Family in Child Development'. In *Playing and Reality*, 111–18. London: Routledge.

———. 1991d. *Playing and Reality*. London: Routledge.

———. 1991e. 'Tailpiece'. In *Playing and Reality*, 151. London: Routledge.

———. 1991f. 'The Location of Cultural Experience'. In *Playing and Reality*, 95–103. London: Routledge.

———. 1991g. 'The Use of an Object and Relating Through Identifications'. In *Playing and Reality*, 86–94. London: Routledge.

Young-Bruehl, Elisabeth. 2011. 'Psychoanalysis and Social Democracy: A Tale of Two Developments'. *Contemporary Psychoanalysis* 47 (2): 179–203. https://doi.org/10.1080/00107530.2011.10746450.

Zournazi, Mary, and Julia Kristeva. 2002. 'Joyful Revolt: A Conversation with Julia Kristeva'. In *Hope: New Philosophies for Change*, 64–77. Annandale, NSW: Pluto Press Australia.

3

Oedipus and Capitalism: Denying Dependence, Effacing Care

Against the idea of the autonomous individual whose concerns revolve around himself and is always hailed as the epitome of social progress and individual freedom, we can ask what this celebration of the individual obfuscates: who does the work to allow for this individual to emerge and thrive? On whose assistive labour does this depend? How and why is this assistive labour so often rendered invisible? (Dowling 2021, 30)

If there is no true recognition of the mother's part, then there may remain a vague fear of dependence. (D. W. Winnicott 1991, 10)

The origins of the tendency to elide care and deny dependence can be traced back to Ancient Greece. Where the myth of Cura underlines relationality and the heteronomous origins of the self, the myth of Oedipus, as recounted in Sophocles *Oedipus Rex*, inaugurates and emblematises a tradition of thinking that centres the individual and the isolated ego. Noting that, in myth and culture, becoming a man means ceasing to be your mother's child, Jean-Joseph Goux explores the significance of Oedipus' encounter with the Sphinx (1993, 42). The Sphinx poses a riddle to Oedipus: what walks on four legs in the morning, two legs in the daytime and three legs in the evening? Using "sheer intelligence," an autodidactic form of knowing that does not call on help from the Gods, Oedipus provides the correct answer: "man" (16). Goux highlights that, for the Greeks, to triumph without help from the Gods represents an act of madness and arrogance (14). Oedipus uses reason alone to defeat the Sphinx, a gesture that sets him on a tragic course towards patricide and incest, whilst concurrently shaping a posture that will come to characterise the modern subject (82). The desire to know the mother anticipates the penetrative logic of modern knowledge, whilst the killing of the father prefigures a form of sovereign power that is answerable to none. Oedipus represents a new Hellenic subject, for whom reason is primary, and a new model of the philosopher, who depends on no one and nothing but himself, and discovers the truth through individual reflection (Goux 1993, 84, 111). His response to the Sphinx places the ego at the centre of knowledge and the world, replacing an aspective relation with the world into a perspectival encounter in which the world is objectivised (119–124). Freud interprets the death of the Sphinx as a substitute for the killing of the father, but Goux foregrounds that Oedipus does not kill the Sphinx—whom Jung links to the figure of the mother—rather she commits suicide following his display of rational mastery. Nevertheless, Oedipus' victory over the monster constitutes a form of matricide. For Goux, "the sphinx…remains uninterpretable in the Freudian code. The Sphinx is the unthought element of Freudian psychoanalysis, a riddle unresolved by the Freudian movement. And one that for structural reasons cannot be resolved, for its solution would threaten the entire Freudian edifice" (23). Matricide, he writes, is "the great unthought element of Freudian doctrine" (27).

It is hard not to read Goux's claims about Oedipus, matricide and the anthropocentring modern subject as a kind of origin story for the denial of dependence and effacement of care that has characterised "Western" modernity. Oedipus' triumph over the Sphinx ushers in a way of thinking that denies heteronomy (the role of others, in this case Gods and mothers), replacing the ideas of dependence and relation with individualised reason and autonomy. The nineteenth-century Swiss scholar, Johann Jacob Bachofen suggests that the identity thinking characteristic of modernity was established by the Greeks, who favoured a patriarchal social organisation in opposition to the matriarchal culture of the

Minoan civilisation of Crete, which flourished before it (Sprengnether 1990). This move, from the maternal to the paternal, signified and enshrined the ascendance of the "masculine" principle of separation and autopoiesis over material dependence (Goux 1993). Drawing on the work of Marilyn Arthur, Linda Nicholson highlights that, in archaic Greek society, "the rise of the Greek city state, the polis, was directly related to the emergence of the oikos or household" (1986, 115). Arthur describes the oikos as "a small holding corporation composed of the male head, his wife, their children, and the slaves who served it and worked the land" (cited in Nicholson 1986, 115). Thus, the ascendance of the principle of reason and separation takes shape in a patriarchal society that secures the power of men by denying heteronomy and dependence on others.

Though the origins of this tendency can be traced to Ancient Greece and linked to the social relations that arose there, its proliferation occurs in the context of modernity. In his early work, Jacques Lacan offers a classic psychoanalytic critique of the autonomous ego, a figure synonymous with the philosophical subject that dominates in modernity. At the beginning of Seminar II, dating from 1953, Lacan asserts that the ego has been "acquired over the course of history" (1988, 4). It emerges with modernity and is articulated in the philosophy of Descartes (6). Lacan sees the ego as the "fundamental illusion of man's experience, or at least of modern man," and his work constitutes a historically grounded critique of the modern ego, which considers itself to be the centre and ground of meaning, creation, and knowledge (4). Theresa Brennan suggests that Lacan provides "a lever for thinking through the trajectory of modernity," as his work foregrounds the psychosocial character of modern discourse and domination (1993, 7).

For Lacan, the work of the French philosopher Rene Descartes serves as synecdoche and inauguration point for the paranoid subject endemic to modern philosophy and modernity itself. In Mladen Dolar's words, "Lacan largely defined his project with the slogan announcing a 'return to Freud,' but subsequently it turned out that this slogan had to be complemented with a corollary: the return to Freud had to pass by way of a return to Descartes" (1998, 14). Cartesian philosophy imagines the relationship between the mind and the world in terms of detachment and mastery. Descartes' view is premised on the idea that the mind is like a mirror, containing representations of the world that can be made more accurate through inspection, repair and polishing (Rorty 1980, 12). Instigating a practice of radical critique, Descartes sought the true foundations for knowledge by stripping away all that could be doubted, including the material world made available via the senses. Negating the external world, and even his own body, Descartes famously arrived at the indubitable: the fact of his own thinking, captured in the famous dictum, "I am thinking, therefore I exist," or cogito ergo sum (Descartes 2006, 29). The capacity to think here offers certainty, foregrounding an anthropocentric conception of both knowledge and subjectivity that can be traced back to Oedipus. The mind—self-present and transparent, rational and certain—comes to be seen as the subject and source of knowledge, and the material world becomes an object that the singular, separate mind contemplates and comes to know.

Given the ways in which the modern subject finds its roots in *Oedipus Rex*, how should we conceptualise the relationship between Oedipus and the effacement of care in modernity? In what follows, this chapter provides a historical account of the privatisation of care and reproduction and charts the psychic mechanisms through which dependence and care are effaced. The family form that comes to the fore in modernity is central to the privatisation of dependence and care. In turn, the family and the Oedipus complex to which it gives rise, are essential to the psychic repudiation of care and the proliferation of the modern subject, as well as the anthropocentric forms of knowledge associated with it. The chapter concludes by exploring the significance of Winnicott's work in providing an alternative to Oedipus that foregrounds the insights held in the myth of Cura that Oedipus both effaces and displaces.

Capitalism, the Family and the Privatisation of Dependence

The development of the idea of the isolated individual, the dominant conception of subjectivity in modernity, cannot be understood without reference to the modern family form, which takes shape in relation to changes in production in the transition from feudalism to capitalism. Opening their account of the "world history" of the family, Jo Maynes and Anne Waltner state that "the family is a historical institution, not a natural one. Families both have a history and make history" (2012, ix). Maynes and Waltner here underscore the dialectical relationship between familial structures and historical change. Not only do ideas of what constitutes a family change over time, families—in whatever form—play a role in shaping history itself. This might be a case of warring dynasties and empires, of shifting territories and allegiances, but from a more materialist perspective, this idea evokes the inherent relationship between the institution of the family and the far-reaching social changes that have taken place over the last six hundred years as part of the development of capitalism.

As Michèle Barrett and Mary McIntosh put it, "there can be no simple history of *the* Western family since the sixteenth century, because there is not, nor ever has been, a single family system" (2015, 81). Nevertheless, the family played a series of important roles in the transition to capitalism. Engels connects the private, monogamous family form to the development of private property, as the necessary mechanism through which inheritance can be guaranteed (2010, 96–97). In Marxian theory, the early stages of capitalism, dating from the fifteenth century, are characterised by a period of primitive accumulation, in which the capital that underwrites the later proliferation of capitalism accrues. For the upper and middle classes, property gave the husband power over his wife and children. Lawrence Stone highlights that, for the upper levels of English society, between 1500 and 1700, the importance of the "nuclear core" increased "not as a unit of habitation but as a state of mind" (1990, 93). The English state in the sixteenth century established its power by transferring the idea of good lordship from its association with the head of the extended kin network to the individual male head of the household, encouraging patriarchy within the family on the basis and principle of ownership (Nicholson 1986, 118). During this period, there was a shift from feudal patriarchy and external religious authority to the authority of the father, as the symbol of patriarchy within the home. In the new and emerging bourgeois family, the husband became the representative of the state, with the role of disciplining and managing the "subordinate" classes, including wives and children. In many ways, the family became a micro-state or micro-church (L. Stone 1990, 104–5).

The status and activities of women were affected in the process, as their behaviour became subject to increasing surveillance and control to ensure the transmission of property to the "rightful" heirs of the male head of the household. Carole Pateman highlights that the new social contract that took shape in this period was premised on a sexual contract that gave men rights over the bodies of women and ownership of their children (1988). At that time, the family began to separate from the public sphere and to acquire connotations as a centre for the reproduction of the family line. Women's role was increasingly restricted to domestic duties, including the reproduction and care of children. A woman in the urban, commercial class in Tudor England was "a socially integrated, socially important individual, whose life experiences were not utterly different from those of a man" (George 1973, 156). She was educated and took an active role in business. However, by the end of the seventeenth century, "middle-class female withdrawal…from business and productive enterprise" had become the norm (156). The institutionalisation of the patriarchal nuclear family led to the restriction of women to the home and to their increasing financial dependence of this class of women on men.

Maria Mies writes that "in the fifteenth and sixteenth centuries…the old European order collapsed and 'there came to be a European world economy based on the capitalist mode of production'" (2014, 79). The process of accumulation, which the upper-class family form safeguarded via inheritance and primogeniture, depended on the expropriation and enclosure of land in Europe and, from the late fifteenth century, colonisation of land in the Americas and beyond (Linebaugh 2014; Linebaugh and Rediker 2012). Ellen Meiksins Wood notes that "for millennia, human beings have provided for their material needs by working the land. And probably for nearly as long…they have been divided into classes, between those who worked the land and those who appropriated the labour of others" (2002, 95). In non-capitalist economies, direct producers, generally peasants, usually control their means of reproduction—the land—and exploiters, landlords, use "extra-economic" powers in order to extract a surplus, through taxation and rents, for instance (95). However,

> Only in capitalism is the dominant mode of appropriation based on the complete dispossession of direct producers, who (unlike chattel slaves) are legally free and whose surplus labour is appropriated by purely 'economic' means. Because direct producers in a fully developed capitalism are propertyless, and because their only access to the means of production, to the requirements of their own reproduction, even to the means of their own labour, is the sale of their labour-power in exchange for a wage, capitalists can appropriate the workers' surplus labour without direct coercion. (96)

Because direct producers in capitalism (workers) lack access to the land, shelter and food that they need to reproduce their lives, they must work in order to secure the means to their own reproduction.

Meiksins Wood links the origins of this practice to the specific political situation in England in the sixteenth century. The English state was fairly centralised by this time, and this depended on alliances between the monarchy and aristocracy, which meant that landlords had less freedom than in other areas of Europe to impose their own taxes and "extra-economic" means in order to extract surplus from the peasants. Therefore, it was necessary for them to find alternative ways of doing so. Given that the majority of land was held by relatively few big landlords, they were able to use their property in new and distinctive ways. In order to increase their wealth, landlords compelled their tenants to produce more and more (99–100). This led to a situation where land was increasingly seized under the guise of "modernisation" and the need for "improvement." In fact, "to improve" land initially meant to cultivate it for profit. In this way, Meiksins Wood argues, the logic of capitalism was born.

Silvia Federici suggests that the enclosure of land, which was underway across Europe by the sixteenth century, was driven by the population crisis that resulted after the Black Death, as landlords frantically attempted to secure their wealth by ostensibly increasing the profitability of their land (2014, 68–75). This desire also spurred the voyages of exploration of the late fifteenth century, through which the European aristocracy sought to grow their wealth and obtain gold to pay the increased wages of the newly powerful, because numerically reduced, peasants. The enclosure of land was also a way, however, to control peasant populations by denying them the means through which to reproduce themselves. Use of the commons and the open field system had allowed peasant populations to sustain themselves and to resist the worst dominations of the lords, who could not starve them into work should the peasants resist their demands. Under the new system of land privatisation, however, the loss of the land meant that the peasants lost their traditional abilities for self-determination. Whilst the peasants had depended on the land as their primary means of sustaining life, enclosure made them increasingly dependent on the wage system in order to have access to the means to reproduce themselves. The process of enclosure produced a propertyless class who no longer possessed the means of their own reproduction, which also led to the growth of vagrancy.

Whilst the accumulation and transmission of property made the control of women a renewed imperative for the wealthy, the institution of the family secured the means of reproduction more broadly. Juliet Mitchell writes that:

> Pre-capitalist society flourishes on individual private property—the peasant has his bit of land, the artisan his tools. Capitalist organisation of work deprives the individual of his private property and takes all the separate pieces of private property (land, tools, etc.) pools them and makes the newly accumulated wealth the private property of a few—the capitalists…However, individual private property for the mass of the people does continue side by said with this new process—it continues in the family. (Mitchell 2015, 153)

Though Mitchell refers to private property rather than the commons and the means of reproduction, her formulation underlines the relationship between the institution of the family and social reproduction, which can be traced to the early modern period.

Similarly to Mitchell, Federici argues that the consent of the disenfranchised and dispossessed male peasants was secured through social changes that extended control over women (2014, 98). The incipient rise of pro-natalist policies effectively brought about "the enslavement of women to procreation" in the service of capitalist accumulation (Federici 2014, 86–89; Mies 2014). Women also lost their legal right to property at this time. During the same period, women were also reconstructed as non-workers, denied access to any but the lowliest roles and increasingly excised from any role in production, as the work they undertook at home came to be cast as "non-work," even if intended for the market (92). When women were allowed to work, their husband received pay for both of their work, a move that led the authority of the husband in the family to increase considerably. Federici identifies this as the first wave of the "patriarchy of the wage" that was to return again in the nineteenth century (Federici 2014; Tilly and Scott 2016; Nicholson 1986). These moves to control women's reproduction and devalue their labour were central to a new gendered division of labour, or sexual contract, according to which women were defined in ways that "hid their status as workers, while giving men free access to [their] bodies, their labour, and the bodies and labour of their children" (Federici 2014, 97).

Perhaps most significantly, Federici writes that "proletarian women became for male workers the substitute for the land lost to the enclosures, their most basic means of reproduction, and a communal good anyone could appropriate and use at will" (97). The development of agrarian capitalism went hand in hand with the institution of the patriarchal conjugal family form because it depended on that form in order to reproduce both property relations and the workers needed to carry out production. Whilst for the upper classes, property gave the husband power over his wife, male workers were compensated for the loss of access to the land and the means to reproduce themselves that it afforded by increasingly being given power over women, whose lives were curtailed and restricted to the home in similar, though also distinct, ways to women in the aristocracy and bourgeoisie. As Horkheimer, puts it, "man, liberated from serfdom in alien households, became master of his own" (1949, 360). However, Federici is also describing here a shift from dependence on the land to dependence on the reproductive work of women which can also be characterised in terms of the privatisation of dependence through the mechanism of the family.

Nancy Fraser and Linda Gordon identify "dependence" as a keyword in political discourse (N. Fraser and Gordon 2013). "To depend" refers to "a physical relationship in which one thing hangs from another" (86). Combining economic, socio-legal and political aspects, in pre-capitalist society, dependency was conceived as a state of subordination to another, but it was a state that was commonplace and normal, constituting the prevailing social relation. In this context "women, however subordinate, shared a condition of dependency with many men" (87). However, in the transition to capitalism, dependency, which had been a state that characterised the experience of the majority, was privatised, taking on a "modern…male-supremacist usage that constructed a specifically feminine sense of dependency" that also "attaches to groups considered deviant and superfluous" (87). Women, but also colonised peoples, came to be identified with dependence, which is both a feminised and a racialised category. As dependence on the land was eroded, and women were rendered dependent on men, the home became its primary locus. As Horkheimer underscores, "when the separation of state and society, of political and private life, was completed, direct personal dependence survived in the home" (1949, 360).

Over time, the idea of dependence was increasingly excised from political and economic discourse in parallel with the coming into being of new conceptions of subjectivity that emphasised the interrelation of autonomy and independence. Fraser and Gordon note that, in the eighteenth and nineteenth centuries, or "in the age of democratic revolutions, the developing new concept of citizenship rested on independence; dependency was deemed antithetical to citizenship" (2013, 90). The burgeoning idea of the independent individual masked and disavowed the ways in which men actually depended on women, not to mention colonised, indentured and enslaved peoples and their labour, for their own reproduction and that of the family line. As Herbert Marcuse notes, the idea of the bourgeois individual necessitates the denial of dependence: "self-sufficiency and independence of all that is other and alien is the sole guarantee of the subject's freedom. What is not dependent on any other person or thing, what possesses itself, is free" (2009, 102). However, how to understand the relationship between the changing structure of social relations that the family form facilitates and the concretisation of specific ideals of subjectivity requires further exploration. How did the emergence of capitalism enshrine the psychic rejection of dependence, and cover over the work of reproduction and care assigned to women in particular?

Subjectivity, Separation and the Denial of Dependence

The intellectual traditions that dominate in modernity are defined by the idea that subjectivity depends on separation from nature and the maternal "other" representing it. In a style redolent of Luce Irigaray's hysterical mimesis, Adriana Cavarero records the views of notable philosophers on the gendered division of labour within the patriarchal family (2016). Whilst the philosophers do not dispute the role of maternal care in the raising of children, subjectivity itself—the achievement of autonomy, understood in terms of freedom from others—depends on the intervention of the paternal figure. For John Locke, for instance, it is inconceivable that the mother would play any role in bringing the child to (what he sees as) the end point of free, rational humanity. The mother remains, Cavarero writes, "a sort of stereotypical figure frozen in a timeless tradition," who "continues to occupy herself with vulnerable and dependent creatures, consigned by her natural inclination to care for the human pups" (24). It is the father, for Locke, who educates the child in discipline, and, in the process, produces the autonomous "I," which exists on the vertical axis. Likewise Kant, who worried about mothers, frightened that they might impede the subject's journey towards rational autonomy (26). The Kantian subject must free himself from the narcissistic relationship with the beautiful realm of the (m)other, journeying towards the phallic law of abstract reason and the experience of the sublime (Eagleton 1990, 90–91). Kantian theory is premised on an isolated and individual "I," offering a key foundation for the "individualistic anthropology of modernity" (Cavarero 2016, 37). Within the tradition Cavarero describes, the maternal represents a sphere of care and relation, of dependence and inclination, either unimportant or dangerous, which must be renounced at all costs.

Such ways of thinking have had a profound effect on the discourse of psychoanalysis itself. As Jessica Benjamin puts it, psychoanalytic theory often trades in the image of the liberating father, who offers protection against the "limitless narcissism" purported to characterise the pre-oedipal period (1990, 135). Freud's famous "oceanic feeling" refers to a putatively primordial experience or merger with, and dependence on, the mother, that must be overcome through a paternal identification that brings both individualisation and the possibility of cultural greatness (1930). Alison Stone highlights a link between material and maternal dependence: "in the West the self has often been understood in opposition to the maternal body, such that one must break away from the mother and maternal care-givers on whom one depends in infancy and childhood to become a full participant in the spiritual, political, or cultural values of one's community" (2012, 1). In his own early work, Jacques Lacan states that the Oedipus myth so beloved by Freud symbolises "the emancipation from matriarchal tyranny" represented by the Sphinx (2001, 58).

Though there is clearly evidence that this tendency has a long history, the cultural fantasy of the all-powerful maternal figure who must be overcome takes on a special significance in modernity, as women are restricted to the home and exclusively associated with childcare (Chodorow and Contratto 1989). Despite its origins residing in antiquity, it is the social relations of modernity that create the conditions for this way of thinking to flourish. The prerequisite for the development of the modern ideal of egocentric subjectivity is the family form, which makes possible the oedipal configuration of familial relations that allow the ideal to spread. Many scholars identify the fundamental link between the changes that take place in social relations in modernity and the development of new forms of subjectivity (Horkheimer 1949; 2002; Poster 1982; Benjamin 1978; Dews 1995; Campbell 2004). Writing in 1936, Horkheimer links the Oedipus complex to the rise of modern capitalism (2002). Similarly, in a text written in 1938, Lacan ties modern psychology to the Oedipus complex, which he links to the development of the conjugal family that "realised itself in the fifteenth century with the economic revolution that produced the bourgeois society and the psychology of modern man" (Lacan 1995, 198; 2001, 69). As already discussed, in the transition to capitalism, symbolic authority shifts from religion and feudal patriarchy to the father, the symbol of patriarchy within the home. In the process, the modern Oedipus complex is born. As Peter Dews puts it, for both Horkheimer, and Lacan, "the Oedipus complex is at the centre of a historically specific type of identity formation which emerges within the context of the patriarchal family" (1995, 55).

Horkheimer and Lacan both emphasise positive aspects of the relationship between the Oedipus complex and the development of individual subjectivity. Though in his first essay on the family, dating from 1936, Horkheimer is generally concerned with the role of the modern family form in instilling authority, he also describes what he considers to be the historical advances that it has brought about:

> At the beginning of the bourgeois age the father's control of his household was doubtless an indispensable condition of progress. The self-control of the individual, the disposition for work and discipline, the ability to hold firmly to certain ideas, consistency in practical life, application of reason, perseverance and pleasure in constructive activity could all be developed, in the circumstances, only under the dictation and guidance of the father whose own education had been won in the school of life. (2002, 101)

Horkheimer here suggests that the family form fosters individual capacities for hard work and self-control, the Protestant work ethic, through identification with the father. Lacan is less ambivalent, emphasising the productive effects of the psychological tensions produced within the conjugal family form, and by the male child's relationship with the paternal figure in particular. The father's double role as both "the agent of prohibition and the example of its transgression" presents the child with a paradoxical injunction: to be and not to be like the father (Dews 1995, 50). This paradox makes possible a mode of identification that fuses sameness and difference, making possible a process of individuation (55). For Lacan, the identity formed through the oedipal configuration is superior to other forms of identity because of the freedom it allows for individual subversion and selection of ideals, and the effect it has on creativity. The constraints dictated by the family "raises the tension of the libido to the highest degree, and increases the scope of sublimation"

(2001, 59). The conjugal family "creates superior successes of character, happiness and creation" (60). Non-patriarchal, or perhaps better non-conjugal, patterns of socialisation lead to stagnation on Lacan's account.

However, both Horkheimer and Lacan insist that, as Dews puts it, "this social form is caught up in a fateful historical dialectic" (1995, 56). For Horkheimer, despite the family's progressive functions in the early stages of capitalist development, as the capitalist formation of society becomes concretised, its role increasingly becomes that is instilling the principle of submission to external authority in its members. In the family "the child's self-will is to be broken, and the innate desire for free development of his drives and potentialities is to be replaced by an internalised compulsion toward the unconscious fulfilment of duty" (2002, 99). Through the internalisation of the paternal super-ego, the bourgeois family seeks "submission to the categorical imperative" (99). Horkheimer pays attention to the diachronic dimension of the family, charting its relation to the emergence and reproduction of capitalism: "the impulse of submission [...] is not a timeless drive," he writes, but a phenomenon emerging essentially from the limited bourgeois family" (111). Dews suggests that the father's authority in the family, "based on superior physical strength and economic power," becomes the representative of "that irrational facticity of the social in the face of which individuals would be 'irrational' to do anything other than submit" (1995, 58). However, the hollowing out of the paternal role eventually undermines his psychic function. The father becomes "an arbitrary power [who] no longer offers possibilities of identification, and the child instead identifies with repressive social instances" (Horkheimer 2002, 127). This results in "direct identification with social power" and "the spread of the malleable narcissistic personality type" (Dews 1995, 58).

By the time he returned to the topic of the family and authority in 1949, Horkheimer was convinced that the failure of the paternal function was to blame for the erosion of the critical capacities of the individual. The earlier piece emphasises the role of paternal authority in inculcating submission, now emphasis falls on the weakening of paternal authority in the context of monopoly capitalism. Horkheimer writes that.

The socially conditioned weakness of the father [...] prevents the child's real identification with him. In earlier times a loving imitation of the self-reliant, prudent man, devoted to his duty, was the source of moral autonomy in the individual. Today the growing child, who instead of the image of a father has received only the abstract idea of arbitrary power, looks for a stronger, more powerful father, as it is furnished by fascist imagery. (1949, 365)

On this analysis, the more the family's mediating role is hollowed out, and the child is directly socialised by the institutions of the state, the more susceptible the younger generation become to *any* form of authority. The older, entrepreneurial father may have forced the son to submit to "duty," but the reflection made possible by the moral law/super-ego was also a resource, the source of an autonomy which Horkheimer still viewed as the key to emancipation. "Where once the agencies of conscience, individual independence, and possible resistance against the pressure of social conformity had their place," Horkheimer laments, "the only yardstick left is that of success, popularity and influence" (369). Horkheimer makes a distinction between instrumental and substantive reason. The former is characterised by "accommodation and conformity" and the later "critical insight into social relations" (Benjamin 1978, 44). In the modern family, identification with the former is achieved, but not the later, because paternal authority has been eroded under the auspices of monopoly capitalism, taking on a merely instrumental function.

For Lacan, at a certain point in time, specifically in the twentieth century, the level of individualism produced by the oedipal structure begins to undermine the by now "highly compacted conditions of oedipal identity formation itself" (Dews 1995, 56).

> This 'anomie,' which made possible the discovery of the complex, gives rise to the degenerated form in which the analyst recognizes it: a form which we could define in terms of an incomplete repression of the desire for the mother, with a reactivation of the anxiety and curiosity inherent in the birth relation; and a narcissistic debasement of the idealisation of the father, which causes the emergence, in oedipal identification, of

the aggressive ambivalence immanent in the primordial relation to the counterpart. (Lacan 2001, 74)

The proliferation of what Lacan conceives as the "ego's era," a time of narcissistic self-absorption, domination and moral failure, is tied to the increasing failure of oedipal identification to produce the tension between identification and prohibition on which the "highest" forms of character purportedly depend. When the paternal imago is weak, as Lacan believes it to be in his own time, the energy of sublimation created by the dual paternal function is diverted from creation (Lacan cites the Enlightenment as a high point for sublimation) into an "ideal of narcissistic integrity" (Lacan 2001, 56).

Kristen Campbell argues that Lacan "repeatedly insists that the decline of the paternal function and the failure of the Oedipus complex characterise modernity" (2004, 153). The father is required to provide the son with a model for social identification and to enforce sexual repression. Yet the father in modernity is at risk of failing to adequately symbolise the paternal law he is supposed to instil. The father is "always in some way deficient—absent, humiliated, divided or false" (Lacan 1995, 200). This potential for failure means that the male child does not identify the father as the agent of repression and thus does not develop a strong paternal super-ego. Instead, the he only takes up half of the paternal law, the relation of identification. He comes to identify with the father and give up the mother not because the father tells him to, but rather in order to gain the social advantage and prestige his father, as a man, represents (Brennan 1993, 58). This form of identification allows a narcissistic, self-aggrandising, attitude to proliferate, unchecked by a moral sensibility. Whilst the masculine subject will, in general, come to identify with the father, he will only take up the ideal dimension of this relation, not its prohibition. Lacan is critical of the form of subjectivity that dominates in his own time, characterised by competition, aggression, self-love and the tendency to dominance. However, his commitment to the Oedipus complex as the main mechanism through which subjectivity is produced means that he seeks a solution in the direction of oedipal identification. "It is this being of nothingness," he writes, "for whom, in our daily task [of analysis], we clear anew the path to his meaning in a discreet fraternity" (2006, 101). As Kristen Campbell puts it, "ultimately, Lacan calls for the father" (2004, 165).

Both Horkheimer and Lacan fall back on a specific aspect of paternal internalisation as the solution to rampant individualism and narcissism. However, as Jessica Benjamin has highlighted, in Freud's work, the distinction between different aspects of the paternal function is never firmly established. She writes that "for Freud the distinction between early fear of authority—and for that matter identification—and the later internalisation of it as super-ego is never hard and fast" (1978, 50). Therefore, the claims that Horkheimer and Lacan both make for the progressive aspects of paternal authority are placed in question. As Benjamin suggests, thinkers like Horkheimer and Lacan are at pains to link critical/moral agency to the paternal function because they are committed to the idea that the father is needed to bring about individuation. They mistake the Oedipus complex's role in gender differentiation for the process of separation-individuation, which actually takes place in early relations of care (51). As a result of this assumption, the maternal function is imagined in opposition to subjectivity, and the maternal figure as one who must, and can only, be escaped through an identification with the father.

Campbell argues that identification with the father also makes possible a new form of social tie. The Oedipus complex produces a fraternal bond between brothers who have symbolically murdered the patriarch and are united by bonds of identification rather than fear and submission (Campbell 2004, 160–61). As Campbell puts it, "the decline of traditional patriarchy does not result in the dissolution of an androcentric Western culture, but instead founds its modern forms. It articulates the shift of discourse from traditional feudal society to its modern bourgeois and capitalist form" (162). The new social order is built on mutual recognition on the part of the brothers, who recognise their shared internalisation of the paternal ego-ideal. This is the liberal bond of equality, liberty and fraternity that comes to the fore in the period. As "fraternity" makes clear, this is a bond between masculine subjects who are tied together through a process of identification with each other on the basis of their shared identification with the social status of the paternal figure.

The "regime of the brother" or "social contract" is a sexuated relation that depends on and produces sexual difference, and it also presupposes a *sexual* contract (MacCannell 1991; Pateman 1988). The social contract is a modern form of authority that replaces the authority of fathers over sons, the original form of authority in society according to John Locke, with a bond between brothers. However, as Pateman points out, the authority of fathers over sons could not have been exercised without a prior sexual encounter that ultimately produced the sons over whom the father was to have authority. "Locke's first husband, like Adam," Pateman writes, "must have exercised conjugal right over his wife before he became a father. The 'original' right or government was, therefore, not paternal but conjugal. Locke had no need to mention the wife when her husband became the family's monarch. Her subjection to his rule had already secured through an earlier agreement" (1988, 93). Eventually, Locke suggests, social conditions meant that the power of father-monarchs was no longer appropriate. The sons symbolically kill the father and institute a new form of authority, the social contract, between them. In this process, the sphere of "natural subjection" is separated out as the "nonpolitical sphere" (93). Familial life is conceptualised as non-political, and the original basis of political right in conjugal right is concealed (94). In an important sense, the modern social contract depends on the effacement of the labour of women. As previously mentioned, Federici links Pateman's description of the sexual contract to the power men gained over women in the transition to capitalism (2014, 97, 129–30). The family form which developed as part of that transition gave fathers increased power, leading to the production of new forms of subjectivity premised on paternal identification. Ultimately, this created the social and psychic conditions for the development of the modern, fraternal, social contract.

At the same time, the Oedipus complex constitutes the psychic mechanism through which the labour performed by women came to be effaced. Benjamin and Campbell both convincingly argue that the modern masculine subject comes into being by repudiating ontological dependence or "lack" (Benjamin 1990, 133–82; Campbell 2004, 59–77). Benjamin argues that, rather than carrying out the task of differentiation it is putatively assigned, the Oedipus complex actually leads to the non-recognition of maternal subjectivity, and the work of care that has been carried out in the early caregiver-child relationship (1990, 135). Benjamin is concerned to account for how the ideas of merger with and separation from caregivers have become so powerful in both philosophy and psychoanalysis. She argues that the idea of merger with the mother is actually a retroactive construction that comes about in response to the oedipal demand that children assume the culturally determined position of man or woman. Rather than producing the differentiation that it is assigned in traditional psychoanalytic theory, the Oedipus complex actually produces the non-recognition of maternal subjectivity (133). At the oedipal moment, the male child not only disidentifies with the mother, but actually repudiates both her and all feminine attributes (135). The repudiation of femininity is embodied in the paternal ideal of separation, formed under the current gender arrangements. The child's fear of the father's power (which is based on social power) is mitigated through identification with him, and the fear that previously attached to that relationship is displaced onto the mother, who becomes a dangerous figure. In order for the masculine ideal of separation to be achieved, all forms of relation have to be repudiated, and what was a relation of mutual recognition with the maternal caregiver breaks down. The rigid splitting between separation and merger takes its place, the latter associated with women and retroactively projected onto early experiences of care, which are no longer conceived as nurturant and capable of playing any role in the development of subjectivity or the achievement of differentiation (168). The female child is called to identify with femininity and henceforth tied to a mode of relatedness that is denigrated within the wider culture, which privileges masculine values of separation and autonomy. This process of splitting also enacts a retroactive failure to recognise and acknowledge the maternal caregiver's subjectivity, and the role of that subjectivity in the process of differentiation and individuation. As Johanna Meehan puts it, "the denial of *the other's* subjectivity becomes a necessary moment and gives rise to the fiction of the bourgeois autonomous subject giving birth to itself, a fiction the psychoanalytic tradition shares with the philosophical one" (1995, 235).

The repudiation of "feminine" qualities, including dependence, nurturance and relation, by the masculine subject allows the illusion of the autarkic, individual subject to come into existence. Similarly to Benjamin, Campbell reconstructs Lacan's social theory in order to demonstrate the link between modern subjectivity and the denial of dependence (2004, 65–77). On her analysis, the masculine subject's capacity to identify with the "unary trait" of the phallus, symbolised by the father's penis, underwrites that subject's sense of its own Oneness, completion and mastery (Lacan 2008, 154). This identification permits the denial of ontological lack, and its projection onto feminised and racialised others. This is a tendency that Brennan identifies as latent in the structures of thinking common in Europe since antiquity, but it is unleashed by the shifting organisation of social relations in modernity (1993).

The proliferation of this tendency is only possible because of the privatisation of the work of reproduction and care that happens during this period. The family form that takes shape in modernity, which secures the appropriation of women's labour and modern gendered relations of power, creates a situation in which the male child seeks to be like *the father*, because *he* holds social power. The character of that identification, however, underwrites a form of subjectivity capable of denying lack and dependence. Identification with the unary trait of the phallus, and with (br)others who have also internalised this ideal, creates an illusion of independence and mastery, one premised on the projection of dependence elsewhere: onto the feminine/private sphere and racialised/colonised others (Benjamin 1990, 187). The modern subject repudiates its dependence on a feminine (m)Other in order to secure its illusory freedom. Masculine dominance in modernity is scaffolded by the family form, which also creates the conditions for the psychic refusal to acknowledge the work of care and reproduction on which capitalism depends.

The Oedipus complex produces specific forms of both subjectivity and knowledge. The repudiation of care, and knowledge of its central role in psychic development, which is the outcome of the Oedipus complex, leads to the proliferation of ideals of subjectivity in which early care becomes invisible. The masculine subject's identification with the unary trait, and with the instrumental qualities of separation, detachment and objectification that are associated with the masculine role, produces a dominant ideal of subjectivity characterised by independence and alienation from others and the world. This way of thinking in turn feeds back into and facilitates the spread of capitalism, which conceives the world and the people who live in it as objects to be exploited. In his later work, Lacan uses his new conception of discourse as social tie in order to theorise the interdependent forms of subjectivity and knowledge characteristic of modernity. For Lacan, the modern subject gives rise to its own unique form of knowledge, one characterised by particular ways of relating. The Discourse of the Master is the discourse of the universal, self-generating and autonomous individual (2008). The modern subject, or Master, sees himself as universal because he can only imagine the world and others as reflections and extensions of himself. This gives rise to the tendency in modern knowledge to universalise from his perspective, the perspective of the masculine subject. Additionally, the Master's sense of his own importance leads to the failure to recognise, and the repudiation of, otherness and difference. The Master seeks to control both objects and himself, and to impose his own image on the world. Campbell writes that:

> While Lacan perceives the modern subject as emerging with the conjugal family of the fifteenth century, his later work ascribes the later emergence of the Discourse of the Master to the sixteenth and seventeenth centuries. Linking these accounts of the emergence of the modern form of the family and the Discourse of the Master, it seems that this discourse emerges in the earlier social shifts of the fifteenth century before it stabilises and then fully develops with the rise of modern imperialist capitalist media society. (2004, 157)

The Discourse of the Master, the contemporary social discourse of competition and domination, is inherently linked to the shifts in social relations tied to the early stages of capitalism and the logic of "improvement" that characterised that period. The enclosure of land, in Europe and beyond, which began in the fifteenth century made new forms of accumulation possible and led to the solidification of new forms of patriarchal authority centred on the home. The family form, premised on the control of women and the appropriation of their labour, produced a new kind of masculine subject characterised by identification with paternal power and the instrumental principles with which the father was associated. The modern masculine subject's repudiation of femininity and relatedness underwrites, in turn, a new norm of objectivising, universalising knowledge. As Benjamin insists, prefiguring Campbell's reconstruction of Lacan, "the structure of gender domination is [...] materialised in the rationality that pervades our economic and social relations" (1990, 187). However, modern forms of gender domination are also intimately linked with the practices of improvement used to justify enclosure in the early modern period.

Ways Out: Towards a New Symbolic

Campbell suggests that the way out of the Discourse of the Master and the society it produces depends on the rearticulation of the relationship between the development of subjectivity and the maternal figure. "We need," she writes, "to represent the relation to the mother as other than a founding sacrifice" (2004, 174). Feminist discourse must reposition the mother not as a "maternal object" but as a "social subject," which in turn facilitates the representation of the maternal relation as "a relation between two speaking subjects, rather than between a subject and an object…so it is not predicated on the sacrifice of the maternal object" (175). For Campbell, this has the advantage of dislodging the maternal figure from the position of lost object, the quest for which structures the knowledge of the Knowing Master, and it also provides women—and others—with a "symbolic relation to the mother" and a "socially powerful maternal identificatory figure" (175–76).

Rehabilitating the mother from "the shadows of our culture" has been a project within feminist psychoanalysis for some time (Irigaray 1991, 35). Theorists such as Luce Irigaray have been keen to point out that "the maternal function underpins the social order" (36). Denied full theoretical consideration, maternal care has been aligned with self-preservation and need, and refused an understanding in terms of desire. In Irigaray's opinion, the paternal law forbids not only the child's desire for the mother, but also the mother's desire itself. In its early dependence on the father, psychoanalysis elided the question of maternal subjectivity and its role in development, colluding in the desubjectivisation, or objectification, of women in the maternal role. Whilst father may wish to be "the sole creator," the potential generative capacity of the mother and maternal subjectivity has become key questions for feminist psychoanalysis (Irigaray 1991, 41; Benjamin 1990; 1994; Jacobs 2007).

Amber Jacobs has asked an important question of psychoanalysis and its investment in myth: why *only* Oedipus? (2007, 47). Jacobs reads Aeschylus's *Oresteia* in search of a supplement to the psychoanalytic preoccupation with *Oedipus Rex*, one that might permit an understanding of the maternal subject position and the possibility of a symbolically mediated mother-daughter relation. *On Matricide* explores the relationship that might pertain between the maternal body and structuration, the possibility of a "maternal structural function" (31). Jacobs concludes that the maternal law haunts us, denied its place through an act of incorporation which leaves intact a fantasy of parthenogenesis—the idea that men can make babies alone (124). However, the maternal law underlines the impossibility of parthenogenesis, reiterating the centrality of others, here mothers in particular, for the possibility of generativity. The care associated with mothers and other primary caregivers might be effaced, as it has been in much modern philosophy and some psychoanalytic theory, but it cannot be escaped. Lisa Baraitser and Alison Stone have also produced accounts of maternal ethics and subjectivity that foreground the vital significance of maternal subjectivity in care and development (Baraitser 2009; A. Stone 2012). Campbell does not discuss Benjamin's work in this context, but her thinking—which draws extensively on Winnicott—contributes towards the creation of a new socio-symbolic capable of recognising maternal figures as subjects.

In his theoretical account of psychic development, Winnicott places immense emphasis on the character of the care that primary caregivers, for him generally mothers, provide to children. This has led some feminist scholars to criticise him for relentlessly associating women with motherhood, whilst leading others to express concern about the potential for his ideas to shore up the existing gendered division of labour by insisting on the naturalness of maternal care, and the benefits of a close relationship with one primary carer (S. Alexander 2013, 154; Doane and

Hodges 1993; Gerson 2004; J. Rose 2004). Jane Flax, whose work has been deeply influenced by object relations perspectives, acknowledges the approach's gender blindness, which, she suggests, "can be accounted for by the fact that the theorists take for granted the existing sexual division of labour in which the mother or other women do primary caretaking" (1991, 121). Similarly, Carolyn Dever criticises Winnicott specifically for his failure to acknowledge the relationship between "women's psychological power and their historical, social and economic struggles" (1998, 73). The near-absolute power that maternal caregivers are perceived to have over their offspring is the flipside of a historical process that restricted women consistently (if unevenly) to the private sphere, and aligned them ideologically with reproduction and caregiving. As Doane and Hodges put it, "object-relations theory...mystifies the construction of the mother–child dyad by defining that dyad as an origin" (1993, 34). For many scholars, the failure to account for the history of the mother–child dyad or the inequality inscribed by the gendered division of labour condemns Winnicott's work, and object relations theory more broadly, as forms of ideological mystification.

It is certainly true that Winnicott does not historicise the mother–child relationship that is at the heart of his theory of subjective development and his conception of flourishing. It is also true that the immense psychic power that Winnicott attributes to mothers cannot be understood in isolation from the social relations of modernity. For some feminist scholars, however, Winnicott's work provides an important supplement to the version of subjectivity that dominates in modernity, characterised by independence, individuality and a rationally grounded autonomy, or, in Adriana Cavarero's ingenious conceptualisation, an isolated and singular "rectitude" (2016). This subject takes shape by repudiating and disavowing care and reproduction; the work of feminised and racialised others, upon the exploitation of whom its existence depends. Winnicott's preoccupation with the maternal role foregrounds the activity of caregivers in infantile development, and brings the labour involved in that care to the fore, contributing to challenging the effect of its concealment on, and in, philosophy and modernity (Chodorow 1978; Irigaray 1985; Benjamin 1990; Flax 1991). As Janet Sayers puts it, though with some obvious reservations about the view, "feminists have been attracted to mother-centred psychoanalysis because it apparently valorises women's work, at least as mothers" (1991, 11).

In place of a Freudian theory that confuses the gender identification that occurs at the oedipal stage with individuation, Benjamin appeals to object relations theory for resources for thinking "a maternal nurturance that actually encourages autonomy" (1978, 51). She writes that:

> Psychoanalysis has shifted its focus since Freud, aiming its sights at ever earlier phases of development in childhood and infancy. This reorientation has had many repercussions: it has given the mother-child dyad an importance in psychic development rivalling the oedipal triangle, and consequently it has stimulated a new theoretical construction of individual development. This shift from oedipal to pre-oedipal—that is from father to mother—can actually be said to have changed the entire frame of psychoanalytic thinking…the last twenty-five years have seen a flowering of psychoanalytic theories about the early growth of the self in the relationship with the other. (1990, 12)

Drawing on Winnicott's ideas, Benjamin provides an account of the development of subjectivity understood as a process of recognition that takes place through early relations of care. Benjamin identifies a variety of aspects of the relationship between the maternal caregiver and child, supplementing the recognised aspects of nursing, feeding and holding with the affective reciprocity, mutuality and attunement that make up an important part of the "the diverse responses and activities of the mother that are taken for granted as the background in all discussions of development" (27, 22). As Meehan puts it, Benjamin "describes the extralinguistic forces that propel the psychic self" (2019, 185). "The mother addresses the baby with the coordinated action of her voice, face and hands. The infant responds with his whole body, wriggling or alert, mouth agape or smiling broadly. Then they may begin a dance of interaction in which the partners are so attuned that they move together in unison" (Benjamin 1990, 27). Significantly, these experiences are capable of creating a "feeling of oneness," but this is specifically an intrapsychic experience for the child that depends on an as-yet unappreciated intersubjective situation between mother and child (27).

For Benjamin, these experiences represent early forms of recognition for the child, but they fundamentally depend on maternal subjectivity. "Recognition," she writes, "is not a sequence of events, like the phases of maturation and development, but a constant element through all events and processes" it begins.

> with the mother's ability to identify and respond to her infant's physical needs, her "knowing her baby," when he wants to sleep, eat, play alone, or play together. Indeed within a few months after birth, this so-called background becomes the foreground, the raison d'être, the meaning and the goal of being with others. As we trace the development of the infant, we can see how recognition becomes increasingly an end in itself—first an achievement of harmony, and then an arena of conflict between self and other. (22–23)

Benjamin emphasises here the acts of intersubjective recognition in which the primary caregiver is engaged from—and even potentially before—the birth of the child. She points up the fact that the period of primary maternal preoccupation is not, from the mother's perspective at least, a state of merger, but is rather a process that depends on recognising the child as an other in their own right, an emerging person with their own needs and wants. The child must come to "recognise the other as a separate person" who is like them yet distinct, but the ability to do so depends on maternal subjectivity: on the mother's individualised capacity to identify, without over-identifying, with the child from the very beginning (23). Benjamin stresses the need to "think about the mother as a subject in her own right" rather than as a "vehicle for growth, an object of the baby's needs" (23). She is, in fact she must be, "another subject whose independent centre must be outside her child if she is to grant him the recognition he seeks" (23). Which is not to say that the mother is not also affected in this exchange.

Whilst the subject develops through the experience of recognition and identification on the part of the caregiver, Benjamin highlights "the need for *mutual* recognition, the necessity of recognising as well as being recognised by the other," an element that "so many theorists of the self have missed" and in itself a "significant…developmental goal"

(23–24). Drawing on Winnicott's work, Benjamin argues that the infant comes to recognise the other through a process of attempted destruction and survival (D. W. Winnicott 1991; Benjamin 1990, 29). Asserting its omnipotence, itself a developmental achievement, the child attempts to negate the other, to make the other no more than its object. If the other survives this attempted annihilation, the child can recognise them as real, as more than their own fantasmatic projection. From this point on, the child will be able to take part in the delicate act of balancing self-assertion with recognition of the other's independent existence. Benjamin is describing the process through which the child learns to mitigate the reduction of the other to the same. But the possibility of recognising the alterity of the other depends on recognising them as a subject: as more than the sum of one's projections. The successful negotiation of this process creates for the subject the "ability to enter into exchange with the outside object," to enter into a meaningful relationship with the world (37).

One of the major significances of this perspective for Benjamin is the alternative account of development that it provides. Rather than construing development on the model of internalisation, the theory of intersubjectivity captures something that eludes the internalisation model "that which is not consumed, what we do not get and take away from others by consumption" (43). This element, which "Winnicott's theory includes," is "the intersubjective aspect of destruction, the recognition of the other, the joy and urgency of discovering the external, independent reality of another person" (43–44). For Benjamin, Winnicott's work offers tools for thinking about "a maternal nurturance that actually encourages autonomy" (1978, 51). Whilst she acknowledges the importance of internalisation, specifically the internalisation of the experience of need gratification and soothing, which "contribute in a major way to faith in the other and a sense of one's own agency," what Winnicott's approach offers—captured in the concept of the facilitating or holding environment—is "an area in which the child is able to develop his innate capacities because the people around him facilitate such development" (46, 45).

Benjamin's turn to Winnicott has to be understood as part of a corrective move to bring to awareness important aspects of the developmental process that are rendered invisible as part of the psychosocial formations of oedipal modernity. As Jane Flax notes, Winnicott was not especially sensitive to gender, but "the stress on the centrality of the mother–child relation...at least enables us to recognise and to begin to undo the repression and distortion of pre-oedipal experience that so pervade the theories of Freud and Lacan" and the philosophical tradition they inherit (1991, 109). Benjamin's work, as well as that of other feminists working with object relations theory (including Chodorow and Dinnerstein), demonstrates how the aim of mutual recognition between subjects breaks down in modern capitalist societies that depend on and reproduce the sexual division of labour, splitting capacities for nurturance and autonomy in falsely gendered ways, and bolstering an understanding of subjectivity premised on separation and independence (1991, 122).

Lynne Layton insists on the fundamental significance of Benjamin's intervention in this context. Benjamin writes in response to, and against, "centuries of Western philosophy and decades of analytical arguing" when she affirms that the Other is not necessarily a hostile presence intent on limiting my freedom (2008, 10). As Layton puts it, Benjamin's work counters "centuries of political philosophy, and psychoanalytic theories that enact and ideologically enforce the split between agency and connection, and devalue connection – a split that works so well for capitalism and patriarchy" (10). The Oedipus complex, the major psychic mechanism for the reproduction of capitalist patriarchy, obscures the fact that we are relational subjects who come into being through relations of care. The narrative of individualism and illusory independence that the oedipal configuration licenses underpins the development of the liberal state (the regime of the brother) and androcentric forms of knowledge. It effaces the link between subjectivity and relationship, and between the psychic and social aspects of development more broadly. As Benjamin puts it, that the "acceptance of powerlessness in the guise of autonomy may deny responsibility to care for others is rationalised by the notion that we can, after all, do nothing to help them" (1990, 179). When subjectivity is conceived to depend on separation from others and dependence is denigrated, then the role of social contexts in shaping subjects and the impacts of forms of social provision are inherently effaced, because the central role of others in human flourishing is denied. Whilst psychoanalytic theory has the potential to collude in and entrench this process, perspectives like Benjamin's and other relational accounts challenge this (Layton 2020; Clarke et al. 2008). As Alison Stone puts it, there are resources within psychoanalysis to "critique the longstanding expectation that we should separate from our mothers to become selves. Psychoanalysis enables us, too, to critique the forms of psyche and society that result from this (attempted) separation," including the ideology of neoliberalism, according to which subjects belong to themselves alone (A. Stone 2014, 339; Michael Rustin 2014). Acknowledging the work of the caregiver, what might be construed as maternal subjectivity, Benjamin's reformulation of intersubjectivity contributes to the creation of a new socio-symbolic not founded on mastery, instrumentality and false universalism. Her work provides tools for laying the path from, in Campbell's words, the "one of the master subject to the other of relational subjects" (2004, 181).

Benjamin's conception of intersubjectivity emphasises the role of the other, of their support and care, in the development of capacities she considers to be innate potentials (Benjamin 1990, 44–45). This view is an important constituent of a feminist politics of care. Whilst Benjamin's intervention cannot be understood outside the social relations of modernity—the need to recover a form of caring labour defined as specifically maternal is inherently linked to the gendered division of labour in modernity—the model of subjectivity that she offers does not necessitate any specific relation between the caregiver and the infant. Though not all aspects of infant development are ungendered (specifically within capitalism), Benjamin is amongst a group of feminist theorists who draw on object relations to attempt to create a post-oedipal account of development wherein subjectivity takes shape through intersubjective experiences grounded in early relationships (Chodorow 1978; Benjamin 1990; 1995; 1998; Flax 1991). Of course, Benjamin's account of subjectivity is itself discursive, the product of a specific time and place, of specific social relations. But her account foregrounds the inherent dependence of subjectivity on the care of an other, not necessarily the person who has gestated us, but someone who is older than us and thus mediates our relationship with the adult world. This is the condition of possibility for psychic development.

Capitalist accumulation, and the Oedipus complex that accompanies it, makes possible the effacement of specific forms of work and practice, namely the work of care and reproduction, and the denial of dependence. As this chapter has set out, capitalism depends on the exploitation of this labour in order to reproduce the workers it needs for production, and the work of reproduction remains an essential and under-acknowledged source of capital accumulation (Vogel 2013; N. Fraser 2016; Bhattacharya 2017). Acknowledging and recompensing this work would have far-reaching consequences. Historically, the Oedipus complex is the mechanism that has made possible the psychic refusal to acknowledge this work. It renders invisible not only the work of care performed by maternal caregivers, but, by association, all of the care and reproductive work that underpins and is exploited by capitalism. Benjamin insists on the radical quality of the demand that society overcome the devaluation care (1990, 183–218). Psychoanalytic theory, like Benjamin's, that foregrounds the significance of care, offers resources for thinking radical forms of social transformation, because it contributes to the production of a socio-symbolic not defined by the illusion of autonomous individualism or forms of knowledge characterised by practices of domination, extraction and exploitation. Once the (maternal) caregiver is no longer understood as an object, but rather as a subject, the social relations in which caring takes place come into focus (Flax 1991, 125). Reaching back to antiquity, concretising a form of subjectivity established in *Oedipus Rex*, the modern oedipal configuration sures up the denial of dependence and the effacement of care. It enacts a matricide that has shaped and continues to shape our societies. The symbolic reconstruction of intersubjectivity, to which Winnicott's work is vital, foregrounds dependence and contains seeds for challenging the privatisation of care that produced the Oedipus complex, which in turn constitutes the psychic mechanism of their effacement. Winnicott's work, and the psychoanalytic feminism it informs, creates a space for Cura, in the wake of the oedipal catastrophe.

References

Alexander, Sally. 2013. 'Primary Maternal Preoccupation: D. W. Winnicott and Social Democracy in Mid-Twentieth-Century Britain'. In *History and Psyche: Culture, Psychoanalysis, and the Past*, edited by Barbara Taylor and Sally Alexander, 149–72. Basingstoke; New York: Palgrave Macmillan.

Baraitser, Lisa. 2009. *Maternal Encounters: The Ethics of Interruption*. Hove, East Sussex; New York: Routledge.

Barrett, Michèle, and Mary McIntosh. 2015. *The Anti-Social Family*. Brooklyn, NY: Verso.

Beauvoir, Simone de. 2011. *The Second Sex*. Translated by Constance Borde and Sheila Malovany-Chevallier. New York: Vintage Books.

Benjamin, Jessica. 1977. 'The End of Internalization: Adorno's Social Psychology'. *Telos* 32: 42–64. https://doi.org/10.3817/0677032042.

———. 1978. 'Authority and the Family Revisited: Or, a World without Fathers?' *New German Critique*, no. 13: 35–57.

———. 1990. *The Bonds of Love: Psychoanalysis, Feminism and the Problem of Domination*. London: Virago.

———. 1994. 'The Omnipotent Mother: A Psychoanalytic Study of Fantasy and Reality'. In *Representations of Motherhood*, 129–46.

———. 1995. *Like Subjects, Love Objects: Essays on Recognition and Sexual Difference*. New Haven; London: Yale University Press.

———. 1998. *Shadow of the Other: Intersubjectivity and Gender in Psychoanalysis*. New York: Routledge.

Bhattacharya, Tithi, ed. 2017. *Social Reproduction Theory: Remapping Class, Recentering Oppression*. London: Pluto Press.

Brennan, Teresa. 1993. *History after Lacan*. London; New York: Routledge.

Campbell, Kirsten. 2004. *Jacques Lacan and Feminist Epistemology*. London; New York: Routledge.

Cavarero, Adriana. 2016. *Inclinations: A Critique of Rectitude*. Translated by Amanda Minervini and Adam Sitze. Stanford, CA: Stanford University Press.

Chodorow, Nancy. 1978. *The Reproduction of Mothering: Psychoanalysis and the Sociology of Gender*. Berkeley, CA: University of California Press.

———. 1989. *Feminism and Psychoanalytic Theory*. New Haven; London: Yale University Press.

———, and Susan Contratto. 1989. 'The Fantasy of the Perfect Mother'. In *Feminism and Psychoanalytic Theory*, by Nancy Chodorow, 79–96. New Haven; London: Yale University Press.

Clarke, Simon, Herbert Hahn, and Paul Hoggett, eds. 2008. *Object Relations and Social Relations: The Implications of the Relational Turn in Psychoanalysis*. London: Karnac.

Descartes, René. 2006. *A Discourse on the Method of Correctly Conducting One's Reason and Seeking Truth in the Sciences*. Translated by Ian Maclean. Oxford; New York: Oxford University Press.

Dever, Carolyn. 1998. *Death and the Mother from Dickens to Freud: Victorian Fiction and the Anxiety of Origins*. Cambridge; New York: Cambridge University Press.

Dews, Peter. 1995. 'The Crisis of Oedipal Identity: The Early Lacan and the Frankfurt School'. In *Psychoanalysis in Contexts: Paths between Theory and Modern Culture*, edited by Anthony Elliott and Stephen Frosh, 53–71. London; New York: Routledge.

Doane, Janice, and Devon Hodges. 1993. *From Klein to Kristeva: Psychoanalytic Feminism and the Search for the 'Good Enough' Mother*. Ann Arbor: University of Michigan Press.

Dolar, Mladen. 1998. 'Cogito as the Subject of the Unconscious'. In *Cogito and the Unconscious*, edited by Slavoj Žižek, 11–40. Durham, NC: Duke University Press.

Dowling, Emma. 2021. *The Care Crisis: What Caused It and How Can We End It?* London; New York: Verso.

Eagleton, Terry. 1990. *The Ideology of the Aesthetic*. Oxford; Cambridge, MA: Blackwell.

Engels, Friedrich. 2010. *The Origin of the Family, Private Property, and the State*. London; New York: Penguin Classics.

Federici, Silvia. 2014. *Caliban and the Witch: Women, the Body and Primitive Accumulation*. New York: Autonomedia.

Flax, Jane. 1991. *Thinking Fragments: Psychoanalysis, Feminism, and Postmodernism in the Contemporary West*. Berkeley, CA: University of California Press.

Fraser, Nancy. 2013. *Fortunes of Feminism: From Women's Liberation to Identity Politics to Anti-Capitalism*. Brooklyn, NY: Verso Books.

———. 2016. 'Contradictions of Capital and Care'. *New Left Review* 100 (August): 99–117.

———, and Linda Gordon. 2013. 'A Geneaology of "Dependency": Tracing a Keyword of the US Welfare State'. In *Fortunes of Feminism: From Women's*

Liberation to Identity Politics to Anti-Capitalism, 1st ed., 83–110. Brooklyn, NY: Verso Books.

Freud, Sigmund. 1930. 'Civilization and Its Discontents'. In *SE 21*, 59–145.

George, Margaret. 1973. 'From "Goodwife" to "Mistress": The Transformation of the Female in Bourgeois Culture'. *Science & Society* 37 (2): 152–77.

Gerson, Gal. 2004. 'Winnicott, Participation and Gender'. *Feminism & Psychology* 14 (4): 561–81. https://doi.org/10.1177/0959353504046872.

Goux, Jean-Joseph. 1993. *Oedipus, Philosopher*. Stanford, CA: Stanford University Press.

Horkheimer, Max. 1949. 'Authoritarianism and the Family Today'. In *The Family: Its Function and Destiny*, edited by Ruth Nanda Ashen, 359–74. New York: Harper & Brothers.

———. 2002. 'Authority and the Family'. In *Critical Theory: Selected Essays*, translated by Matthew J. O'Connell, 47–128. New York: Continuum.

Irigaray, Luce. 1985. *Speculum of the Other Woman*. Translated by Gillian C. Gill. Ithaca, NY: Cornell University Press.

———. 1991. 'The Bodily Encounter with the Mother'. In *The Irigaray Reader*, edited by Margaret Whitford, translated by David Macey, 34–46. Cambridge, MA: Basil Blackwell.

Jacobs, Amber. 2007. *On Matricide: Myth, Psychoanalysis, and the Law of the Mother*. New York: Columbia University Press.

Lacan, Jacques. 1988. *The Seminar of Jacques Lacan. Book II, The Ego in Freud's Theory and in the Technique of Psychoanalysis 1954–1955*. Translated by Sylvana Tomaselli. New York: Norton.

———. 1995. 'The Oedipus Complex'. In *Polysexuality*, edited by François Peraldi, translated by Andrea Kahn, 190–200. New York: Semiotext(e).

———. 2001. 'Les Complexes Familiaux Dans La Formation de l'individu'. In *Autres Écrits*, edited by Jacques-Alain Miller, 23–84. Paris: Editions du Seuil.

———. 2006. 'Aggressiveness in Psychoanalysis'. In *Écrits: The First Complete Edition in English*, translated by Héloïse Fink and Bruce Fink, 82–101. New York: W.W. Norton & Co.

———. 2008. *The Seminar of Jacques Lacan: Book XVII: The Other Side of Psychoanalysis, 1969–70*. Edited by Jacques-Alain Miller. Translated by Russell Grigg. New York; London: Norton.

Layton, Lynne. 2008. 'Relational Thinking: From Culture to Couch and Couch to Culture'. In *Object Relations and Social Relations: The Implications of the Relational Turn in Psychoanalysis*, edited by Simon Clarke, Herb Hahn, and Paul Hoggett, 1–24. London: Karnac.

———. 2020. *Toward a Social Psychoanalysis: Culture, Character, and Normative Unconscious Processes*. Edited by Marianna Leavy-Sperounis. Abingdon, Oxon; New York, NY: Routledge.

Linebaugh, Peter. 2014. *Stop, Thief! The Commons, Enclosures and Resistance*. Oakland, CA: PM.

———, and Marcus Rediker. 2012. *The Many-Headed Hydra: Sailors, Slaves, Commoners, and the Hidden History of the Revolutionary Atlantic*. London: Verso.

MacCannell, Juliet Flower. 1991. *The Regime of the Brother: After the Patriarchy*. London; New York: Routledge.

Marcuse, Herbert. 2009. 'Philosophy and Critical Theory'. In *Negations: Essays in Critical Theory*, translated by Jeremy J. Shapiro, 99–118. http://mayflybooks.org/wp-content/uploads/2010/07/9781906948054Negations.pdf.

Maynes, Mary Jo, and Ann Beth Waltner. 2012. *The Family: A World History*. Oxford; New York: Oxford University Press.

Meehan, Johanna. 1995. 'Autonomy, Recognition, and Respect: Habermas, Benjamin, and Honneth'. In *Feminists Read Habermas: Gendering the Subject of Discourse*, edited by Johanna Meehan, 231–46. New York: Routledge.

———. 2019. 'Intersubjectivity on the Couch: Destruction and Recognition in the Work of Jessica Benjamin'. In *Transitional Subjects: Critical Theory and Object Relations*, edited by Amy Allen and Brian O'Connor, 185–208. New York; Chichester: Columbia University Press.

Mies, Maria. 2014. *Patriarchy and Accumulation on a World Scale: Women in the International Division of Labour*. London: Zed Books.

Mitchell, Juliet. 2015. *Woman's Estate*. London: Verso

Nicholson, Linda J. 1986. *Gender and History: The Limits of Social Theory in the Age of the Family*. New York: Columbia University Press.

Pateman, Carole. 1988. *The Sexual Contract*. Stanford, CA: Stanford University Press.

Poster, Mark. 1982. *Critical Theory of the Family*. London: Pluto Press.

Rorty, Richard. 1980. *Philosophy and the Mirror of Nature*. Princeton, NJ: Princeton University Press.

Rose, Jacqueline. 2004. *On Not Being Able to Sleep Psychoanalysis and the Modern World*. London: Vintage. http://www.vlebooks.com/vleweb/product/openreader?id=none&isbn=9781446418413.

Rustin, Michael. 2014. 'Belonging to Oneself Alone: The Spirit of Neoliberalism'. *Psychoanalysis, Culture & Society* 19 (2): 145–60. https://doi.org/10.1057/pcs.2014.7.

Sayers, Janet. 1991. *Mothering Psychoanalysis*. London: Penguin.

Sprengnether, Madelon. 1990. *The Spectral Mother: Freud, Feminism, and Psychoanalysis*. Ithaca: Cornell University Press.
Stone, Alison. 2012. *Feminism, Psychoanalysis, and Maternal Subjectivity*. New York; Abingdon: Routledge.
———. 2014. 'Psychoanalysis and Maternal Subjectivity'. In *Mothering and Psychoanalysis: Clinical, Sociological and Feminist Perspectives*, edited by Petra Bueskens, 325–42.
Stone, Lawrence. 1990. *The Family, Sex and Marriage in England 1500-1800*. London: Penguin.
Tilly, Louise A., and Joan Wallach Scott. 2016. *Women, Work and Family*. London; New York: Routledge.
Vogel, Lise. 2013. *Marxism and the Oppression of Women: Toward a Unitary Theory*. Leiden: Brill.
Winnicott, Donald W. 1991. *The Child, the Family and the Outside World*. London: Penguin
Wood, Ellen Meiksins. 2002. *The Origin of Capitalism: A Longer View*. London: Verso.

4

Caring States: Maternal Care, Holding and Social Provision

The recognition that care receives in Winnicott's work constitutes a critique of the "ego's era" and his thinking has contributed to attempts to "humanise" the capitalist mode of production that is part of it, supporting and shaping policies that emphasise the importance of social provision (Richards 1984; Lebeau 2019). Specifically, Winnicott's work informed the ethos and character of the post-war welfare state in Britain (N. S. Rose 2005; S. Alexander 2013; Shapira 2015). The attempts to humanise capitalism that took shape around the mid-century had an inherently "maternalist" character, as thinkers, including Winnicott, contributed to reimagining the relationship between the private and public spheres, advocating for more socialised forms of support that reconceived care as a collective responsibility (Bar-Haim 2021). The recognition of the value of care and the fact of human dependence draw attention to aspects of existence—and forms of labour—that are occluded in dominant conceptions of subjectivity and society. It underpins an idea of ethical responsibility towards others that was an important if implicit element of the philosophy of social provision in the post-war period (Hoggett 2000). However, though admirable for recognising dependence and the need for care (Michael Rustin 2015), the post-war welfare state also entrenched a gendered division of labour and was replete with fault lines of racialised exclusion, not to mention its economic imbrication with, and dependence on, British imperialism (Wilson 1980; Pitcher 2016; Bhambra and Holmwood 2018). The post-war social settlement, for instance, served to interpellate caregivers, and mothers in particular, in ways that valorised the privatised family, and Winnicott's ideas were implicated in this process. Nevertheless, Winnicott's work, and the tradition of "maternal thinking" of which it is part—which can be traced from the eighteenth century into contemporary feminist theory—does more than reinscribe the family form associated with modern capitalism. It imagines and demands the social dissemination of forms of experience and ways of being that have been privatised and feminised in modernity. It demands the production of "caring states" in both the individual and the institution, which exist in fundamental interrelation.

Maternal Thinking and the Longing for Care

Winnicott's interest in maternal care, and its role in the development of subjectivity and human flourishing, does not, of course, develop in a vacuum. His maternal preoccupations are part of a growing interest in the social, political and ethical significance of care taking shape in modernity in a complex and often critical relation with capitalist society. Though Winnicott's view takes its distance from the ideas of separation and individualism that come to dominate in modernity, his thinking takes shape in dialectic with the vicissitudes of modernity and forms of social critique evolving from the eighteenth century. Evident in the work of Rousseau and the Romantics, as well as the maternalism of the nineteenth century, the tendency to esteem and laud the practices of care that are privatised and feminised in modernity constitutes a critique of existing capitalism and reflects a desire for more public forms of nurturance: for increased social provision for meeting need. Nevertheless, the lives and needs of primary caregivers, often mothers, are not always at the centre of such approaches.

Concern with the relationship between nurturance and society is evident in the work of Rousseau, who laments, in *Emile*, that mothers do not care for their children, linking a perceived absence of morality in modern society to contemporary mothering practices (1979, 46). Modern mothers, he suggests, do not look after their children, preferring instead to employ wet nurses and put infants out until the age of two. As a result, he claims, "the whole moral order degenerates" (46). Were mothers to "deign to nurse their children," however, Rousseau thinks that "morals will reform themselves, nature's sentiments will be awakened in every heart, the state will be repeopled" (46). Rousseau here walks a precarious line that at once esteems nurturance and polices the behaviour of women. The private sphere is imagined to contain the potential for forms of feeling and sympathy that might play a role in ameliorating public life, but Rousseau's account concurrently positions women as mothers who are—or should be—"specifically there to care for the child," preparing the citizen for entry and activity in the public sphere (Kaplan 1992, 20). The values of care and nurturance are conceived to be relevant to public life, but they remain decidedly private concerns. Though the public and private are related on his account, they remain distinctly separate. *Emile* was widely read in England and, though Stone argues that it had little "practical influence," at the time, it shaped understandings of subjectivity, and ideas about mothers and children, in the proceeding centuries (L. Stone 1990, 256; Kaplan 1992, 20). Social historians, Anne Mellor writes, "have all argued powerfully for the emergence during this century of a more emotionally charged "affective" nuclear family and an idealised mother who remained at home in more sustained and intimate contact with her children" (1993, 81). Rousseau's comments provide support for this private and intensive conception, which valorises care as a means of specifying the behaviours and activities appropriate for women.

In the late eighteenth century, inspired by Rousseau, male romantic writers also developed an interest in the feminine and the maternal, as well as a growing esteem for the qualities of feeling and empathy associated with the private sphere. Richardson notes that, during the "'ages' of Sensibility and Romanticism," the patriarchal tradition was qualified by a widespread revaluation of the feminine, of the emotions, and of relationality," a tendency that he describes as a form of colonisation (Richardson 1988, 14). Whilst also foregrounding the tendency for male romantic authors to laud the feminine whilst concurrently profiting from, and failing to challenge, the assignment of domestic labour of women, Meena Alexander also links their attentiveness to care to a desire for social change:

> Drawing on the sentimental tradition, enlarging it, Romantics redefined the limits of moral knowledge. They drew on the powers of intense feeling, empathy and nurturing care. This was implicitly a validation of femininity and the functions previously reserved for women. A revolutionary age needed to provide its own visible indices for the longing for change, and the feminine could at times satisfactorily stand for this longing. (1989, 23)

The romantic celebration of the intimate and the particular, often articulated via the figure of woman, symbolised a desire for something different to the isolated individualism of capitalist society. Though the private sphere was itself a product of capitalist modernity, rather than a timeless realm untouched by it, the romantic appeal to the maternal-feminine offers a strategy—though not an unproblematic one—for, in the words of Herbert Marcuse, "confronting the inadequacies of the present with images of the fulfilled promises of childhood" (cited in Calhoon 1992, 72). In this instance, the appeal to feminised qualities discloses a wish for nurture, connection and care, desires that "were initially social," but were privatised and feminised in the transition to capitalism as the occluded other of the alienating, individualised, public sphere (Calhoon 1992, 72). Informed by Rousseau, the child becomes for the Romantics a symbol of potential and possibility, a being whose existence can be nurtured or thwarted by the world in which they find themselves. Wordsworth's famous rendering of the mother and "infant Babe" in Book Two of *The Prelude* is emblematic (1959). Wordsworth's infant "drinks in the feelings of his Mother's eye," an image of connection and possibility very different to the relational norms of modernity, which Eric Santner conceptualises as a space "in which one is systematically trained not to return the gaze of the other" (1990, 123). However, whilst male

Romantic writers lauded the qualities assigned to the modern private sphere as an alternative to the alienation of modern life, they did not fundamentally challenge the division of labour or the separation of the spheres.

Denise Riley discusses the growth of interest in child development in the nineteenth and early twentieth centuries, which saw scientists and philosophers demonstrate a new level of awareness and appreciation of the significance of maternal care (1983). At the end of the nineteenth century, philosophy and the emergent discipline of psychology seized on child development in order to try to clarify speculation about the nature of the mind through direct observation (43–44). In an article on "Babies and Science," published in 1881, the evolutionist James Sully emphasises the effect that the long period of infantile helplessness has on human sensibilities and development, calling up "tendance [and] protection…on the part of the parent; only in this condition could the family, the community or the race be preserved." It is the "period of infancy which produces…the germs of altruistic sentiments, affection and sympathy," he writes, before falling victim to prejudice: this period is "longer in the case of civilised man than in the savage" (cited in Riley 1983, 46). Sully emphasises the effect of encountering a young infant on the caring sensibilities of adults, and the role of care in fostering the sentiments of children, whilst also subscribing to a Eurocentric fantasy of superiority. However, he also asserts that, by showing an interest in infancy, science "has constituted itself the avenger of a whole sex (women)." Through its observation of infancy, science is giving due recognition to the importance of the work of care women have been assigned, he suggests.

As Riley points out, the observation of infancy had both positive and negative consequences. Firstly, observation soon led to the giving of advice, as male scientists assessed and theorised the "best handling of infants" and the "effects of 'ignorance' of the child's needs" (1983, 52). At the same time, scientists also became interested in the role played by historical and social conditions in shaping children's development. Writing in 1914, Williams Stern advised that more observational studies of working-class children were needed in order to adequately assess the influence of situation and circumstance on development. Though he thought that most of the developmental features of upper-class and working-class children were likely to be the same, "in details such as the relative time of development or the influence of certain conditions of environment, it is but reasonable to suppose that amongst the lower classes, variations will be found which so far are but little known and which offer a wide and important field for future enquiry" (cited in Riley 1983, 58). There was a developing idea that historical and social conditions might colour the relationship between the mother and the child, affecting their sensibilities and development. Therefore, a growing sense of the significance of early care fostered awareness of the relationship between ostensibly private early relations and the wider social world.

Concurrent with the burgeoning of scientific interest in child development, the nineteenth century witnessed the growth of specifically "maternalist" approaches to politics and state provision, often spearheaded by women (Koven and Michel 1993, 2). Koven and Michal define maternalism as a diverse set of "ideologies and discourses that exalted women's capacity to mother and applied to society as a whole the values they attached to that role: care, nurturance, and morality" (4). Whilst some maternalists celebrated women's role within the home, and others sought to support their capacity to work outside of it, maternalism was characterised by a "thoroughgoing reevaluation" of women's work and its relationship with political economy, state and society (2). Maternalists drew attention to the role of the social environment in shaping relations between caregiver and baby, and some believed that "their values should be applied universally to transform the very foundations of the social order" (2–3). Koven and Michal foreground the role of maternalist campaigners in laying the foundations for welfare provision from the late nineteenth century and into the twentieth. Maternalism intuitively asserts the idea that the state should care for its citizens, especially mothers and children. Interest in mothers and care was a significant feature of British culture in the first half of the twentieth century, and it often played a role in calls for social change. Before the First World War, the figures of mother and child were central to feminist campaigns for maternity services, family allowances, slum clearance and the abolition of homework, as well as calls for a minimum wage and National Insurance for married women (Rowbotham 2010, 106). However, a focus on maternal figures did not have an inherent connection with progressive politics. Shaul Bar-Haim highlights that maternalism had both patriotic and progressive forms during and after the First World War, which saw some women identify with the project of preserving the "race" by creating future generations of workers and soldiers, and others cleave to a maternally inflected pacifism (Bar-Haim 2021; Koven and Michel 1993; Davin 1978).

Gal Gerson identifies a preoccupation with the mother–child relation in the reformist liberalism that characterised British social thought in the early twentieth century, which found in maternal care a resource for justifying forms of state support (2017, 312). Combining elements of liberalism and socialism, this loosely configured political inclination furnished basic arguments that informed the creation of the welfare state. Critical of materialism and the selfishness of capitalism, though increasingly unable to draw on religious authority to support this critique, reformist liberals sought an alternative sphere of value outside material fulfilment, which might provide the rationale for increasing state intervention and provision (Gerson 2017, 316). In 1924 the liberal philosopher L. T. Hobhouse appealed to maternal care and its role in shaping the sociability of future citizens in order to argue for increased state provision. Gerson notes that Hobhouse highlights that individuals are cared for by others from the time of their birth, and that humans require an extended period of nurture, meaning that "the maternal care that makes infants' subsistence possible is humanity's essential condition" (318). The behaviour of individuals was conditioned by the experience of love in childhood and its anticipation in the future. Children therefore needed to be afforded opportunities for sociability and the experience of a specific attitude of care on the part of a primary caregiver. Progressive liberals focused on the nuclear family as a place where sociability could be fostered and expressed, a private realm in need of support and protection by a welfare state. In many ways, this perspective anticipated the British middle-classes' move "from an ideology of self-reliance to one of solidaristic interdependence," which Richard Titmuss identified as developing through the experience of the Second World War (Hoggett 2000, 193).

By the 1930s, and in the wake of the Wall Street Crash of 1929, a preoccupation with maternal figures was widespread within British culture and society and characteristic of much psychoanalytic thought and social critique. The anthropological fieldwork of Malinowski in the Trobriand Islands demonstrated the provisionality of Freud's father-centred Oedipal theory, as did the fertility myths collected in James Frazer's *The Golden Bough* (Zaretsky 2005, 253). Jane Harrison's study of matriarchy in Greek myth also did much to unpick the centrality of *Oedipus Rex*. Freud's view was also challenged by psychoanalytic thinkers on the left, such as Otto Gross, Wilhelm Reich and Erich Fromm, who criticised "Freud's patriarchal world view" and embraced modified versions of maternal theories found in the work of Bachofen, Engels and Briffault, amongst others (Burston 1996, 74). Zaretsky suggests that this prevailing interest in the mother and appreciation of the role of care "symbolised a wish for nurturance, peace, and security amid the dangers and disappointments of the time" (2005, 250). Interest in mothers was piqued by a desire for forms of experience at odds with the unpredictability and insecurity that characterised life in the interwar period.

The entry of more women into psychoanalysis also affected its theoretical preoccupations. Zaretsky ties the interest in childhood exhibited by female analysts to the British romantic poets and Victorian novelists (2005, 253). In addition, no doubt the fact that many of these women were mothers informed their perspectives. During the interwar period, female analysts brought to light the maternal role that had been so "spectral" in Freudian theory, the figure, Freud came to admit, he had overlooked (Sprengnether 1990). "Everything in the sphere of this first attachment to the mother," he wrote late in his career, "seemed to me so difficult to grasp in analysis—so grey with age and shadowy and almost impossible to revivify—that it was as if it had succumbed to an especially inexorable repression" (Freud 1931, 226). From the time of the second typography, in the early 1920s, he had begun to recognise the importance of the pre-oedipal period—proposing that the mother implanted the super ego in the child—but his growing appreciation of the role of others in the early development of subjectivity was influenced by the work of women-analysts, including Helene Deutsch and Melanie Klein

(Freud 1923). Janet Sayers has demonstrated that Deutsch and Klein were amongst the first psychoanalytic thinkers to insist on the importance of the maternal relation, pointing out its centrality in their own psychic constellations and those of their female analysands (1991). The pre-oedipal period of development increasingly became the focus of theoretical interest, and Zaretsky suggests that British object relations theory therefore "resonated with the deepest currents in the culture" (2005, 249). By 1930, Freud himself was emphasising infantile helplessness and the need for care as a basis for an orientation towards others and the development of community (1927; 1930).

Paul Hoggett suggests that it really only became possible to take psychoanalysis out of the consulting room when Klein and object relations theorists developed its theories away from the drive model, towards the encounter—real and phantasmatic—with others in the world (1992, 73). Though the mother was an important focus of consideration in object relations theory, there were considerable differences in approaches. Melanie Klein and Anna Freud both pioneered child analysis, but they disagreed on a number of significant points. These included the extent to which children's play constitutes a parallel to adult free association—which Klein thought it did—and whether children's on-going attachments to their parents interfered with them forming a transferential relationship with the analyst—which Freud thought it did (King and Steiner 1991, 14–15). Where Freud advocated analysts working with children endeavour to educate them in how to master their drives and urges, given that their super-egos are yet to fully form, Klein dated the Oedipus complex to much earlier in life and saw Freud's educative methods as constituting interference with real psychoanalytic treatment. Shapira connects the differences between Klein and Freud's approaches to their differing "backgrounds and political commitments" (2015, 103). Freud generally identified the sources of the child's suffering as "stemming from a deprived environment that was unable to meet the infant's emotional needs" (103). Freud was a committed teacher who mixed in the circles of socially conscious analysts, whilst Klein "was neither a teacher nor a social reformer" whose ideas "developed mostly out of her engagement with psychoanalytic theory" (103).

The theorists of the independent group, which emerged out of the "controversial discussions" that took place at the Institute of Psychoanalysis during the Second World War, insisted on the social significance of maternal care (King and Steiner 1991). Ian Suttie, often considered a prototypical influence for the independents, emphasised the role of care in the late 1920s, stressing that the mother's usual status as the first companion that a newborn meets, means that the relationship with her conditions the future development of the child's personality (Suttie 1999). Eschewing Freud's instinctual understanding of the connection between mother and child, Suttie emphasised the emotional character of attachment, and the ability for maternal care, Gerson writes, to "heal whatever rifts were created in early childhood" if the family was located in "a culture that assigns dignity and agency to mothers" (Gerson 2017, 314). Other theorists, including Roger Fairbairn, developed this perspective. Fairbairn wrote, in 1940, that "the child's oral relationship with his mother is the foundation upon which all his future relationships…are based. It also represents his first experience of a social relationship; and it therefore forms the basis of his subsequent attitude to society" (1994, 24). Whilst these theorists emphasised relationships and the role of (m)others, recognising care's status as a source of sociability that requires support, it was in the work of Winnicott that this perspective achieved its fullest expression. Winnicott's thinking was also pivotal in shaping how social provision both during and after the war was conceptualised.

Holding and Society

Winnicott's interwar work with mothers and children, and his wartime experience of hostel care, informed the form and character of the post-war welfare state. As Bar-Haim has recently demonstrated, psychoanalysis was central to the maternalism of the mid-century, playing an important role in shaping the post-war social settlement and the welfare state (2021). Winnicott's work in particular was both aligned with and influential in moulding the "structure of feeling" that characterised the forties and fifties, which emphasised maternal care and foregrounded the state's responsibility to care for its citizens. Noting that the task of excavating the social history of Winnicott's thinking is only now in its early stages, Alexander asserts his status, along with Klein, as the psychoanalyst of the welfare state, locating the experience that facilitated this influence in the interwar period (2013). Winnicott's first-hand experience with mothers and children led to his recognition of need and dependence, as well as informing a developing sense of the relationship between environmental provision and emotional well-being. In time, this provided a blueprint for forms of state care, contributing to bringing the values and capacities associated with the feminised private sphere into public life.

Through his interwar work with mothers and children, Winnicott formulated an original appreciation of the significance of the environment of care for emotional well-being, as well as the emotional effects of deprivation. Winnicott discovered psychoanalysis in 1919, whilst studying medicine at Cambridge (Rodman 2003, 41). He would go on to become the first paediatrician to train as a psychoanalyst, remaining an "isolated phenomenon in the field" for several decades (D. W. Winnicott 1990a, 171). In the early years of his career, which began in 1920, Winnicott worked in a variety of public hospital settings, as well as in private practice. He ran open clinics for mothers and children in Paddington Green and Hackney from 1923. The clinics revealed a "vast mass of indefinite and chronic unwellness" that called out for psychoanalytic understanding (cited in S. Alexander 2016, 121). Here Winnicott came to appreciate the relationship between the experiences of children and their emotional well-being, a way of thinking that would shape his specific contribution to psychoanalysis (D. W. Winnicott 1958a). Working with working-class women and their children, who exhibited a variety of symptoms but had "nothing really wrong with them," Winnicott developed an interest in the lives and inner worlds of his patients (cited in S. Alexander 2013, 163). Alexander links this to "a wider curiosity about the recently literate and enfranchised people in the aftermath of total war" (152). Winnicott's ideas, then, developed in the context of public and social forms of provision, which shaped his appreciation of the environmental contribution in turn.

The role of the early environment in shaping emotional development is laid out in the case histories that Winnicott recorded, a practice that also illustrates his willingness to listen attentively to the working-class parents and children who consulted with him in the free clinics. In an early paper based on his experiences in the clinics, Winnicott notes the "profound effect" that his "careful history-taking" had on his outlook (1958b, 33). Through this practice, "the doctor gets from the parents as clear a picture as he can of the child's past life, and of his present state, and he tries to relate the symptoms for which the child is brought to the child's personality, and to his external and internal experiences" (D. W. Winnicott 1958c, 130). The stories Winnicott heard from his patients and their parents often told of separation and loss, of maternal pregnancies and sibling births that brought on experiences of depression or anxiety in the form of headaches, pounding hearts, night terrors and swollen limbs. The physical symptoms exhibited by the children who consulted Winnicott were often linked to their emotional experience with family members and caregivers. Famously, Winnicott developed what came to be known as the "spatula game," which gave the consulting doctor the chance to infer the history of an infant's emotional development from their response to, and interaction with, the wooden spatula with which they were presented (1958b). The practices of history-taking and the spatula game, which Winnicott describes as a "film strip" through which the child's emotional development can be observed, foreground the effects of early relationships on the form taken by the self and foretell of the persistent implications of early experiences across the life course. Alexander highlights that Winnicott's studies of the mother and infant from the 1920s demonstrated how closely inner feeling and the external world were linked (2013, 149).

Winnicott's work as a paediatrician made him uniquely placed to appreciate the relationship between the care the child received and their psychic constitution in previously unexplored ways. He began his psychoanalytic training in 1929, and it was around this time that he gradually came to realise that the babies and young infants he saw in his consulting room were human beings (Abram 2012, 79). Andre Green is no doubt correct that Winnicott's analysis "enabled him to see the child with the eyes of the analysed adult who has rediscovered the child in himself" (cited in Abram 2012, 79). However, Abram highlights that "alongside his daily analytic sessions as alternating patient and analyst,

Winnicott is confronted with the infant or young child on the mother's lap in his paediatric work," a particular situation that invariably had an effect on his understanding (79). In both his personal analysis and his work in the clinics, Winnicott was in touch with forms of infantile experience unavailable to many, including the vast majority of men (who were not engaged in childcare) and anyone who had not experienced the kinds of regression that psychoanalysis facilitates. His position was unique, and it produced unique insights. As "a paediatrician with a knack for getting mothers to tell me about their children and about the early history of their children's disorders," he soon became aware of both "the insight psycho-analysis gave into the lives of children" and "a certain deficiency in psycho-analytic theory" (1990a, 171). If his interest in psychoanalysis had taught him that "it is in the years between one and five that the foundations of mental health are laid," the clinics led Winnicott to realise that disorders and symptoms manifesting in adolescence and adulthood often find their origins in infancy, "even…earliest infancy" (1958a, 7; 1958b, 33). Whilst other theorists acknowledge the significance of care, what distinguishes Winnicott's approach is his concern with a "stage of human development that *precedes* object relations" (Abram 2012, 73). The infant is not only "object-seeking," but cannot come to exist at all without suitable care from others, without what he would come to describe as the experience of "holding" (1990c).

A holding environment involves identification and good enough adaptation to need, as well as respect for the cared-for other as a separate human being (Abram 2007, 196). It makes the initiation of the developmental process possible. Such an environment begins with the mother and the infant, and grows outwards towards other groups in society (195). The idea of holding, which calls attention to the vital significance of early development and the role of the caregiver's attitude in fostering emotional well-being, connects the dyad of infant and caregiver to the broader institutions of social life. Abram asserts that the concept was present from the beginning of Winnicott's career, although he didn't use the word until the 1950s, in relation to antisocial children (2007, 194). Joel Kanter suggests that the term was originally coined by Winnicott's second wife, Clare Britton Winnicott, a psychoanalytic social worker with whom he worked in the Oxfordshire hostels during the war (2000, 256). Kanter acknowledges the intricate cross-fertilisation most likely at play between Donald and Clare's thinking during their work together, but the idea that social work influenced the concept only further emphasises its broad social significance.

The influence of psychoanalytic thinking in shaping ideas about forms of public care is inseparable from the circumstances of the Second World War. The outbreak of war brought interest in the mother and child to a head, and generated circumstances—the need for women to work outside the home and the risks of air raids—that called attention to the state's responsibility to care for children. The reconfiguration of relationships during this period, as children were separated from their parents and more women entered work, proved amenable to psychoanalytic reflection and intervention, arguably leading to a high point of psychoanalytic influence on welfare and public policy in Britain (Hollway 2006a, 450). The war itself, as Hollway notes, "produced a natural experiment on a grand scale when many children were displaced from their positions in the traditional gender-differentiated family" (451). What Winnicott describes as "the wartime feeling that any cost could be borne" led to massive extensions in the social provision of forms of care, for both children and adults, during the war (D. W. Winnicott 2012b, 54). In addition to day-care services, there were also residential nurseries and, in time, hostels for children who did not adapt well to their evacuation billets. "British Restaurants" were also set up to help people bombed out of their homes or otherwise in need. The new childcare provisions functioned as laboratories for observation that drew on and fed into psychoanalytic thinking. Shapira describes the Hampstead war nurseries, run by Anna Freud and Dorothy Burlingham, as aiming to provide "substitute mothering" for those in their care (2015, 67). The nurseries, then, actualised society's responsibility to care for children, extending the practices and values associated with mothering beyond the private home. However, support for social forms of care was far from universal. Nursery provision was criticised before and after the war for imperilling children by providing impersonal forms of attention, and arguments proliferated that insisted on the child's need for the personal warmth of the family (Riley 1983, 115).

Winnicott's interwar work with young children informed both his response to government policy concerning the care of children during the war and, in time, his contribution to shaping it. Proposals for the evacuation of children from inner-city London after the outbreak of war led Winnicott to write, with colleagues Emanuel Miller and John Bowlby, in a well-cited letter of December 1939, to the *British Medical Journal*. Drawing on Bowlby's work, the authors cautioned against the evacuation of young children, highlighting the significance of early relationships and their importance for emotional development. "One important external factor in the causation of persistent delinquency," they wrote, "is the small child's separation from his mother," arguing that sustained separation of young children from their mothers was likely to lead to serious psychological disorders (2012a, 13). Though the stance taken in this letter might suggest the need to maintain the assumed sanctity of the mother–child bond, reinforcing established gender roles, from another perspective the letter draws attention to the importance of care and advises government ministers to think seriously about the needs of children. Though aligned with Bowlby in this instance, the emphasis Winnicott placed on the constructive function of maternal failure demonstrates that he was not working with a simple deprivation paradigm (Hollway 2006a, 453). Where Bowlby, mistakenly, endorsed the idea that any form of separation was bad for the child, Winnicott emphasised continuity of care over continual care (455). He insisted that the child's capacity to tolerate maternal absence and failure was related to age and development, and increased quickly after an initial period of absolute dependence. Winnicott's perspective, then, did not preclude the idea of forms of social provision capable of supplementing and supporting the care work performed by the primary, often maternal, caregiver.

Winnicott's work, during the war, on the Government Evacuation Scheme in Oxfordshire, developed his understanding of the parallels between "private-maternal" and "public-social" forms of care. The hostels placed him in a "unique position to assess the relative importance of what he called the 'environmental provision'" (A. Phillips 2007, 63). The evacuation of children made their care an increasingly social concern, and children who were unable to adapt to life in foster care were accommodated in hostels. Here, Winnicott came to appreciate that these "difficult children" had something to teach about the needs of children, environments of care and the effects of deprivation on psychic life (2012b). Writing about the hostel scheme in 1947, Winnicott described the "psychiatrist's task" in terms of drawing "direct attention" to

> the fact that these children were seriously affected by evacuation and that nearly all had personal reasons why they could not find good billets to be good; to show, in fact, that these evacuation breakdowns occurred for the most part in children who had originally come from unsettled homes, or in children who had never had in their own homes an example of a good environment. (52)

What these children needed was not "substitutes for their own homes," but rather "*primary home experiences* of a satisfactory kind," which meant the "experience of an environment adapted to the special needs of the infant and little child, without which the foundations of mental health cannot be laid down" (2012b, 52, emphasis in the original). Examples of things that might make a home unsuitable include "a parent who is a psychiatric case, certified or uncertifiable, or a dominating or antisocial brother or sister, or housing conditions that are in themselves a persecution" (58). Emotional development is not, then, the sole responsibility of the mother, but relates to the total environment in which primary care takes place. Clare Britton Winnicott writes that "the children [Winnicott] worked with in the hostels had reached the end of the line; there was nowhere else for them to go and *how to hold them became the main preoccupation of all those trying to help them*" (Britton Winnicott 2012, 2, emphasis added). Through the hostel work, Winnicott was forced to turn his attention to the "problem of care and management" (2).

Though the concept of holding appears intermittently in Winnicott's lectures from the 1950s, it did not become a central focus of his work until the 1960 paper, "Theory of the Parent-Infant Relationship" (Kanter 2000, 256). Writing in 1955, Britton Winnicott describes social work itself as the provision of a "reliable environment" in which "people can find themselves or that part about which they are uncertain" (cited in

Kanter 2000, 256). The social worker is able to "hold a consistent idea of the client as a person," as well as "the difficult situation which brought him to us by tolerating it until he either finds a way through it or tolerates it himself." The word "hold" is here "deliberately used" because it includes both acceptance of the client and "what we do with what we accept." Similarly, the work required in the hostels involved holding the difficulty of the child's situation and experience. In order to develop "a working relation to external reality," an infant requires "someone specifically orientated to his needs" (D. W. Winnicott 2012b, 52). Without "one person to love and hate," the infant "cannot come to know that it is the same person that he loves and hates, and so cannot find his sense of guilt, and his desire to repair and restore" (52). The child needs "a limited human and physical environment" in which they learn about the extent and limits of their aggression, and sort out "the difference between fantasy and fact" (52). What the unbilletable children needed was an environmental experience capable of facilitating the development of the capacity for concern, by providing a form of holding, an experience of continuity.

Britton Winnicott highlights that Winnicott's experience in the hostels "affected his basic concepts on emotional growth and development" (2012, 3). His work with deprived children led him to realise and emphasise the need for a reliable environment in which emotional development can take place. The relationship between the infant and their primary caregiver is a vital part of this, but success in this area is made possible by forms of social provision that supplement and support primary relationships. Alexander gives a clear account of the implications of Winnicott's thinking for social policy:

> Winnicott's vision is social—the maternal environment, the two-body relation inaugurates subjectivity; the space between them both instils what he calls the "maturational process," and forms the basis of creative life and culture. But Winnicott always kept part of his mind on the institutions that formed civil society and in which he worked. Town planning, public health and housing, hospitals, schools (including nursery schools) staffed by reliable and tolerant professionals were the necessary context of mental landscapes. (2013, 151)

The institutions of society take on, in both his thinking and in visions of a post-war welfare state, an analogous role to the maternal holding environment. As Winnicott puts it, "these ever-widening circles" of support are "the mother's lap and her arms and her concern" (2006, 130). Alexander describes Winnicott as one of the "intellectual architects of the welfare state," and his thinking drew attention to the importance of the relationship between the mother and child and shaped social provision in turn (2013, 154). Britton Winnicott also emphasises the significance of his ideas for society. Not only are they of "historical interest," they also belong to the "ever-present encounter between the antisocial elements in society and the forces of health and sanity which reach out to reclaim and recover what has been lost" (2012, 4).

This is a comment that reveals a deep investment in health and a hopefulness about what social provision might achieve. From another perspective, the desire to overcome the antisocial tendency might be read as a mode of control that attempted to produce productive members of society. Shapira, for instance, understands the work of the hostels as a process of normalisation designed to contain emotions that were seen as a problem for society and mould the children into democratic citizens (2015). Alexander, however, emphasises that preoccupations with emotional development and the democratic tendency were framed by fears about the rise of fascism (2016). Winnicott's work with evacuee children "deepened his understanding of unconscious feeling and the environment—maternal or if necessary institutional—which might strengthen or repair the potential for democracy by developing concern and the capacity for creative living in the child" (115). Winnicott understood the antisocial tendency as a response to deprivation. Without adequate environmental provision—maternal, institutional or social—insecurity and deprivation can lead to splitting—the failure to develop the capacity for concern—and the risk of submission to authoritarianism. The psychic threat of fascism was to be mitigated by social environments capable of holding anxiety and aggression so that others can be recognised and cared about. Forms of social provision, then, were not to be designed to inculcate subservience, but to facilitate thinking, deliberation and concern.

Young-Bruehl argues that psychoanalysis provided social democracy with a theory of human development and basic needs, and she sees psychoanalysis as contributing to the Freud-Marx synthesis of the post-war period (2011, 186). First published in 1942, the Beveridge Report paid considerable attention to meeting the needs of the population, mothers and children in particular, and offered the revolutionary vision of a society organised to fight the "Five Great Evils," that plagued society, namely want, disease, ignorance, squalor and idleness. The report set out radical and comprehensive proposals for social insurance, a safety net that would ensure families never again lacked "the means for healthy subsistence" due to a lack of work or money (Beveridge 1942). Though the report received a lukewarm response from Churchill and his inner circle, 95% of the general population were in favour of the initiatives it proposed, which included child and unemployment benefits, maternity care, pensions and funeral allowances (Day 2017). The social research project, Mass Observation, recorded public reactions to the report, which brought "the sudden realisation of how insecure one's own life really is" (D. Fraser 2017, 243). Winnicott and Britton Winnicott gave evidence to the Curtis Committee of 1946, on the rights of children in group homes to a family life and personal attention, and their ideas informed the Children Act of 1948 which set out the responsibilities of local authorities in relation to children who could not be cared for by their parents. Barry Richards suggests that object relations theorists offered "the translation of war-time practices into wide-ranging civil objectives to reform capitalism by applying theoretical insights into the infantile dimension of adult psychology to practices in welfare and industry; in short to humanise capitalism according to psychoanalytic principles" (1984, 13). From theories of infantile attachment (Bowlby) and maternal care (Winnicott), and an awareness of the splitting and "unthinkable anxiety" that insecurity might bring about, could be inferred the need for institutions that might hold the citizen and facilitate their "going-on-being" (D. W. Winnicott 1990b, 57, 60). Winnicott disseminated his idea to the public through his broadcasts on the BBC during and after the war (Farley 2012). He was also part of the network of professionals—including doctors, social workers, teachers and child guidance workers—who brought the post-war social settlement into being and made it work (S. Alexander 2016, 116).

Riley highlights that the claim that psychoanalytic ideas were popularised both during and after the war suggests that the theory itself existed independent of context and reveals nothing about why certain ideas capture the public imagination at any particular time (1983, 85). As the foregoing discussion suggests, the experiences of insecurity and loss which were intensified during the war no doubt contributed to a public desire for nurturance and support, which was to be met by the social implementation of psychoanalytic ideas taking shape in the same context. The war brought awareness of the importance of care and relationships to the fore. More critically, scholars highlight that the emphasis that the new psychology placed on the vital significance of early care made parents increasingly responsible for creating normal subjects (N. S. Rose 2005, 159). As a result, a new way of thinking developed that stressed the role of parenthood, and specifically motherhood, in promoting emotional stability and healthy maturity (Shapira 2015, 65–66). Object relations theories valorised the child-centred family and informed the creation of social services designed to safeguard it, wherever possible (N. S. Rose 2005, 160). Indeed, "the main activity for promotion of [the] democratic tendency is a negative one: avoidance of interference with the ordinary good home," Winnicott wrote in 1957, in his article on the meaning of democracy (1986a, 259). "The future of democracy and the possibility of cooperation amongst citizens," Shapira writes, "rested on such values of care" (2015, 64). However, for Winnicott the potential for psychic development was always intimately connected with the context of social provision. Winnicott insists that the stability children need in order to develop their emotional capacities is "passed down, from the community in general, to the children," a comment that challenges the idea of solely parental responsibility (2012b, 59).

For Winnicott, the caregiver's capacity to care depends on a stability facilitated by the wider society. However, object relations theories and the welfare state did tend to conceptualise this in line with the traditional gendered division of labour, which led to the development of social forms of holding that supported the nuclear family. In the home, the paternal breadwinner functions as "the protecting agent who frees the mother to devote herself to her baby" (D. W. Winnicott 1986a, 248). Healthy families are for Winnicott, Gerson writes, "organised to meet the child's demand to be held," which implies the presence of a caregiver (most often the mother) dedicated to caring for the child and supported by a breadwinner (assumed by Winnicott to be the father) who mediates and softens the insecurities of the external world (2017, 326). The need for stability in the caregiver-child dyad would make reliable social institutions necessary, institutions capable of sheltering the family unit from extremes of poverty and insecurity, through social insurance and children's allowances. If the primary caregiver is to provide the child with a good-enough holding environment, then the home itself must have a similar holding environment, provided by the welfare state. Gerson writes that for Winnicott "a stable home that is relatively free from anxieties is where individuality forms [...] government should draw away from primary relationships, as such relationships are the condition for human flourishing" (2005, 115). Social services should be on hand to meet the family's need for holding in the form of medical, educational and accommodation services, extending to the family "the same pattern of care that the family gives to the child" (Gerson 2017, 326). It is important to reiterate, however, that for Winnicott the care the child receives needs to be continual, not continuous (Hollway 2006a). The primary caregiver is not required to be always at home, nor does care have to be provided by the child's biological mother. Winnicott's ideas do not preclude the development of more socialised forms of provision.

Nevertheless, Gerson's concerns about the gender politics of Winnicott's thinking echo longstanding feminist analyses, which balance critique of Winnicott's maternal preoccupations with estimation of the value of his thinking. Mitchell stresses the social conservatism of the post-war period, which led to the closure of nurseries and communal restaurants, and the restriction of women to the home: "instead of national workers, they were to be private wives" (1974, 228). Commenting on the relationship between this trend and object relations theory, she argues that "it does not amount to an estimation of the intrinsic merits or otherwise of the work if one points out that the development of child psychoanalysis contributed very neatly to the demands of the epoch" (229). Riley, however, demonstrates the falsity of the common view that psychoanalytic discourse supported the return of women to the home after the war because its emphasis on the needs of children for their mothers fitted seamlessly with government desires to re-establish a male labour force and post-war pronatalism. Whilst "a widespread pronatalist appeal" sat comfortably with Winnicott and Bowlby's ideas (Riley 1983, 91), it was wrong to suggest "there was any kind of concerted effort at the level of government policy to get women back into the home" (Wilson 1980, 181). Certainly, women's domestic role was "reinforced by the progressive currents of thought of the period," but Wilson suggests that the basis of their popular appeal lay in "the flowering of love for children in a war-torn world," and a celebration of working-class maternal spontaneity and warmth in opposition to austere forms of upper-class child-rearing (190). In fact, as Riley shows, though mothers were indeed "the true target of post-war social philosophy," it was the absence of government policies designed to support working caregivers—i.e. specific public forms of holding designed with their needs in mind—that led them to forego work (1983, 170). The provision of public forms of holding could have facilitated liberation from the home as well. Though John Bowlby did insist on the negative impact of any form of maternal separation prior to the age of two, Bowlbyism only gained purchase on the policy imagination in the 1950s, and at this point made the idea of the provision of childcare for working mothers unaskable. What, amongst other factors, really drove the government decision to retrench support for working mothers, including the provision of the war nurseries, was the desire to retain the idea of maternal responsibility for childcare, and head off any developing sense that childcare should be a social provision (118). Nevertheless, Winnicott's sustained association of women with motherhood and his preoccupation with women's apparently "intuitive" mothering when in a state of "health" (never guaranteed, however) certainly did little to challenge traditional gender roles. The post-war welfare state depended on women keeping up this unpaid care work, and Winnicott's idea of the "ordinary good home"—protected by, yet separate from, the outside world—did seem to naturalise this arrangement. Winnicott was definitely a product of his time in this regard. In his paper on "The Mother's Contribution to Society" he writes that "ordinary good parents do build a home and stick together, thus providing the basic ration of child care and thus maintaining a setting in which each child can gradually find the self and the world, and a working relationship between the two," a comment that demonstrates his adherence to the norms of his time (1986b, 124). As Shapira puts it, the heterosexual family was envisioned as "the healthy environment for children" (2015, 64).

Maternal Attitudes and Caring States

However, as Mitchell writes, the "paeans to the family" that peppered Winnicott's early work "obscured its more interesting content" (1974, 229). Winnicott's thinking may have eulogised wishfully about the importance of the heterosexual nuclear family and failed to challenge the division of labour characteristic of it, but it also contains valuable insights into the environmental prerequisites for emotional development, and the relevance of values and practices associated with maternal care for public life. Winnicott may have emphasised the importance of the "intact family" for emotional growth, but his reminder that "social provision is very much an extension of the family" makes it possible to imagine the caring functions that have condensed in the maternal role over the course of modernity as disseminated and distributed across the institutions of collective life (2006, 133, 136). This is partially a case of acknowledging that a child requires care in order to foster their capacities and relations with others. It also involves acknowledging the needs of caregivers for support if they are to be able to care. However, seeing social provision as an extension of the family is also about the ways in which the mother–child relationship, and Winnicott's account of holding, functions as a model for both the ethos and character of social provision. "If we examine," he writes, "the ways in which people provide for young children and for older children, and if we look at the political institutions of adult life, we find displacements from the home setting and the family…the home and the family are still the models on which is based any sort of social provision which is likely to work" (136). The family, wherein forms of relationality and dependence are privatised in modernity, provides a model for forms of public holding and support that aim to mitigate the anxieties and insecurities that capitalism manufactures.

Bar-Haim highlights that the popularisation of Winnicottian thinking in the post-war period should not be understood simply as a tool for entrenching traditional gender roles, but as a central part of an ideological attempt to bring the maternal into the public sphere (2021, 135). This might well refer to the surveillance and policing of the family through the dissemination of advice and the institution of social services but, more positively, it offers a way of describing the ways in which the state adopted a maternal attitude towards its citizens in the post-war period (136). Certainly, psychoanalytic knowledge existed in complex relation with power both during and after the war. However, as Layton notes, a Foucauldian approach that emphasises governmentality, whilst important, sidesteps the question of whether or not there are basic human needs that must be met for a democratic society to function (2013). Layton is rightly critical of an ahistorical understanding of need, but dependence on others—including caregivers and the planet itself—can arguably be conceived as a universal state whilst preserving the idea of historical variation in how it is met. The post-war welfare state may have bolstered the family, but the principles that informed it could have informed proposals for more socialised forms of care.

Object relations theorists took dependence seriously and sought to foster the emotional development of children, as well as providing a model which had implications for adults too. The post-war welfare state evolved in relation to, whilst also actualising, Winnicott's sense of the response that dependence demands: holding. As Michael Rustin puts it, the post-war welfare state involved "recognition of the realities of unavoidable and universal human dependency" (2015, 3). Vicky Lebeau writes that "the post-war welfare state was also a 'socially sanctioned settlement for the management of our knowledge of social suffering and conflict'; in other words, it was a settlement, at once material and symbolic, that made human need and human vulnerability a properly social concern (from 'cradle to grave' in the classic formulation: you can't birth or bury yourself)" (2019, 166). Paul Hoggett suggests that the sense that humans are dependent, vulnerable and prone to adversity informed the philosophy of the post-war welfare state which "tacitly assumed the existence of a community of interdependent strangers sharing together an experience of actual or imminent vulnerability" (2000, 202).

The consensus on social justice and the welfare state that briefly held after the war took the reproduction of human beings seriously. As Carolyn Steedman records, the period of relative stability produced a generation born in the 1940s and 1950s who enjoyed social freedom and educational access unavailable to their parents. She writes that:

> The 1950s was a time when state intervention in children's lives was highly visible, and experienced, by me at least, as entirely beneficent. The calculated, dictated fairness of the ration book went on into the new decade, and we spent a lot of time [...] picking up medicine bottles of orange juice and jars of Virol [...] I think I would be a very different person now if orange juice and milk and dinners at school hadn't told me, in a covert way, that I had a right to exist, was worth something. My inheritance from those years is the belief (maintained always with some difficulty) that I do have a right to the earth. (1986, 121–22)

The expansion of public provision in the post-war period licensed forms of government intervention in citizens' lives, but Steedman suggests that at least some of these interventions were experienced as a form of public concern that facilitated a sense of personal existence and the right to be alive. For her, the belief that her existence mattered was bestowed by the state and this demonstrates "what a fully material culture might offer in terms of physical comfort and the structures of care and affection that it symbolises, for all children," and for adults too (123).

Rose links the subsequent erosion of forms of public provision to the critique of object relations psychoanalysis, which gained ground from the mid-60s (2005, 180–81). In addition to feminist critiques, psychologists also questioned the bases of psychoanalytic knowledge, whilst libertarians challenged the rationale of welfare bureaucracies and social work. "Out of all of this," he writes, "would gradually emerge a new strategy for the government of social life centred on the privacy of the family; the responsible, autonomous family was its emblem" (181). Such approaches locate the source of inequality and social malaise in an isolated family unit and disavow the state's responsibility for care. In a recent iteration of this view, David Cameron, for instance, has asserted that "what matters most to a child's life chances is not the wealth of their upbringing but the warmth of their parenting" (cited in Jones 2012, 77). The primary relationships a child experiences are obviously of central significance, and material circumstances are not determinative, but intimate relationships also cannot be understood in complete isolation from the social contexts in which they occur. The idea of the autonomous family makes that institution alone responsible for children's care and development. As a result, the inequality reproduced through networks of privilege and inheritance is rendered invisible, and the holding function of forms of social provision is eclipsed. That the erosion of social provision can be linked to the critique of theories like Winnicott's, demonstrates how central those theories and their principles of care were in "maternalising" the post-war public sphere. Winnicott's work brought values and practices associated with maternal care, specifically the idea of holding, into public life. The welfare state provided a collective holding environment for citizens.

Holding, however, can also be considered an ethic of care. Describing a way of relating and responding to the dependence of an other, a child in the first instance, it involves, in Fred Alford's words, "a subtle combination of otherness and identification" that fosters the continuity of being, allowing the other to grow in their own way (2000, 246). Without reference to Winnicott, the term "holding" has also been employed by Ruddick to describe a "fundamental attitude of protectiveness" developed by those providing maternal care (1995, 78–79). Holding, for Ruddick, is "a way of seeing with an eye toward maintaining the minimal harmony, material resources, and skills necessary for sustaining a child in safety" (79). Julie Stephens emphasises that Ruddick's concept has a metaphysical aspect that extends beyond kinship ties to wider communities and the non-human world (2011, 39). The capacity develops in the act of childcare and can then be put to work in other contexts. It has broad social significance. Winnicott foregrounded the idea that institutions can hold. Whilst holding can lapse into degenerative forms of over and under-protection (Ruddick 1995, 79), a maternal model of social provision calls attention to protection and meeting need as characteristic of an ethical response to dependence.

The idea that human dependence and vulnerability confront those who encounter them with an ethical decision about how to act is a feature of many of the perspectives discussed thus far. That the encounter with the young child calls up "tendence" and "protection" on the part of the caregiver is there in Rousseau and Sully. Winnicott, confronted with the child on the mother's lap in his consulting room, or with the evident distress of the child in hostel care, whilst also in touch with his own inner child through his personal analysis, was called to both formulate and think about dependency and the response it demands. Adriana Cavarero uses Arendt's idea of natality to highlight that the newborn represents human potential, the potential for action, but she insists that the realisation of potential depends on nurturance (2016, 116). Potential is realised through relationship; faced with the vulnerable and dependent other, the caregiver has the choice of whether to care or harm (Cavarero 2011). Without dwelling on the encounter between the mother and child, Judith Butler has famously discussed the relationship between human vulnerability and responsibility, arguing that our inherent relationality and precariousness constitute the basis of our ethical obligations towards others (2004, 2009). As Erinn Gilson puts it, "vulnerability carries with it…normative force; it calls for response and, moreover, for particular kinds of response…[namely] to try to prevent vulnerability from being turned into harm or being unequally distributed" (2014, 15–16).

In recent decades, the ethos of policymaking has eschewed knowledge of dependence and vulnerability. Stephens suggests that holding, as conceived by Ruddick, is the antithesis of the ideals of neoliberalism, which actualises forms of planned abandonment rather than care, and is characterised by what Hoggett describes as "hatred of dependency" (Stephens 2011, 39; Hoggett 2000, 159–80). Recently, Butler has suggested that humans are "born into a condition of radical dependency" that we may seek to disavow as we grow (2020, 41). "As we reflect back on that condition as adults," she writes, "perhaps we are slightly insulted or alarmed, or perhaps we dismiss the thought. Perhaps someone with a strong sense of individual self-sufficiency will indeed be offended by the fact that there was a time when one could not feed oneself or could not stand on one's own." Liberal individualism tends towards this kind of disavowal, which has again become hegemonic in the wake of the long, slow dismantling of the welfare state. A refusal to think about need, dependence and vulnerability shapes public policy in ways that reproduce the perspective of the rational liberal contractor.

Virginia Held, however, proposes that knowledge of dependence could have positive implications for designing policy provision. "Those thoughtfully involved in the work of bringing up children or caring for the dependent," she writes, "may design better public institutions for child care, education, health care, welfare, and the like" (2006, 78). Those with experience of caring for children and others are well-positioned to recognise dependence—that of those in their care and their own—and the kinds of responses that facilitate growth. Held does not advocate that welfare services infantilise adults, but rather suggests that we consider what is best for the very young or very old, the highly dependent, seriously ill or heavily medicated by imagining what we would have wanted of our carers *if we were children* (77). Such values, she suggests, may be relevant for fostering relations between welfare states and their beneficiaries. In ways that resonate with the ethos of the welfare state Winnicott helped shape, she writes that "political institutions that have the task of governing activities in which the value of care is more obviously relevant may also be greatly improved by considering their design from the perspective of mother–child relations rather than only from the perspective of the liberal rational contractor" (78). Doing so requires being able to think about dependence in ways that the dominant ideals in our society disavow.

Overtly invoking the relevance of Winnicott's thinking for contemporary policymaking, Nussbaum writes that "we should not ask about the 'facilitating environment' for development by looking to the family circle alone," and she insists on the need for public institutions to "provide what Donald Winnicott called a 'facilitating environment' for lives of trust and reciprocity" (2004, 225, 223). A facilitating environment, Nussbaum reiterates, is one in which total helplessness and dependence are acknowledged and met (2001, 186). It is a space capable of resisting the tendency to flee from vulnerability into a state of defensive narcissism, a space capable of holding neediness and difficulty so that a way through might be found. These ways of thinking, which Ruddick and Hollway argue are available to primary carers, were also available to Winnicott through his work with children (Ruddick 1995; Hollway 2006b). These experiences permitted Winnicott to model a vision of social provision based on early care that involved holding: the recognition and meeting of dependency needs. Attending to the early relations of care through which selves are formed, the practices of holding that shape our capacities, represents a necessary corrective to the forms of subjectivity, policy and politics that have dominated social life in modernity. Winnicott offers a model for social provision very much like the one Held advocates. His work invests in and advocates for "caring states" at both an individual and collective level, whilst foregrounding the relationship between them. The development of the capacity for concern, a caring state, depends on the ability of caregivers—individual and institutional—to enter into caring states, acknowledging and meeting dependence. Winnicott's work, then, contributes to the process of "cultivating and prioritising the social, institutional and political facilities that enable and enhance our capacities to care for each other" (The Care Collective 2020, 26).

References

Abram, Jan. 2007. *The Language of Winnicott a Dictionary of Winnicott's Use of Words*. London: Karnac.

———. 2012. 'The Evolution of Winnicott's Theoretical Matrix: A Brief Outline'. In *Donald Winnicott Today*, edited by Jan Abram, 73–112. The New Library of Psychoanalysis. London; New York: Routledge.

Alexander, Meena. 1989. *Women in Romanticism: Mary Wollstonecraft, Dorothy Wordsworth, and Mary Shelley*. Women Writers. Savage, MD: Barnes and Noble.

Alexander, Sally. 2013. 'Primary Maternal Preoccupation: D. W. Winnicott and Social Democracy in Mid-Twentieth-Century Britain'. In *History and Psyche: Culture, Psychoanalysis, and the Past*, edited by Barbara Taylor and Sally Alexander, 149–72. Basingstoke; New York: Palgrave Macmillan.

———. 2016. 'D. W. Winnicott and the Social Democratic Vision'. In *Psychoanalysis in the Age of Totalitarianism*, edited by Matt Ffytche and Daniel Pick, 114–30. London; New York: Routledge.

Alford, C. Fred. 2000. 'Levinas and Winnicott: Motherhood and Responsibility'. *American Imago* 57 (3): 235–59.https://doi.org/10.1353/aim.2000.0015.

Bar-Haim, Shaul. 2021. *The Maternalists: Psychoanalysis, Motherhood, and the British Welfare State*. Philadelphia: University of Pennsylvania Press.

Beveridge, William. 1942. 'Social Insurance and Allied Services'. https://archive.org/stream/in.ernet.dli.2015.275849/2015.275849.The-Beveridge_djvu.txt.

Bhambra, Gurminder K., and John Holmwood. 2018. Colonialism, Postcolonialism and the Liberal Welfare State. *New Political Economy* 23 (5): 574–587. https://doi.org/10.1080/13563467.2017.1417369.

Britton Winnicott, Clare. 2012. 'Introduction'. In *Deprivation and Delinquency*, by Donald W. Winnicott, edited by Clare Winnicott, Ray Shepherd, and Madeleine Davis. London; New York: Routledge.

Burston, Daniel. 1996. 'Conflict and Sociability in Hegel, Freud, and Their Followers: Tzvetan Todorov's "Living Alone Together"'. *New Literary History* 27 (1): 73–82.

Butler, Judith. 2004. *Precarious Life: The Powers of Mourning and Violence*. London; New York: Verso.

———. 2009. *Frames of War: When Is Life Grievable?* London; New York: Verso.

———. 2020. *The Force of Nonviolence: An Ethico-Political Bind*. London; New York: Verso.

Calhoon, Kenneth Scott. 1992. *Fatherland: Novalis, Freud, and the Discipline of Romance*. Detroit: Wayne State University Press.

Cavarero, Adriana. 2011. *Horrorism: Naming Contemporary Violence*. New York: Columbia University Press.

———. 2016. *Inclinations: A Critique of Rectitude*. Translated by Amanda Minervini and Adam Sitze. Stanford, CA: Stanford University Press.

Davin, Anna. 1978. 'Imperialism and Motherhood'. *History Workshop Journal* 5: 9–65.

Day, Chris. 2017. 'The National Archives—The Beveridge Report and the Foundations of the Welfare State'. The National Archives Blog. The National Archives. 7 December 2017. https://blog.nationalarchives.gov.uk/beveridge-report-foundations-welfare-state/.

Fairbairn, W. Ronald D. 1994. *Psychoanalytic Studies of the Personality*. London; New York: Routledge.

Farley, Lisa. 2012. 'Analysis On Air: A Sound History of Winnicott in Wartime'. *American Imago* 69 (4): 449–71.

Fraser, Derek. 2017. *The Evolution of the British Welfare State: A History of Social Policy since the Industrial Revolution*, 1st ed. London: Palgrave Macmillan Education.

Freud, Sigmund. 1923. 'The Ego and the Id'. In *SE 19*, 3–66.

———. 1927. 'The Future of an Illusion'. In *SE 21*, 1–56.

———. 1930. 'Civilization and Its Discontents'. In *SE 21*, 59–145.

———. 1931. 'Female Sexuality'. In *SE 21*, 223–43.

Gerson, Gal. 2005. 'Individuality, Deliberation and Welfare in Donald Winnicott'. *History of the Human Sciences* 18 (1): 107–26.

———. 2017. 'Winnicott and the History of Welfare State Thought in Britain'. In *D.W. Winnicott and Political Theory: Recentering the Subject*, edited by Matthew H. Bowker and Amy Buzby, 311–32. New York: Palgrave Macmillan.

Gilson, Erinn C. 2014. *The Ethics of Vulnerability: A Feminist Analysis of Social Life and Practice*. New York: Routledge.

Held, Virginia. 2006. *The Ethics of Care: Personal, Political, and Global*. Oxford: Oxford University Press.

Hoggett, Paul. 1992. *Partisans in an Uncertain World: The Psychoanalysis of Engagement*. London: Free Association Books.

———. 2000. *Emotional Life and the Politics of Welfare*. Houndmills, Basingstoke, Hampshire; New York: Macmillan Press; St. Martin's Press.

Hollway, Wendy. 2006a. 'Family Figures in 20th-Century British "Psy" Discourses'. *Theory & Psychology* 16 (4): 443–64. https://doi.org/10.1177/0959354306066200.

———. 2006b. *The Capacity to Care: Gender and Ethical Subjectivity*. London; New York: Routledge.

Jones, Owen. 2012. *Chavs: The Demonization of the Working Class*. London; New York: Verso.

Kanter, Joel. 2000. 'The Untold Story of Clare and Donald Winnicott: How Social Work Influenced Modern Psychoanalysis'. *Clinical Social Work Journal* 28 (3): 245–61.

Kaplan, E. Ann. 1992. *Motherhood and Representation: The Mother in Popular Culture and Melodrama*. London; New York: Routledge.

King, Pearl, and Riccardo Steiner. 1991. *The Freud-Klein Controversies 1941-1945*. London: Tavistock/Routledge.

Koven, Seth, and Sonya Michel. 1993. 'Introduction: "Mother Worlds"'. In *Mothers of a New World: Maternalist Politics and the Origins of Welfare States*, edited by Seth Koven and Sonya Michel, 1–42. New York: Routledge.

Lebeau, Vicky. 2019. 'Feeling Poor: D.W. Winnicott and Daniel Blake'. *New Formations* 96 (96): 160–76. https://doi.org/10.3898/NEWF:96/97.07.2019.

Layton, Lynne. 2013. 'Psychoanalysis and Politics: Historicising Subjectivity'. *Mens Sana Monographs* 11 (1): 68–81. https://doi.org/10.4103/0973-1229.104493.

Mellor, Anne K. 1993. *Romanticism and Gender*. New York: Routledge.

Mitchell, Juliet. 1974. *Psychoanalysis and Feminism: A Radical Reassessment of Freudian Psychoanalysis*. London: Allen Lane.

Nussbaum, Martha C. 2001. *Upheavals of Thought: The Intelligence of Emotions*. Cambridge; New York: Cambridge University Press.

———. 2004. *Hiding from Humanity: Disgust, Shame, and the Law*. Princeton, NJ: Princeton University Press.

Phillips, Adam. 2007. *Winnicott*. London: Penguin.

Pitcher, Ben. 2016. 'Race, Debt and the Welfare State'. *New Formations* 87 (87): 47–63. https://doi.org/10.3898/NEWF.87.3.2016.

Richards, Barry. 1984. 'Introduction'. In *Capitalism and Infancy: Essays on Psychoanalysis and Politics*, edited by Barry Richards, 7–21. London; Atlantic Highlands, NJ: Free Association Books; Humanities Press.

Richardson, Alan. 1988. 'Romanticism and the Colonization of the Feminine'. In *Romanticism and Feminism*, edited by Anne K. Mellor, 13–25. Bloomington: Indiana University Press.

Rieff, Philip. 1966. *The Triumph of the Therapeutic: Uses of Faith After Freud*. London: Chatto and Windus.

Riley, Denise. 1983. *War in the Nursery: Theories of the Child and Mother*. London: Virago.

Rodman, F. Robert. 2003. *Winnicott: Life and Work*. Cambridge, MA: Perseus.

Rose, Nikolas S. 2005. *Governing the Soul: The Shaping of the Private Self*. London: Free Association Books.

Rousseau, Jean-Jacques. 1979. *Emile: Or, On Education*. Edited and translated by Allan Bloom. New York: Basic Books.

Rowbotham, Sheila. 2010. *Dreamers of a New Day: Women Who Invented the Twentieth Century*. London; New York: Verso.

Ruddick, Sara. 1995. *Maternal Thinking: Toward a Politics of Peace*. Boston, MA: Beacon Press.

Rustin, Michael. 2015. 'A Relational Society'. Edited by Stuart Hall, Doreen Massey, and Michael Rustin. *Afterneoliberalism? The Kilburn Manifesto*. https://www.lwbooks.co.uk/soundings/kilburn-manifesto.

Santner, Eric L. 1990. *Stranded Objects: Mourning, Memory, and Film in Postwar Germany*. Ithaca, NY: Cornell University Press.

Sayers, Janet. 1991. *Mothering Psychoanalysis*. London: Penguin.

Shapira, Michal. 2015. *The War inside: Psychoanalysis, Total War, and the Making of the Democratic Self in Postwar Britain*. Cambridge: University of Cambridge Press.

Sprengnether, Madelon. 1990. *The Spectral Mother: Freud, Feminism, and Psychoanalysis*. Ithaca: Cornell University Press.

Steedman, Carolyn. 1986. *Landscape for a Good Woman: A Story of Two Lives*. London: Virago.

Stephens, Julie. 2011. *Confronting Postmaternal Thinking: Feminism, Memory, and Care*. New York: Columbia University Press.

Stone, Lawrence. 1990. *The Family, Sex and Marriage in England 1500–1800*. London: Penguin.

Suttie, Ian D. 1999. *The Origins of Love and Hate*. London: Routledge.

The Care Collective. 2020. *The Care Manifesto: The Politics of Interdependence*. London; New York: Verso Books.

Wilson, Elizabeth. 1980. *Only Halfway to Paradise: Women in Postwar Britain, 1945–1968*. London; New York: Tavistock Publications.

Winnicott, Donald W. 1958a. 'A Note on Normality and Anxiety'. In *Collected Papers: Through Paediatrics to Psycho-Analysis*, 3–21. London: Tavistock.

———. 1958b. 'Appetite and Emotional Disorder'. In *Collected Papers: Through Paediatrics to Psycho-Analysis*, 33–51. London: Tavistock.

———. 1958c. 'The Manic Defence'. In *Collected Papers: Through Paediatrics to Psycho-Analysis*, 129–44. London: Tavistock.

———. 1986a. 'Some Thoughts on the Meaning of the Word "Democracy"'. In *Home Is Where We Start From: Essays by a Psychoanalyst*, 239–59. Harmondsworth: Penguin.

———. 1986b. 'The Mother's Contribution to Society'. In *Home Is Where We Start from: Essays by a Psychoanalyst*, 123–27. Harmondsworth: Penguin.

———. 1990a. 'A Personal View of the Kleinian Contribution'. In *The Maturational Processes and the Facilitating Environment: Studies in the Theory of Emotional Development*, 166–70. London: Karnac and the Institute of Psycho-Analysis.

———. 1990b. 'Ego Integration in Child Development'. In *The Maturational Processes and the Facilitating Environment*, 56–63. London: Karnac and the Institute of Psycho-Analysis.

———. 1990c. 'The Theory of the Parent-Infant Relationship'. In *The Maturational Processes and the Facilitating Environment: Studies in the Theory of Emotional Development*, 37–55. London: Karnac and the Institute of Psycho-Analysis.

———. 2006. 'The Family and Emotional Maturity'. In *The Family and Individual Development*, 128–38. London: Routledge.

———. 2012a. 'Evacuation of Small Children'. In *Deprivation and Delinquency*, 11–19. London; New York: Routledge.

———. 2012b. 'Residential Management as Treatment for Difficult Children'. In *Deprivation and Delinquency*, 49–64. London; New York: Routledge.

Wordsworth, William. 1959. *The Prelude*. Edited by H. Darbishire. Oxford: Clarendon Press.

Young-Bruehl, Elisabeth. 2011. 'Psychoanalysis and Social Democracy: A Tale of Two Developments'. *Contemporary Psychoanalysis* 47 (2): 179–203. https://doi.org/10.1080/00107530.2011.10746450.

Zaretsky, Eli. 2005. *Secrets of the Soul: A Social and Cultural History of Psychoanalysis*. New York: Vintage.

5

Care, Power, Justice

> We must learn to see the ethics of justice and care as complements rather than rivals. The challenge is to integrate the project of human emancipation, the search for a society which can give expression to the fullness of human powers, with the passive and tragic dimensions of human life. Anything else will sell us all short. (Hoggett 2000, 180)

> The task is to think through [humans'] primary impressionability and vulnerability with a theory of power and recognition. (Butler 2004, 45)

Since the 1970s, there have been various different approaches to understanding the relationship between care and justice. One of the first areas to receive attention was the scale of informal care. Feminists, for instance, highlighted the sexual division of labour, drawing attention to "the exploitation of women's unpaid labour as carers and the role of the state in maintaining this" (Williams 2001, 475). Central to this was a political demand for increased recognition of unpaid care work, as well as an appreciation of its role in reproducing capitalism. In 1972, Selma James proposed the idea of Wages for Housework at the National Women's Liberation Conference in Manchester, as a means of highlighting the dependence of the sphere of production on the unacknowledged and uncompensated domestic sphere of reproduction. Here, justice was predicated on the recognition of the fundamental and disavowed centrality of care within society. Achieving social justice would depend on acknowledging the importance of care and allowing that knowledge to transform social policy and social relations.

In the 1980s, however, care and justice came to be conceived as opposing moral principles. Carol Gilligan's account of care as an ethical principle, one more commonly evident in the ethical deliberations of women because of the caring labour that was assigned to them, was pivotal in transforming understandings of the relationship between ethics and gender (1990). For Gilligan, care represents a feminine ethical principle that stands in contrast to the masculine principle of justice. Whilst a justice perspective emphasises universal principles in making ethical and moral judgements, from the perspective of the ethic of care, situation, circumstance and particularity inform decision-making, eschewing a monolithic account of right and wrong. Gilligan has been criticised for seeming to naturalise the heterosexual nuclear family, and for failing to consider the ways that 'race,' class, disability and sexuality intersect with and complicate gendered relations of care. As a result of these critiques, subsequent work has sought to do justice to marginalised perspectives, exploring the implications of difference for thinking about care, in particular how differences in terms of disability, 'race,' ethnicity and sexuality inflect understandings, practices and sites of caring (Williams 2001, 476).

Joan Tronto was amongst the first scholars to take the principle of the ethic of care into the field of political theory, exploring the value of the concept outside of the private sphere to which it had been consigned (Okin 1989; Tronto 1993). Tronto argues that care, as both practice and principle, needs to be understood as central to all aspects of human life, including politics, and that care is itself a political concept. As Marion Barnes highlights, the Rawlsian idea of distributive justice is based on a contractual understanding of social relations (the regime of the brother) that assumes forms of equality and autonomy that are disputed by care theorists (2012, 28). A care perspective, however, emphasises the inherent relationality of subjectivity, and the (inter)dependence of subjects on the care of others. As a result, Tronto claims, it makes it possible to see the "achievement of equality as a political goal" because it draws attention to how "inequalities of resources prevent citizens from equal power" (1993, 164–65). A care perspective sidesteps the artificial split between public and private life that obscures certain aspects of lived experience (especially for women and minoritised groups) and falsely establishes the idea that some concerns are private responsibilities (165). An awareness of care allows discussions of public life to proceed not on the presupposition of an autonomous individual, but rather with a view of people as interdependent actors who both need and provide care, as well as having other interests (168). Thinking about who cares for whom highlights the relations of power within society, and the ways in which care relations are intersectionally structured (169). Existing arrangements can then be judged against a normative idea of what a just distribution would look like. Whilst welfare can be conceived as a "public form of 'taking care,'" it is still very capable of fostering repressive patterns of private caretaking in which care is individualised, privatised, marketised and racialised (173).

Whilst Tronto clearly asserts the importance of the principles of care for collective life and justice, she also foregrounds the fact that there is a relationship between the ethical principle of care and lived experiences of care (167). We become "adept at caring" via "practices of giving and receiving care" (167). The experiences we have of care—as both providers and receivers—have the potential, she suggests, to make us better citizens in democracy, because through them, we learn to think and act with care towards others. Sevenhuijsen agrees with Tronto that care aids the development of civic capacities (1998). Williams writes that, for Sevenhuijsen:

> Rather than simply being counterposed to justice, we should see care as a social process engendering important elements of citizenship. The processes of caring for or being cared for make one aware of diversity, of interdependence, of the need for acceptance of difference, which form an important basis for citizenship (and are as likely, or more likely, to be learned through care as through paid work practices). (2001, 477)

These thinkers identify experiences and practices of care as important prerequisites for the development of an attitude of care relevant to political deliberation and participation. However, as Hollway notes, they do not explore the intersubjective processes through which the capacity to care develops (2006). Tronto and Sevenhuijsen are reluctant to employ the caregiver-child model of care—Tronto, for instance, is rightly wary of infantilising all care-receivers—however, the decision to avoid this paradigm means that their theories neglect the locus and process through which caring selves develop: a radical asymmetrical relationship between an infant and a caregiver that makes possible the development of subjectivity and self. In what follows, I draw in the work of Hollway and others to explore what attending to early intersubjective relationships adds to Tronto's account of the relationship between care, power and justice. How does such an approach impact the way that we think about how "inequalities of resources prevent citizens from equal power" and how we pursue "equality as a political goal" (Tronto 1993, 164–65)? What is the relationship between early experiences, capitalism—and its exploitation of care—and justice? Overall, this chapter sets out to demonstrate that the inequalities endemic to the capitalist system skew and inhibit the development of relational and caring capacities in fundamentally unjust ways.

Capacities, Care and Justice

Iris Marion Young has proposed an alternative to the "distributive paradigm" of justice, which understands justice to be co-extensive with the distribution of material goods. Young conceives justice as involving the provision of the conditions in which capacities can develop. She argues that whilst "any conception of justice must address the distribution of material goods…many public appeals to justice do not concern primarily the distribution of material goods" (1990, 19). In addition to distribution, Young suggests a range of other values relevant to social justice including "learning and using satisfying and expansive skills in socially recognised settings; participating in forming and running institutions, and receiving recognition for such participation; playing and communicating with others, and expressing our experience, feelings, and perspective on social life in contexts where others can listen" (37). Justice, however, is not identical with the realisation of these values in individual lives, it is "not identical with the good life as such." Rather, it "concerns the degree to which a society contains and supports the institutional conditions necessary for the realisation of these values" (37). The good life involves "developing and exercising one's capacities and expressing one's experience" and "participating in determining one's action and the conditions of one's action." Social justice relates to the extent to which a society contains institutional structures capable of facilitating the good life, understood in these terms.

In a related vein, Nussbaum has developed a version of capability theory that provides a useful list of the "capacities political communities should develop and support" (Nussbaum 1995b; cited in Threadcraft 2016, 24). Nussbaum makes a distinction between a threshold level of capacities for distinguishing what counts as a human life and another threshold for what counts as a good life, a life of flourishing, a life worth living (1995b, 76–85). The latter threshold is the most significant for thinking about public policy, "for we don't want societies to make their citizens capable of the bare minimum" (81). The list of capacities required for human flourishing includes:

1. Being able to live to the end of a human life of normal length, not dying prematurely, or before one's life is so reduced as to be not worth living.
2. Being able to have good health; to be adequately nourished; to have adequate shelter; having opportunities for sexual satisfaction, and for choice in matters of reproduction; being able to move from place to place.
3. Being able to avoid unnecessary and non-beneficial pain, so far as possible, and to have pleasurable experiences.
4. *Being able to use the senses; being able to imagine, to think, and to reason...*
5. *Being able to have attachments to things and persons outside ourselves*; to love those who love and care for us, to grieve at their absence...
6. Being able to form a conception of the good and to *engage in critical reflection about the planning of one's own life...*

7. *Being able to live for and to others, to recognise and show concern for other human beings*, to engage in various forms of social interaction; *to be able to imagine the situation of another and to have compassion for that situation*; to have the capability for both justice and friendship…
8. Being able to *live with concern* for and in relation to animals, plants and the world of nature.
9. Being able to laugh, to play, to enjoy recreational activities.
10. Being able to *live one's own life* and nobody else's…
    10a. Being able to live one's own life in one's own surroundings and context. (83–85, emphasis added)

Nussbaum holds that a life that lacks any of these capabilities cannot be deemed a good human life, and she advocates for taking these things as the "focus for concern" in assessing the quality of life in a country and considering the role of public policy and institutions in meeting human needs (85). Nussbaum's list of capabilities includes the conditions for bodily life and health, but it also includes a range of subjective capacities that are intimately connected with relations of care, including the capacity to imagine; to think; to have attachments; to plan and live one's own life (to have autonomy); to feel concern. The work of object relations theorists, and philosophers informed by their theories, foregrounds the fact that these capacities develop initially (or don't develop) in the early intersubjective relationships in which selves take shape, relationships that are inherently related to the social world in which they are located.

In object relations-based accounts of the development of subjectivity, the formation of the self, and its capacities, is inherently relational. As Alison Stone glosses, "the core self is a core self-*with-another*," or, in Winnicott's famous words, "there is no such thing as a baby!" (A. Stone 2019, 96; D. W. Winnicott 1958a, 99). Axel Honneth foregrounds the centrality of relation in the development of the self. "In the first months of life," he writes, "infants are so dependent on practical extension of their behaviour via the care they receive that it is a misleading abstraction…to study the infant in isolation from all significant others" (1996, 98). He continues: "the care with which the 'mother' keeps the newborn baby alive is not added to the child's behaviour as something secondary but is rather merged with the child in such a way that one can plausibly assume that every human life begins with a phase of undifferentiated intersubjectivity," from the child's perspective at least (98). Hollway emphasises that subjectivities are inherently intersubjective, which means they are formed and reformed through "a set of ongoing dynamic processes" that "originate in early infant-mother connectedness" (2006, 63). Though it begins in infancy, the intersubjective relationality of the self is a lifelong aspect of our existence.

Developing a synthetic account of the development of the self and the capacity to care that draws on a range of object relations-based approaches, Hollway demonstrates that intersubjectivity is the condition of possibility for us to come into being as subjects, and to develop into subjects capable of relating to others with care. Hollway suggests that Winnicott "was probably the first to develop an idea of intersubjectivity which radically parted company with the idea of two interacting individuals," and she characterises the early relation between caregiver and child in terms of a "unity" (66). What unites the caregiver and the infant at this stage is the absolute need for the caregiver to adapt to the infant, which Winnicott held to be of paramount importance: "the mother's failure to adapt in the earliest phase does not produce anything but an annihilation of the infant's self" (1958c, 304). This is the stage during which the child does not have their own "psyche-soma," but rather depends on that of the caregiver. In early development, the other is a regulating and attuned presence, providing a form of "primary relationality" through which the self takes shape (Benjamin 1990). As discussed in Chapter 3, Benjamin identifies forms of intersubjective "recognition" in the early relationship between caregiver and child, specifically affective reciprocity, mutuality and attunement, which are significant elements of "the diverse responses and activities of the mother that are taken for granted as the background in all discussions of development" (27, 22). Ogden suggests that the way of organising experience available to the newborn baby can be described as an "autistic-contiguous" mode (1989). This form of relating is a "sensory-dominated, presymbolic area of experience in which the most primitive form of meaning is generated on the basis of the organization of sensory impressions, particularly at the skin surface" (4). The infant's contact with objects, as well as encounters that occur through other modalities such as smell and sound, provide the basic material through which the infant begins to organise sense experience. Hollway writes that "the contiguous appearance, disappearance and reappearance of the mother figure who is familiar to the baby's senses by her smell, voice tone, skin texture and gestures provides the baby with some location in time and therefore some sense of the ongoing nature of its own being" (2006, 45). This is an "unconscious organising process" that "does not belong to the realm of self-conscious awareness" but continues to be present throughout life in the form of what Christopher Bollas calls "the unthought known" (Hollway 2006, 45; Bollas 1987, 3). Ogden draws attention to "a hidden, taken-for-granted, largely unconscious dimension of care," one tied to the earliest period of life (Hollway 2006, 42).

Intersubjectivity is also central to the development of subjective capacities, including the capacity to care about others. Drawing on Wilfred Bion's theories of reverie and containment, Margot Waddell seeks to understand how the disorganised experiences of infants become manageable in the unconscious space that the maternal figure creates for them (2002; Bion 1988). In Bion's account, the primary caregiver acts as a container for the threatening feelings the baby experiences and wishes to get rid of. There are a range of things that can happen to these feelings, but one possibility is that the baby can receive them back from the caregiver in a "detoxified" form, which permits the baby to think. Waddell describes the specific character of this process: "the mother's relationship to her infant is not one simply of reflecting moods and impulses, and thereby enabling the baby to get to know himself by a process of mirroring, of recognition of self-in-other, but rather one of having an actively participatory role in doing something with the projected emotions" via "an unconscious processing of the baby's instinctive communications" (2002, 37). For the baby to be able to "turn the sense data of experience into his own reflexive mind" there needs to be "a primary experience of active holding by his mother's mind" (37). Waddell describes Bion's theory of "reverie," which involves not the reflection of the mental states the caregiver perceives in the child but, as Hollway puts it, an active process of "engaging with the distress rather than explaining it, tolerating not knowing its source, restraining herself from imposing a solution reactively" (2006, 49). However, Waddell also uses the term "holding" which is of course Winnicott's. Adam Phillips notes that Winnicott's "holding" and Bion's "reverie" are the "two formative paradigms of analytic technique in the British School," a point Ogden supports when he argues that they offer "two vantage points from which to view an emotional experience" (A. Phillips 1994, 113; Ogden 2004, 1349).

Through such encounters, babies learn about themselves, coming to understand their own experiences of needs and feelings, as well as their incipient agency through their own attempts at communication. If the carer is not able to think about and contain the infant's distress, the child is likely to come to misunderstand their own feelings and needs. "The baby's reliance on accurate recognition of its needs," Hollway writes, "is a reminder of why the carer needs a sense of a separate self so that she does not confuse the baby's feelings with her own, even when—especially when—she is containing them" (2006, 52). The absence of an experience of adequate holding and containing in the child's early development has significant consequences. Such failures can lead to confusion about which are one's own feelings and which are those of someone else, "imposed from outside" (52). These kinds of experiences form the basis of what Winnicott described as the "false self," an inauthentic sense of self that is based on having to respond and adapt to the feelings of a caregiver.

Object relations perspectives like those of Winnicott, Benjamin, Ogden, Waddell and Hollway emphasise that the capacity to recognise and respond to the other, which constitutes an important part of a "baby's difficult development towards understanding and accepting difference" (A. Stone 2019, 98), evolves out of a prior relationship of dependence and care in which the caregiver's capacity to recognise and respond to the child paves the way for the development of the infant's own capacities. "The mother's active understanding of her infant's needs is…vitally important in the early stages," Hollway writes (2006, 52). If this has been well-accomplished, then in time, the infant can benefit from frustration and de-adaptation. Faced a growing sense of their own dependence, the infant attempts to assert their omnipotence and denies their vulnerability through the manic defences of the paranoid-schizoid position. The caregiver needs to withstand the child's destructive attacks in order for recognition of the caregiver as an independent subject to occur (53). When they survive, the child comes to realise that "his illusions are not omnipotent." This is a significant achievement, and the key mechanism through which differentiation from the primary caregiver occurs. It is this capacity that distinguishes between "narcissistic caring and the caring that recognises the cared-for person's separate self," a distinction that gets to the heart of what, for Hollway, constitutes "good-enough" care: the capacity to identify the other's needs, recognise them as distinct from one's own and respond to them as such.

The capacity to care enables both care for others and for the self, an important aspect of becoming autonomous. On Hollway's analysis, the capacity for autonomy develops in the relationship with the primary caregiver and is linked to the intersubjective processes through which the capacity to care develops. Just as caring depends on being able to differentiate between one's own needs and desires and those of the cared for person, so autonomy also requires the ability to recognise oneself as an individuated subject with one's "own desires, pleasures and aspirations" (Hollway 2006, 31). This is both a relational and a developmental achievement. Recognition by a caregiver, and their care, makes it possible to enter into subject-subject relations, or in popular speech, to "be my own person" (32). Experiences including torture, rape and physical or emotional neglect affect the subject's ability to develop self-confidence, damaging their sense of self/other boundaries (Petherbridge 2013, 148).

The capacities formed through intersubjective relationships in infancy have implications for adult life. Honneth argues that the process of self-formation that takes place in infancy provides the basis for the capacity to enter into relations of mutual recognition in adulthood and represents the pre-condition for the capacity to demand recognition in the spheres of legal rights and social esteem (1996). Early relationships are the genealogical origin of the capacity for political action in the world. Discussing Honneth's interpretation of object relations theory, Danielle Petherbridge notes that "because infants establish their identities in relationships with certain significant others, the nature of these relationships structures the formation of identity, and more mature forms of relationality" (Petherbridge 2013, 147). Subjectivity and the capacity to "recognise, offer and demand respect" develop in relations with primary caregivers, who care for the bodily and psychological needs of the infant and recognise them (148). As a result, "an individual's future ability for the articulation of his or her needs and desires is understood to be dependent on conditions of support and care from significant others" (148).

Additionally, the capacities formed in early relationships have other political implications. Hollway focuses on how the capacities developed in the early situation of care can serve the ends of justice (2006, 115). She explores the role that capacities central to caring—the ability to identify with the other without blotting them out and reducing them to a mirror of the self—have and can play in institutional contexts. In order to demonstrate how the capacity to care can be put to work in such contexts to facilitate institutional change (with the ultimate aim of contributing to social justice), Hollway explores the work of the campaigners James and Joyce Robertson, who mounted a campaign in Britain in the post-war years to allow parents and their hospitalised children to have more contact than was permitted under existing regimes. Informed by attachment theory, the Robertsons demonstrated that long periods of isolation from their caregivers had the potential to cause serious problems for hospitalised children. James Robertson was "able to identify with the children he met there, despite the distress this caused him" (115). Through this process of identification, Robertson actualised an "emotional form of knowing" that did not "function in a determinist way to 'other' the children that he met" (115). The Robertsons campaigned for the fair and reasonable treatment of hospitalised children. Hollway writes with regard to their work: "that it was based on an ethic of care, dependent on James Robertson's capacity to care across difference and therefore to challenge an uncaring institutional regime, illustrates how the dichotomy of care and justice ethics can be transcended. His capacity…had a basis in his openness to identification with difference" (116).

On this basis, Hollway suggests that global social justice can be facilitated by a cosmopolitan vision founded on identification with difference. This way of thinking, she suggests, can be encouraged by employing similar methods to those of Robertson, namely by bringing the plights of distant others nearer through the representation of specific cases in their particularity (117). The capacity to identify with others without mistaking one's own needs for theirs can play a vital role in institutional and global change. Similarly, Nussbaum foregrounds the capacity to imagine the other as a central component in justice and citizenship (Nussbaum 1995a, 2001, 2004). Our society, she writes, "is full of refusals to imagine one another with empathy and compassion" (1995a, xvii). The ways of thinking and imagining that dominate modern politics often do not include the capacity to recognise other people as fully human. Therefore, she argues, there is a need to foster the ability to imagine the concrete ways in which people different to us grapple with disadvantage (xiii). On this analysis, the capacity to care, which generally develops through early intersubjective relations of care, has a role to play in bringing about social justice, because it represents a particular attitude towards others which involves both the recognition of, and a response to, their needs.

Hollway focuses on the role of early relations in fostering capacities with political value. The work of Young and Nussbaum, however, prompts reflection on the institutional conditions in which subjective capacities take shape (Young 1990; Nussbaum 1995b). Stone highlights that early relationships are so important because they "*form* our selves" (2019, 98). Subsequent relational experiences are only capable of reforming selves that are already formed. Our first relationships have "a formative power that no later relationships can equal" (98). Whilst part of the reason that these relationships are so important is that they happen first, it is the fact of our fundamental dependency on the care of others in early life that makes their effects so significant. An infant cannot survive or develop alone, our selves are inherently relational and intersubjective from the start. However, the relationality through which the self is formed in intersubjective encounters with caregivers is only one dimension of our relationality. Stone highlights other dimensions of relationality that have been emphasised by philosophers. For Hegel, the norms of our culture and society, its institutions and beliefs, shape who we are. For Marx, the social relations that organise society's material production of the means of subsistence are crucial (99). For Heidegger, our very being is inherently related to the objects in the world, which only become meaningful in relation to our projects and plans. The fact of our birth and dependence, and the significance of our early relationships in shaping our selves, can enhance these accounts. As Stone succinctly puts it, "on the one hand…our first relationships mediate the social and cultural world to us. On the other hand, they do this because these relationships themselves are already shaped by and occur in that social and cultural world" (99–100). The subjects we develop into, and the capacities we have, are shaped by the relational contexts in which we are born and live. Contemporary existence is inseparable from the system of capitalism. How does this system influence and skew the development of capacities in ways that are fundamentally unjust, from the perspective of Young and Nussbaum's theories?

Subjectivity and Power

Lois McNay articulates a forceful critique of object relations-based approaches to theorising the development of subjectivity and its relationship with structures of power (2008a). McNay takes issue with the account of power relations in Benjamin's work, where "power is motivated by conflicts to do with desire for omnipotent control and recognition" (Hollway 2006, 126). Drawing on Winnicott, Benjamin offers an intersubjective account of recognition as a process that involves a "*constant tension* between recognising the other and asserting the self" (Benjamin 1995, 38). From this perspective, power is located in the intersubjective dynamics of demanding, needing, denying and extending recognition to another. However, McNay argues that Benjamin's focus on the vicissitudes of recognition between an infant and their caregiver configures the early dyad as the primordial location in which subjectivity develops. According to McNay, Benjamin's analysis does not account for the relationship between this "interpersonal"—perhaps better intersubjective—model of power and the complex ways in which hierarchical identities are constituted (48). On this analysis, "Benjamin does not recognise that recognition might in fact be a psychic disposition induced by social circumstance" (58). As Simon Thompson notes, the Hegelian motif in recognition theory leads to problems for McNay, because it represents an idealised account of the formation of the subject in intersubjective relations where power is seen as merely secondary and as having a distorting effect on such relations, rather than shaping such relations in the first place (2009).

In order to illustrate her position, McNay turns to Steedman's *Landscape of a Good Woman*, which explores "the impact social deprivation has upon the psyche" (1986, 57). Steedman offers an account of her childhood relationship with her mother, which for McNay provides an exploration of how, "in circumstances of dispossession, the affectual dynamics of the mother–child relationship are often dictated by economic calculations" (2008a, 57). Paraphrasing Steedman's position, McNay writes that "the effects of poverty on working-class women like [Steedman's] mother were such that having children was regarded as a form of traffic with the future. In the absence of any other resources or power, working-class women realised that their reproductive capacity was an object that they might use to acquire security in the form of marriage." The sense of disregard Steedman felt from her mother was related to the fact that "having children had not brought her mother the material security she craved." McNay suggests that whilst "it is undoubtedly possible" to describe the relationship between Steedman and her mother "in terms of withheld recognition where economic deprivation destructively skews the primal dynamic between mother and child," this would be to misread Steedman, whose point is actually to "throw that causality into question; it is social circumstances which shape the psyche rather than simply reinforcing its primal dynamics" (57).

McNay wants, I think, to problematise the idea that the mother–child dyad is outside of politics. In the example from Steedman, the very fact of her birth has to be understood as a consequence of the power relations that shaped her mother's decision to have children. The mother–child dyad has to be located within the framework of capitalist modernity, rather than as a primal and universal origin of subjectivity that is impinged on, but not shaped by, the outside world. McNay has also applied a similar critique to Honneth's recognition paradigm, arguing that its "most insuperable difficulty" is "that power relations are always viewed as a posteriori effects of a fundamental psychic dynamic" (2008b, 276). Honneth's failure to position the caregiver-child dyad/family unit within the historical and economic frame of capitalist modernity results in his adherence to a "normative view of the family" that "overlooks the extent to which the family and its internal dynamics are contingent historical structures shaped by the forces of money and social control" (277). What Honneth takes to be the original, non-political instance of a recognitive process that only later becomes public and politicised in the spheres of rights and esteem is, in fact, an inherently political space that must be understood as an important part of the social relations of capitalist modernity. Honneth is not wrong in identifying a connection between early relationships and the development of specific subjective capacities, but his early work in particular downplays the fact that these relationships are part of, not simply a model and prerequisite for, socio-political life.

Is it possible to reconcile McNay's point, that babies are conceived— or not conceived—in a social world that shapes the very form and character of early relationships with a commitment to the vital importance of intersubjective experience for the development of the self? I think it is. First it is necessary to acknowledge and accept that the idea the mother/caregiver-child dyad is a primal locus outside of society is a fallacy. This has hopefully been demonstrated in previous chapters, which have set out a history of the "modern" family as part of the structure of capitalist social relations. Secondly, I agree with McNay that there are "specific class dynamics of the mother–child relation which cannot be adequately captured in the idea of recognition" (2008a, 57). I am not committed to the idea that the concept of recognition can satisfactorily explain all forms of interaction and all relations of power. Intersubjective relationships are shaped by the social world and the power relations in which they take place. However, we are formed through relations with others. As a tool for thinking about the character of "good-enough" early care, and the capacities for concern, care and autonomy that develop in early relationships, recognition is an important idea, and one that need not commit us to a belief in a primordial dyad that necessarily includes an infant and a biological mother and is outside of the social world. Infants need someone to care for them, they cannot, and will not, develop alone. The kind of self/subject one becomes is inherently related to the character of the intersubjective experiences one has as a child, specifically as an infant. To claim this does not necessitate the concurrent dismissal of the fact that "the emotional impact of deeply internalised class differences complicates the treatment of motherhood as a psychologically undifferentiated and universal role" (McNay 2008a, 57). In fact, to the extent that object relations theories like those of Winnicott, Benjamin and Hollway emphasise the caregiver as an active subject rather than an object, the significance of social relations for subjective development comes into view (Flax 1991, 125). The caregiver is undeniably a psychosocial creature with a history of experience and identity, as well as a social position, that cannot be subtracted or bracketed out of the interaction they have with the infant/other they care for.

Given the emphasis object relations theorists place on the fact of dependence and the inherent relationality of the self, such perspectives explicitly acknowledge the asymmetry of capability and power between the caregiver and the child and provide tools with which to explore the effects of power relations on the development of subjectivity. Stone defines power relations as: "members of group A have power over or relative to members of group B when those in A are more able than those in B (i) to steer the course of their own actions, desires, and lives; (ii) to affect how the other group's members act, desire, and live; and (iii) to shape arrangements that embody and prolong this state of affairs" (2019, 100). Stone emphasises that we are born into power relations, including the inequality of power between a caregiver and a child; the gendered norms of language and bodily comportment characteristic of any given society; and divisions of economic and global power (100). Both the power relations of the socio-cultural world into which we are born and the powers of caregivers stamp us markedly. Our "first relations mediate the social and cultural world to us," to the extent that "when we were children, power came right into ourselves" (99, 102). Laplanche's idea of the enigmatic signifier is useful in the context, as a tool for understanding the unconscious and enigmatic cultural messages that caregivers communicate to their children unwittingly (1989).

Stone lists examples of the ways that power enters us through our relations, including our bodily comportment, our way of speaking and accent, the personalities that we develop through identifications with others as we grow, and our capacity to exercise autonomy. Theorists of relational autonomy emphasise how social conditions, including our personal relations, can foster or hinder the development and ability to exercise such capacities. Catriona Mackenzie and Natalie Stoljar write that "an analysis of the characteristics and capacities of the self cannot be adequately undertaken without attention to the rich and complex social and historical contexts in which agents are embedded" (2000, 21). Nussbaum makes a similar point that the development of our capacities is inherently related to the material conditions in which we live our lives (Nussbaum 1995b, 95). Mackenzie and Stoljar also highlight the need to think of autonomy as "a characteristic of agents who are emotional, embodied, desiring, creative, and feeling, as well as rational, creatures; and they highlight the ways in which agents are both psychically internally differentiated and socially differentiated from others" (2000, 21). In order to develop the capacity to act autonomously, we need to experience the right kind of socialisation. "Only through their relationships with others do humans become capable of making choices, and…the quality of those relationships will help or hinder one's capacities…Human autonomy is an achievement, not a starting premise, and it is an achievement that requires many years," as Tronto puts it (2013, 124–25). Autonomy depends on a range of lower-level functions, for instance the capacity to regulate sleep which is internalised from our caregivers and depends on their intergenerational experiences (A. Stone 2019, 104). However, it also depends on the kinds of intersubjective experience previously discussed, namely the experiences of holding, containment, recognition and reverie through which one learns to differentiate oneself from others, have a mind of one's own and be one's own person. Intersubjectivity captures something that eludes the idea of internalisation, "that which is not consumed, what we do not get and take away from others by consumption" (Benjamin 1990, 43).

One of the factors that likely shapes the "affectual dynamics" between the caregiver and child is the character of the holding provided by the social order (McNay 2008a, 57). As Winnicott highlights, the facilitating environment the caregiver provides is located within the broader holding environment of the society in which they are located (2006). Meehan suggests that Benjamin doesn't offer an account of what social environments might produce the best conditions for recognitive capacities and, by implication, the capacity for autonomy, to develop (1995). Though aware that pre-oedipal processes are not gender-neutral, Benjamin's analysis doesn't address the ways in which what the caregiver brings to their interaction with the child might be shaped by the socio-economic circumstances in which they find themselves. Emma Downing emphasises that because "care is deeply emmeshed within power relations…We must not lose sight, therefore, of the structural conditions that impede or facilitate the availability of and access to sufficient care" (2021, 44).

Feminists and philosophers have long noted how gender norms and inequalities underpin and are reproduced by the differential development of capacities between those identified as men and women (Wollstonecraft 1985; Beauvoir 2011; Mitchell 1974; Chodorow 1978). Historically, women have been encouraged to develop caring and relational capacities, and men have been pushed in the direction of defensive forms of autonomy and abstract reasoning, and this has been a key mechanism through which capitalism has reproduced itself. In her famous account of the genesis of gendered forms of subjectivity, *The Reproduction of Mothering*, Nancy Chodorow emphasises the pull of identification between mother and daughter, and the consequences of this for the development of the daughter's subjectivity (1978). "The mother," Chodorow writes, "does not recognise or denies the existence of the daughter as a separate person, and the daughter herself then comes not to recognise, or to have difficulty recognising, herself as a separate person" (103). The intensity of the mother's bodily identification with her daughter has consequences for the female child's psychic development: "she experiences herself, rather, as a continuation or extension of […] her mother in particular, and later of the world in general" (103). The persistence of closeness and attachment between mother and daughter leads women to identify more consistently with the feminine qualities they associate with her: care, emotionality and relatedness specifically. Chodorow suggests that the bodily difference between the mother and a son, however, makes it easier for the mother to distance herself, which encourages the development of "masculine" characteristics including separation and defensive autonomy. On Chodorow's analysis, the gendered division of labour skews the development of capacities. Benjamin suggests that the demand that boys give up identification with their mothers during the oedipal stage is key to a retroactive distortion of capacities along the lines of gender difference (1990).

For both Chodorow and Benjamin, the normative social relations of capitalist society have a distorting effect on the development of capacities. However, gender is only one dimension of the structures of power and inequality that organise the social world. In recent years, important work on the unequal distribution of caring responsibilities and its effect on capacities has been undertaken by black feminists in the USA (S. A. Ferguson and King 2014; Threadcraft 2016). Shatema Threadcraft highlights the historical expectation that black women undertake tough and exploitative "women's work" in white households in order to "meet the bodily needs of white families often at the expense of care for the bodily needs of their own" (2016, 9). Such work might well have freed white women to focus on the care of their children. Chodorow and Benjamin's accounts assume a mother who is there to care for a child, a situation that may well mask inequalities that pool along the axes of 'race' and class difference. Threadcraft emphasises the "longstanding inhibition of black women's intimate—that is sexual, reproductive, and caretaking—capacities under successive systems of racial domination" (8). She highlights how the social order, and specifically the inequalities built into the capitalist political economy of care and reproduction, interact with and inhibit a range of capacities, including the capacity for caretaking. Lynch, Baker and Lyons develop the idea of "affective inequality" to describe aspects of human experience and development that have received insufficient attention. Affective inequality involves the experience of "being deprived of the capacity to develop supportive affective relations of love, care and solidarity, or [being deprived] of the experience of engaging in them when one has the capacity" (2009, 1). The concept also occurs when "the burdens and benefits" of affective work are "unequally distributed, and when this unequal distribution deprives those who do the love, care and solidary work of important human goods, including an adequate livelihood and care itself" (1).

Black women in the USA have long been deprived of the experience of engaging in "supportive relations of love, care and solidarity," because they have been subjected to intergenerational experiences of oppression in which they are expected to perform productive labour and secondary-care labour for white families in a political economy unjustly structured along the fault lines of gender, 'race' and class. Threadcraft also describes this as a situation that is intergenerationally inflected: "today, to be born black is to be born less likely to have the physical and emotional needs of one's body met adequately *and* to be more likely to have those needs met by someone who was less likely to have had them adequately met and so on" (158). This is obviously not to suggest that black people in the United States are incapable of meeting those needs or developing specific capacities, but rather to insist on the significance of the legacies of enslavement and inequality, as well as the "natal alienation" that was the result of enslaved people's estrangement from historical memory and the ties of kinship, culture and economic inheritance (Patterson 2018). Tronto writes that "the condition of being oppressed often makes even seemingly simple virtues, such as the possession of hope, difficult and rare" (Tronto 2013, 124). The intersubjective processes through which capacities develop are likely to be inflected by the injustice and inequality of the historical and contemporary organisation of social relations and welfare support within capitalism, precisely because these processes are relational, asymmetrical and part of the social world.

The absence of adequate social provision bears intensely on these experiences. Threadcraft describes how African Americans' caring has taken place in "pathogenic" environments, characterised by "health disabling resources" and "excess death," and how their caring has been inadequately supported by a "malfare" state that has "disproportionately taken the black body as its object, and disproportionately brings harm and not security to that body" (2016, 156). These, she rightly notes, are not "enabling social contexts for emotional development" but rather blight black lives with "fear and anxiety" which has the capacity to negatively affect caring relationships and reproduce affective inequality (157). From Threadcraft's analysis, it is clear that the US state fails in its duty to provide a holding environment for black caregivers and those they care for. Tony Talevski describes the attitude of welfare states towards "mothers at the margins" as paranoid-schizoid (2014, 200). In the US context, Black people's care needs are often inadequately supported, which affects the development and expression of the capacity to nurture emotional attachments in the same way that more privileged groups (whites) are more easily able to (Threadcraft 2016, 166). Evoking Winnicott's account of the need for nested holding environments, Stone writes that "those who care for others—mothers of babies, for instance—are often so occupied with caregiving that they need others to care for them in turn" (2019, 90). However, Threadcraft suggests that in the USA, the "nested dependencies" needed to support black life are not provided (Kittay 1999, 132). Threadcraft writes that "the body politic has helped white women a great deal in their efforts while at the very least neglecting black women in their efforts to do the same...whites have...hoarded opportunities to produce healthy infants" (153).

Threadcraft does not focus on the psychosocial co-ordinates of the processes she describes, but her intervention raises questions about the development of psychic capacities. Of course, if parents are not around to care for children, this does not mean that they will not have opportunities to develop other nurturing relationships, but Threadcraft's emphasis on the amount of time certain groups are forced to spend "working and commuting," and her description of the high levels of "fear and anxiety" that African Americans are forced to endure, calls attention to the inherent relationship between psychic capacities and social environments (166). What happens when histories of injustice and violence, condensed in contemporary inequalities of labour and support, impact the intersubjective processes through which psychic capacities for imagination, thinking, relationship, concern and autonomy develop? Does the social order then have a chance to succeed in reproducing existing power relations? Is this, in fact, an aspect of the mechanism through which it reproduces itself? Alease Ferguson and Toni King explore the effects of "diverted mothering" in African American families, the "sense of loss" that "results when a mother is paid to provide care and affection to others and subsequently becomes absent to varying degrees within her own family" (2014, 177). They describe encountering a particular psychic constellation in many of the African American women they have worked with, characterised by career success coupled with a circumscribed personal life and relational self, and they theorise this to be a response to and rejection of the relational sacrifices their mothers were forced to make in order to earn a living (188). Rochelle, for instance foregrounds that "there is a horrible cost associated with what Black women must do to keep their families afloat. Overall, I have been left with a life-long sense of futility, mistrust, and cynicism. My rage has made it hard to date, and keep friendships" (189). Ferguson and King's analysis illustrates how the social order is able to channel psychological processes, and potentially shape capacities, in ways that bolster existing social relations and in fact provide the very means through which those relations are lived psychically.

Though Hollway does not explore the more social aspects of the intersubjective exchanges she describes, she acknowledges the significance of the wider environment in shaping capacities. The child's capacity to care depends on the caregiver's capacity for reverie, holding and recognition. These are abilities that are likely to be called forth by the experience of becoming a caregiver for a newborn child, but they are also historically conditioned capacities with intimate ties to the caregiver's intergenerational experience of care in their own infancy. Hollway therefore draws attention to the factors in the caregiver's experience that affect and influence the development of the capacity to care. She doesn't only focus on the child, she insists that the caregiver must have a "facilitating environment" too (2006, 80). She writes that "the development of the capacities to care [in the caregiver is] not guaranteed…but the infant does communicate a demand for them and good-enough conditions (*external and internal*) make their development likely in those who are positioned to receive them" (80, emphasis added). Here, Hollway acknowledges that the ability of caregivers to provide good-enough care depends on their own historically and experientially constituted abilities (internal conditions) and the wider environment in which practices of care are located (external conditions). Hollway, however, is critical of what she terms "sociological reductionism" (6). She notes that when there is a breakdown of care, "material and social factors are emphasised as causative," for instance insufficient time or money, competing demands, women's dual role in the home and at work, or failures of training and safeguards. She criticises this approach because it neglects the intersubjective experiences through which capacities develop. Capacities are not simply *there* provided there are adequate resources, they require cultivation.

Hollway's articulation must be taken seriously by any psychosocially informed investigation seeking to theorise the relationship between care and justice. She denaturalises care, demonstrating that the capacity to care about and for people, including ourselves, is a psychic achievement that depends on intersubjective experience. It is not enough to assume that, with the necessary financial and environmental supports, good care will simply happen. Developing and facilitating the ability to care involves psychic work, a form of labour that has been insufficiently recognised. Hollway is aware that the capacity to care is shaped by "gendered power relations" that are part of the implication of "the family" in the capitalist social relations of modernity and intersect with the vicissitudes of class, 'race,' ethnicity, sexuality, identity and disability (75). Her account of caregiving remains focused on caring as a complex and difficult process, characterised by ambivalence and hatred from the start, and made more difficult when institutional supports are lacking (Hollway 2006; D. W. Winnicott 1958b; Parker 2005). Recently, members of the Care Collective have emphasised this aspect of caring in order to foreground an appeal for social justice: "it is because of the complexity and profound challenges of care, as capacity and practice, that we must provide and ensure the necessary social infrastructure that enables us to care for others, both proximate and distant" (2020, 28).

Other scholars highlight the inherent relationship between the development of capacities and the contexts of care. Young points out that today, "hundreds of millions of children in the world…are not afforded the opportunity for childhood" in the sense of a "period when caregivers nurture in a person a stable sense of self, and the ability to reflect on one's own action and position in a complex social structure, to interact with others with cooperation and generosity, and to develop intricate physical and cognitive skills" (2007, 206–7). The reasons for this are often related to the fact that "the adults around them lack the material and experiential means to provide it" (207). Young does not assume that caregivers will have the psychic capacities or material resources needed to provide the care a child requires. She insists that the needs of caregivers require attention (208). Nussbaum also draws attention to the interrelation between psychic development and the social world in which caring practices take place, identifying "mature interdependence" as the norm of emotional health (2004, 223). Whilst in a state of infantile dependence, the child is needy, helpless and wants to control and incorporate sources of the "good," in a state of mature interdependence, a child has accepted that those they need and love are separate beings, not just instruments to be used. They are able to allow themselves to depend on their caretakers without insisting on omnipotence, and they also allow their caretakers to depend on them, which suggests they are able to care about and possibly for others (224). However, Nussbaum notes that the "this state of health is a precarious achievement…and is highly prone to destabilisation by forces both personal and social" (224). Nussbaum acknowledges the role of society in structuring the facilitating environment in which the capacities for recognition, care and autonomy develop. "The impact," she writes, "of institutions on child development goes deep. It is crucial not to think of children as if their development takes place in the "private sphere" until they are adult citizens. At every stage, it is affected, for better or worse, by laws and institutions" (225). She acknowledges that public institutions play a role in child development (225). Norms of "gender, sexuality, and discrimination" affect the "lives of parents, hence those of their children" in a range of different ways (225). They are "transmitted by parents and peers to children against the background of social…institutions" (226). Social norms and institutional structures influence the development of selves and subjective capacities in multiple ways, demonstrating the inherent relationship between ourselves, our capacities and the structure of, and support provided for, social relations. The often-dyadic caregiving structures in which our sense of self and subjective capacities develop are part of the political realm. They are thoroughly political spaces—constituted historically, discursively, socially and economically—that possess their own claims to justice.

Subjectivities and capacities are shaped by power and the social world, specifically by the fact of inequality. Stone notes that we are "vulnerable to being born into the world in disadvantaged locations, and that vulnerability is heightened the greater are the inequalities in the world we are born into" (2019, 205). The fact that our development as subjects depends on relationships with others means that we are vulnerable to suffering the harmful and damaging effects of the power relations and inequalities that affect us in our early lives. We can be born into disadvantaged locations and social groups, we are subject to the unequal distribution of wealth and access to the means to sustain ourselves and reproduce life, our caregivers will experience more or less precarity, and our access to care itself will not necessarily be equally distributed. As Tronto highlights, thinking about who cares for whom illuminates power relations in society and demonstrates how care is intersectionally structured (1993, 169). The unequal distribution of goods, including the intersubjective relations through which selves and capacities develop, can prevent citizens from equal power. How, given these circumstances, can we pursue equality as a political goal?

Justice, Capacities and the Organisation of Care

Given the central significance of early experiences in shaping ourselves and our capacities, one important aspect of achieving social justice involves thinking about the kinds of care, the forms of holding, that would provide for their realisation. Stone, Young and Nussbaum suggest a specific way of thinking about the relationship between capacities, care and justice, namely that their interrelation be understood by focusing on how the distribution of care affects access to the intersubjective relationships in which subjects can experience and practice forms of care that facilitate the development and exercising of specific subjective capacities. For Young, justice refers to the provision of the institutional conditions that facilitate the development of one's capacities, including the capacity to participate in determining one's actions (1990, 37). Recognising, and theorising, the role of care in the development of subjective capacities contributes to the process of revaluing care, and the sphere of intimate relations that has historically been coded as feminine and aligned with women. It provides a way to critically analyse the kind of environments of care that are possible within the current organisation of care and reproduction, and it prompts reflection on what just conditions, those capable of facilitating the development of capacities, might look like. To ask this question is in many ways to ask about how care work can and should be organised, returning to the questions posed by feminists in the 1970s and the 1990s. What way of organising care work could best support human capacities, and how might this be related to the struggle for justice and equality?

Emphasising the vital importance of intersubjective relationships in the development of capacities might be taken to imply that the best way of organising care is to turn to the ideological ideal of the modern patriarchal family form, comprised of a caregiver at home in the feminised private sphere, taking care of children, and supported by a breadwinner who provides for the family through employment in the masculine public sphere. However, as already discussed in this and previous chapters, the model of the heterosexual nuclear family, and the gendered division of labour that accompanies it, does not lead to the equal development of the capacities that comprise human flourishing. Rather, historically, it has skewed the development of capacities, encouraging girls and women to adopt caring capacities (an ethic of care) and boys to tend towards a more defensive autonomy (an ethic of justice). Additionally, this family form took shape and has been maintained in complex relation with the oppression and domination of racialised and minoritised others, whose opportunities to develop and employ their own capacities have been inhibited and curtailed in unjust ways. The modern patriarchal family, then, does not provide the social conditions for human flourishing and is not the be preserved as a locus of justice.

Nancy Fraser proposes a range of alternative models for organising care, discussing their relative success and failure as means to achieve gender justice. I want to explore her accounts and draw out their consequences for the intersubjective relationships I have been emphasising as key to justice. Firstly, Fraser discusses the "universal breadwinner" model for organising care (2013, 124). This is a model in which the market and the state take on the work of care, enabling all of those with caring responsibilities to become fulltime breadwinners. In this model, care is esteemed and well-paid. However, Fraser asks whether it is possible to shift all forms of care work to the market/state. Fraser doesn't focus on the intersubjective aspects of care, but she does note that "much parenting work cannot be shifted" (128). Whilst we may well want to ask about the extent to which ideas of parenting, and the current organisation of childcare, is socially constructed and historically contingent, it remains the case that subjectivities and capacities form in intersubjective relationships that depend on some sense of continuity and concern, aspects that are likely to be more difficult to replicate in institutions provided by the market or state. The universal breadwinner approach thus fails to adequately recognise the significance of care in development, and it continues to treat it androcentrically and instrumentally, as "something to be sloughed off in order to become a breadwinner" (128).

The second model that Fraser explores is the "caregiver parity" model, which characterises the policy approach of many contemporary welfare states. This model aims not to overcome the differences between men and women in the gendered division of labour, but to make these differences costless, by providing caregivers with allowances for childcare and promoting workplace reforms, like paid maternity leave (129). This is a model that keeps the caregiver in the home, at least for certain periods of their lives when they are taking care of young children, and supports them with public funds. Again, it might seem like this model would support the intersubjective relationships through which subjective capacities develop but, in reality, the work of care remains inherently gendered, and the development of capacities is likely to be skewed. Additionally, the caregiver parity model is likely to discriminate against women who do work, and the time-limited character of support for those in employment makes necessary care chains that impact on the intersubjective relationships of care workers.

Finally, Fraser proposes the model of the "universal caregiver" as a solution to the injustice built into other ways of organising care work (134). This model proposes that there is a need to encourage men to take on more of the caregiving tasks that, historically, have been feminised. On this approach, all jobs would be designed for workers who are also presumed to be caregivers. There would be a shorter working week and support services for all. In this formulation, not all care work is shifted to the market or the state, some is performed in households, but these households in no way need to be heterosexual families. Care work in the household is publicly supported; it is esteemed on par with paid work in a single social-insurance system and supported by institutions in the community. This way of organising care work would promote justice by revaluing the "feminine" and not separating it from breadwinning. It would also support the intersubjective relationships through which capacities develop, because it would support households without reproducing the gendered division of labour that skews capacities. Recognising care and imagining a universal caregiver, and providing financial and institutional support for caregiving, would facilitate a more equal redistribution of care, addressing the "inequalities of resources" that "prevent citizens from equal power" (Tronto 1993, 164–65). The model of the universal caregiver draws attention to the fact that care workers are also often primary caregivers, and these relationships need to be supported and recognised as part of a system that currently functions through their attenuation.

In terms of the distribution of material goods, so central to the Rawlsian conception of justice, taking the work of care seriously would involve a confrontation with capitalism itself. Johanna Brenner writes that

> Social responsibility for care depends on the expansion of public goods, which in turn depends on taxing wealth or profits. Compensating workers for time spent in caregiving (e.g., paid parenting leave) expands paid compensation at the expense of profits. In addition, requiring (either by regulation or by contract) that workplaces accommodate and subsidise employees' caregiving outside of work interferes with employers' control over the workplace and tends to be resisted in the private sector, where jobs continue to be organised as if workers have very little responsibility for care. (2014, 36)

Brenner advocates the increased socialisation of care, which would see capitalism forced towards recognising the role that the privatisation of care has played in the accumulation of capital and extraction of profit. It may well be that the inequalities inherent to the capitalist system inhibit the development of capacities in fundamentally unjust ways. Increasing social responsibility for care, which would involve acknowledging dependence, would go some way towards providing the institutional conditions that would support the early intersubjective relationships in which the subjective capacities necessary for human life can flourish. With this normative idea in mind, existing organisations of care can be assessed, in order to identify whether they foster oppressive patterns of caretaking and inhibit the development of capacities, this is the focus of the following chapter.

References

Barnes, Marian. 2012. *Care in Everyday Life: An Ethic of Care in Practice*. Bristol: Policy.
Beauvoir, Simone de. 2011. *The Second Sex*. Translated by Constance Borde and Sheila Malovany-Chevallier. New York: Vintage Books.
Benjamin, Jessica. 1990. *The Bonds of Love: Psychoanalysis, Feminism and the Problem of Domination*. London: Virago.
———. 1995. *Like Subjects, Love Objects: Essays on Recognition and Sexual Difference*. New Haven; London: Yale University Press.
Bion, Wilfred. 1988. 'A Theory of Thinking'. In *Melanie Klein Today: Developments in Theory and Practice*, edited by Elizabeth Bott Spillius, 1: 174–82. London: Routledge.
Bollas, Christopher. 1987. *The Shadow of the Object: Psychoanalysis of the Unthought Known*. New York: Columbia University Press.
Brenner, Johanna. 2014. '21st Century Socialist-Feminism'. *Socialist Studies/Études Socialistes* 10 (1). http://www.socialiststudies.com/sss/index.php/sss/article/viewArticle/355.
Butler, Judith. 2004. *Precarious Life: The Powers of Mourning and Violence*. London; New York: Verso.
Chodorow, Nancy. 1978. *The Reproduction of Mothering: Psychoanalysis and the Sociology of Gender*. Berkeley, CA: University of California Press.
Dowling, Emma. 2021. *The Care Crisis: What Caused It and How Can We End It?* London; New York: Verso.
Ferguson, S. Alease, and Toni C. King. 2014. 'Dark Animus: A Psychodynamic Interpretation of the Consequences of Diverted Mothering Among African-American Daughters'. In *Mothering and Psychoanalysis: Clinical, Sociological and Feminist Perspectives*, edited by Petra Bueskens, 177–96. Canada: Demeter Press.

Flax, Jane. 1991. *Thinking Fragments: Psychoanalysis, Feminism, and Postmodernism in the Contemporary West*. Berkeley, CA: University of California Press.
Fraser, Nancy. 2013. *Fortunes of Feminism: From Women's Liberation to Identity Politics to Anti-Capitalism*. Brooklyn, NY: Verso Books.
Gilligan, Carol. 1990. *In a Different Voice: Psychological Theory and Women's Development*. Cambridge, MA: Harvard University Press.
Hoggett, Paul. 2000. *Emotional Life and the Politics of Welfare*. Houndmills, Basingstoke, Hampshire; New York: Macmillan Press; St. Martin's Press.
Hollway, Wendy. 2006. *The Capacity to Care: Gender and Ethical Subjectivity*. London; New York: Routledge.
Honneth, Axel. 1996. *The Struggle for Recognition: The Moral Grammar of Social Conflicts*. Translated by Joel Anderson. Cambridge, MA: MIT Press.
Kittay, Eva Feder. 1999. *Love's Labor: Essays on Women, Equality, and Dependency*. Thinking Gender. New York: Routledge.
Laplanche, Jean. 1989. *New Foundations for Psychoanalysis*. Translated by David Macey. Oxford; New York: Basil Blackwell.
Lynch, Kathleen, Maureen Lyons, and John Baker. 2009. 'Introduction'. In *Affective Equality: Love, Care, and Injustice*, edited by Kathleen Lynch, John Baker, and Maureen Lyons, 1–11. Houndmills, Basingstoke; New York: Palgrave Macmillan.
Mackenzie, Catriona, and Natalie Stoljar. 2000. 'Introduction: Autonomy Refigured'. In *Relational Autonomy: Feminist Perspectives on Autonomy, Agency, and the Social Self*, edited by Catriona Mackenzie and Natalie Stoljar, 3–31. New York: Oxford University Press.
McNay, Lois. 2008a. *Against Recognition*. Cambridge: Polity.
———. 2008b. 'The Trouble with Recognition: Subjectivity, Suffering, and Agency'. *Sociological Theory* 26 (3): 271–96.
Meehan, Johanna. 1995. 'Autonomy, Recognition, and Respect: Habermas, Benjamin, and Honneth'. In *Feminists Read Habermas: Gendering the Subject of Discourse*, edited by Johanna Meehan, 231–46. New York: Routledge.
Mitchell, Juliet. 1974. *Psychoanalysis and Feminism: A Radical Reassessment of Freudian Psychoanalysis*. London: Allen Lane.
Nussbaum, Martha C. 1995a. *Poetic Justice: The Literary Imagination and Public Life*. Boston, MA: Beacon Press.
———. 1995b. *Women, Culture, and Development: A Study of Human Capabilities*. Edited by Jonathan Glover. Oxford; New York: Oxford University Press.

———. 2001. *Upheavals of Thought: The Intelligence of Emotions*. Cambridge; New York: Cambridge University Press.

———. 2004. *Hiding from Humanity: Disgust, Shame, and the Law*. Princeton, NJ: Princeton University Press.

Ogden, Thomas. 1989. *The Primitive Edge of Experience*. London; Northvale, NJ: J. Aronson.

———. 2004. 'On Holding and Containing, Being and Dreaming'. *International Journal of Psycho-Analysis* 85: 1349–64. https://doi.org/10.1516/T41H-DGUX-9JY4-GQC7.

Okin, Susan Moller. 1989. *Justice, Gender, and the Family*. New York: Basic Books.

Parker, Rozsika. 2005. *Torn in Two: The Experience of Maternal Ambivalence*. London: Virago.

Patterson, Orlando. 2018. 'Authority, Alienation, and Social Death'. In *Critical Readings on Global Slavery*, edited by Damian Alan Pargas and Felicia Roşu, 90–146. Leiden; Boston: Brill.

Petherbridge, Danielle. 2013. *The Critical Theory of Axel Honneth*. Lanham: Lexington Books.

Phillips, Adam. 1994. *On Kissing, Tickling, and Being Bored: Psychoanalytic Essays on the Unexamined Life*. Harvard University Press.

Sevenhuijsen, Selma. 1998. *Citizenship and the Ethics of Care: Feminist Considerations on Justice, Morality, and Politics*. London; New York: Routledge.

Steedman, Carolyn. 1986. *Landscape for a Good Woman: A Story of Two Lives*. London: Virago.

Stone, Alison. 2019. *Being Born: Birth and Philosophy*. Studies in Feminist Philosophy. Oxford: Oxford University Press.

Taveleski, Toni. 2014. 'Mothers at the Margins: Psychodynamic Therapy with Mothers in the Welfare System'. In *Mothering and Psychoanalysis: Clinical, Sociological and Feminist Perspectives*, edited by Petra Bueskens, 197–212. Canada: Demeter Press.

The Care Collective. 2020. *The Care Manifesto: The Politics of Interdependence*. London; New York: Verso Books.

Thompson, Simon. 2009. 'Against Recognition'. *Contemporary Political Theory* 8 (2): 248–50. https://doi.org/10.1057/cpt.2008.55.

Threadcraft, Shatema. 2016. *Intimate Justice: The Black Female Body and the Body Politic*. New York: Oxford University Press.

Tronto, Joan C. 1993. *Moral Boundaries: A Political Argument for an Ethic of Care*. New York: Routledge.

———. 2013. *Caring Democracy: Markets, Equality, and Justice*. New York: New York University Press.
Waddell, Margot. 2002. *Inside Lives: Psychoanalysis and the Growth of the Personality*. London: Karnac.
Williams, Fiona. 2001. 'In and Beyond New Labour: Towards a New Political Ethics of Care'. *Critical Social Policy* 4: 467–93.
Winnicott, Donald W. 1958a. 'Anxiety Associated with Insecurity'. In *Collected Papers: Through Paediatrics to Psycho-Analysis*, 97–100. London: Tavistock.
———. 1958b. 'Hate in the Countertransference'. In *Collected Papers: Through Paediatrics to Psycho-Analysis*, 194–203. London: Tavistock.
———. 1958c. 'Primary Maternal Preoccupation'. In *Collected Papers: Through Paediatrics to Psycho-Analysis*, 300–305. London: Tavistock.
———. 2006. 'The Family and Emotional Maturity'. In *The Family and Individual Development*, 128–38. London: Routledge.
Wollstonecraft, Mary. 1985. *Vindication of the Rights of Women*. London: Penguin.
Young, Iris Marion. 1990. *Justice and the Politics of Difference*. Princeton, NJ: Princeton University Press.
———. 2007. 'Recognition of Love's Labor: Considering Axel Honneth's Feminism'. In *Recognition and Power: Axel Honneth and the Tradition of Critical Social Theory*, edited by Bert van den Brink and David Owen, 189–212. Cambridge; New York: Cambridge University Press.

6

Attacks on Holding

> The visible consequences of our failure to provide socially organised nurturance—a safe holding environment—intensify our distance and disidentification from those who require support. (Benjamin 1990, 202)

> The fluctuating and complex modern economy does not constitute a caring environment. (Gerson 2004, 788)

> When there is nothing to depend upon, when social structures fail or are withdrawn, then life itself falters or fails: life becomes precarious. (Butler 2020, 50)

There is a crisis of care at the centre of contemporary capitalism. In the UK, health and social care services are at breaking point, and the government's latest proposal to resolve this situation through an increase in National Insurance contributions will disproportionately affect low-paid workers, including many care workers. We live in a society where, as the Care Collective puts it, "carelessness reigns," a situation that has not been significantly challenged by the rolling out of care packages in the wake of Covid, nor by the rhetoric of care that increasingly characterises a capitalism in the process of realising the benefits of *carewashing* (2020, 1, 11). This state of affairs is the product of the forty-year hegemony of neoliberal ways of thinking and doing. David Harvey defines neoliberalism as "a theory of political economic practices that proposes that human well-being can best be advanced by liberating individual entrepreneurial freedoms and skills within an institutional framework characterised by strong private property rights, free markets, and free trade. The role of the state is to create and preserve an institutional framework appropriate to such practices" (2005, 2). In the sphere of care, neoliberalism has involved the rolling back of welfare states, the attenuation of government responsibility for caring for citizens and the attendant marketisation of public provision, as well as a persistent emphasis on care as a personal and private responsibility, rather than a collective one.

However, although neoliberalism is often seen as a theory of political economy, David Chandler and Julian Reid suggest that it is better understood as a theory and practice of subjectivity (2016, 4). Neoliberal forms of governance function through specific technologies of the self, producing particular kinds of subjects, characterised by "resilience, adaptivity and vulnerability" (7). In what follows, I explore the relationship between neoliberal thinking and practice, structures of care and subjective capacities. What are the effects of the erosion and attenuation of holding structures on the subjectivities and capacities of individuals? How does the destruction of collective forms of support—the erosion of welfare conceptualised in terms of concern—affect the kinds of subjects we have the potential to become? Additionally, how does the organisation of care in contemporary society, and the inequalities that characterise it, impact subjectivities and affect the opportunities subjects have to develop and employ the capacities for spontaneity, creativity, care and autonomy, qualities that Winnicott and other object relations theorists consider central to human flourishing? What are the psychosocial effects of the attacks on holding that have taken place over the last forty years?

Changing Structures of Care

Contemporary society is characterised by forms of governance and policy that took root in the 1970s and 1980s. Margaret Thatcher and Ronald Reagan are often identified as the ideologues behind a new social settlement that emphasised personal responsibility in contrast to the solidaristic sentiment of the post-war welfare state. Thatcher's famous line that there is "no such thing as society" has become a kind of shorthand for the shift towards individualism that took place at that time, but in the interview from which the quote is taken, Thatcher went on to say that

> There is a living tapestry of men and women and people and the beauty of that tapestry and the quality of our lives will depend upon how much each of us is prepared to take responsibility for ourselves and each of us prepared to turn round and help by our own efforts those who are unfortunate. (Thatcher 1987)

As Emma Dowling highlights, "it is not individualism per se, but private or personal responsibility" that has been central to neoliberal ideology (2021, 9). Thatcherism stressed the rationality of self-interest and mobilised divisive arguments that pitched "tax-payers" against a workless "underclass" with the aim of eroding social solidarity. Political, social and economic inequality was reconceptualised as a matter of individual responsibility, and the obligation to help and support others less-advantaged than oneself was recast as a voluntary action grounded in charity or obligations conferred through relations of kinship. Helping others was decidedly not a matter of public or collective responsibility enshrined in the rights of citizens.

Thatcher's governments of the 1980s set about dismantling the collective institutions of care that made up the welfare state, returning responsibility to individuals under the guise of increasing individual agency and autonomy, and the rationale of personal responsibility has played an important role in shaping welfare provision in the intervening forty years. If citizens are responsible for their lives and for their fortunes, then they have no inherent right to support and the state has no ethical responsibility to provide it. Hoggett discusses the development, since the late 1970s, of the "enterprise state" (2000, 199). This is a state that is not geared towards meeting need, because the idea that the state should meet needs is antithetical to the idea of personal responsibility. Rather, on this model, the role of the welfare state is understood in terms of its contribution to the economy, as a driver of growth. Thatcher's government in the early 1980s introduced markets into the welfare state, justified by a perceived need to improve efficiency. "By shaping the new forms of production to their own political strategy," Hoggett writes, "the neoliberals were able to fuse decentralisation with competitive individualism and thereby fragment the welfare state into a sea of tiny public enterprises which, as they were drawn into the embrace of the market, were forced to go touting for customers" (199). Additionally, since the late 1970s, there has been a consistent move to outsource public services as the flipside of the retrenchment of the welfare state (Dowling 2021, 12). In the UK, a decade of austerity in the wake of the financial crisis of 2008 has posed limits to the previously dominant models of privatisation, as the guaranteed revenue streams of public funding have been significantly reduced. However, new forms of financialisation are developing that, despite emphasising social values and an ethos of community, continue to be driven by market logics and the desire for profitability (12).

Hobsbawn suggests that the 'triumph of the individual' characteristic of the 1960s cultural revolution supplied the intellectual apparatus necessary for the dismantling of social institutions that got underway in the 1980s (1995). The cultural changes of the 1960s, he writes, created a society where "human beings lived side by side but not as social beings" (341). Writing on the situation in France, Luc Boltanski and Eve Chiapello claim that the new spirit of capitalism evident in the 1980s and 1990s took inspiration from the critiques of state-organised capitalism that flourished after the events of May '68 (2007). Fraser suggests that feminist critiques of the welfare state also unwittingly contributed to the anti-state ethos of the period (2013). Fraser uses Boltanski and Chiapello's argument to structure her own controversial claim that "the diffusion of cultural attitudes born out of the second wave has been part and parcel of another social transformation, unanticipated and unintended by feminist activists—a transformation in the social organisation of post-war capitalism" (211). Second wave feminism (broadly conceived) took issue with welfare-state capitalism and attacked it. Fraser argues that this attack, however, unwittingly provided discursive tools that governments could mobilise in order to weaken and erode the welfare state (212–14). Second wave feminists critiqued the androcentrism and paternalism of the welfare state, arguing that it worked to maintain existing relations of inequality between men and women by valorising work from which many women were excluded. Whilst the idea that both before and after the war women did not work is a myth, the critique of the family wage centred on women's desire to be given equal rights to work as men. Women demanded not only access to jobs, but the possibility of flexible and part-time work that could be organised around caring responsibilities. Fraser argues that the critique of the family wage "now supplies a good part of the romance that invests flexible capitalism with a higher meaning and moral point" through its claim to be meeting demands for freedom and gender equality (220). "It seemed a short step," she writes, "from second-wave feminism's critique of welfare-state paternalism to Margaret Thatcher's critique of the nanny state" (221).

However, whilst second wave feminism and neoliberal ideology may both have harboured reservations about the welfare state, Fraser can be criticised for downplaying political arguments and emphasising the cunning of capital as the driving force behind these changes. The rolling back of the welfare state was facilitated by ideas of individuality and personal responsibility that won out over the commitment to social solidarity. These were widespread cultural attitudes, not the product of feminism. Neoliberal ideology enshrined a dichotomy between ideas of dependence/welfare/the feminine and independence/laissez faire/the masculine, one at odds with the more radical demands of second wave feminism that care be taken seriously (Hall 2011; N. Fraser 2013). By valorising personal responsibility and championing the efficiencies of privatisation, government policy in the Thatcher era worked to undermine the post-war ethos of solidarity, which had provided the rationale for a welfare state that implicitly constituted a "socially sanctioned system of concern" (Cooper and Lousada 2011, 21). Neoliberalism has involved a sustained attack on the welfare state and the recognition of care and dependence that characterised it (Hall 1988, 1990, 2003). However, Hobsbawm highlights the contradictions at work in this shift. For instance, the policy of closing mental hospitals and replacing them with care in the community, implemented in the UK from 1983, faltered because a structure of feeling characterised by individualism and personal responsibility meant that "there was no longer a community to care" (1995, 337).

Dowling notes that whilst "retrenching the state's material responsibility for social welfare has been a key project of neoliberalism, the cementing of care as a private or personal responsibility is scarcely less important" (2021, 9). The reprivatisation of care, however, coincided with the increased entry of women into paid employment. The entry of more women into the labour market from the 1980s brought about changes in the character of working practices, which have become increasingly precarious (Philipson 1994). As women have entered work at all levels, wages have fallen and job security has gradually eroded. Additionally, "prestigious" professions, formerly populated by men, have come to be seen as "women's work," suffering a concurrent fall in esteem. Jobs for life, if they ever existed, have been replaced by part-time, insecure positions. Irene Philipson describes this as a process of "feminisation" (1994). For Fraser, women's entry into work has also served "to intensify capitalism's valorisation of waged labour" (2013, 221). Of course, entry into the workplace did not result in the disappearance of reproductive and caring labour. Though the fact of the "second shift" did not originate at this moment in time, many women, especially the working-class and people of colour, having been forced into this situation before, it became a reality for many white middle-class women in ways it had not previously been. Whilst there has been a move to increased flexibility in working arrangements since the 1970s, to allow women to juggle the competing demands of caring and career, there has not been a concurrent rebalancing of the gendered distribution of caring labour. The onus continues to fall on women to perform this work, in their own homes and/or for others. As Nancy Folbre succinctly puts it, it is still women who largely "pay for the kids," as well as the grandkids and ageing parents, in terms of additional labour and loss of earnings

(1994). Though inequalities in the distribution of care did not begin in the 1970s, the freedom granted to some women to enter the job market in the last half century has produced a "care deficit" that requires the low-paid work of less affluent, often female, 'others,' reinscribing and re-inflecting long-standing structures of inequality (Hochschild 2003, 214; Tronto 2002). As state provision has been eroded and more women have entered work, there has been a tendency to reject caring roles, and in turn this has supported the increased commodification of caring in "new spaces of marketised domesticity" (M. Green and Lawson 2011, 646). Privatised forms of care, such as care homes and nannies, have increasingly replaced state provision, and the work of care has been globalised: performed by women and low-paid migrant workers who take on the management of needs for those able to pay. Global care chains are part of the care crisis that has developed as a result of the neoliberal policies of recent decades, which have sought to erode the welfare state through processes of marketisation, austerity and financialisation and increasingly shift the responsibility for providing care onto citizens (Ehrenreich and Hochschild 2003).

In Winnicott's terms, neoliberalism represents an attack on the structures of holding within society. Care is progressively privatised, whilst work (in the care sector and beyond) is increasingly underpaid and precarious. As Dowling suggests, care chains represent an attempt at a "care fix" designed to address the care deficits that have resulted from both the increased entry of women into the world of work in the last forty years and the concurrent erosion and marketisation of forms of welfare provision in societies in the global north (2021, 10–14). As previously mentioned, as care services are removed, access to care increasingly depends on one's capacity to pay. Dowling identifies a global care crisis in which "the restructuring of welfare states in Europe and North America is but one facet…a growing number of the world's population cannot access the care and support they require" (4). There are currently estimated to be over two billion people worldwide in need of care, with children making up the overwhelming majority, and the number is growing. However, as Dowling highlights, "care for these recipients is increasingly difficult to ensure" (4).

Traumatogenic Environments and Careless Subjects

Bonnie Honig writes that "holding environments are part of the infrastructure of human development and of the active human life" (2017, 85). For Winnicott, they constitute the conditions of possibility for the development of capacities and a life worth living. However, capitalism as such, and its neoliberal iteration in particular, erodes the structures of care and holding in which selves take shape and thrive. Honig describes "public things" as constituting "a kind of *democratic holding environment*, a laboratory for citizenship in which we experience lifelong the attachments and play that form and re-form all of us into individuated and resilient persons, capable of aggression, concern, and the self-collection they postulate" (54). Honig has in mind the infrastructures of collective life, including parks, libraries and bridges, but her ideas apply equally well in the context of thinking about the character and effect of recent forms of welfare provision. Living in "a fluid world of object impermanence" can lead a people to "lack the 'liveness' to which Winnicott repeatedly refers as an ideal," leaving them "prone to mere compliance and inauthenticity" (8). Without the structures of holding that facilitate going-on-being, the sense that life is worth living can fail to develop, or be eroded by the anxiety that consumes when holding fails.

For Winnicott, the infant resides "on the brink of unthinkable anxiety" (1990, 57); never far from disintegration, or the loss of self, which can only be managed through the form of care that is holding. If the ego-coverage provided is good-enough, the "new human person" can "build up a personality on the pattern of going-on-being" (1990, 60). Failures capable of producing "unthinkable anxiety" call for "a reaction of the infant" that "cuts across the going-on-being," producing, in time, the conditions for "a pattern of fragmentation" (60). Unthinkable anxiety takes a small range of experiential forms: "going to pieces," "falling forever," "having no relationship to the body" and "no orientation" in the world (58). Later Winnicott added "complete isolation because of there being no means of communication" (1987, 99). This is the stuff of "psychotic anxieties," each form bearing a trace of a specific element of growth that has been distorted. Failures in care can lead to distortions in ego organisation, resulting either in unthinkable anxiety or in self-holding: the formation of a false self, a defence based on reaction to external impingements (Winnicott 1990, 58–59). Unlike the true self which Winnicott believes adequate maternal care to nurture, "the false self cannot [...] experience life or feel real" (D. W. Winnicott 1958, 297).

The production of subjects "on the brink of unthinkable anxiety" has been central to governance in recent decades. As Layton puts it, since the rise of neoliberal ideology in the 1970s, "government has increasingly retreated from providing any functions that might contain anxiety and trauma" (2008, 71). Hollander and Gutwill describe such an environment as "traumatogenic" (2006, 81). The destruction of social support structures constitutes a kind of "relationally inflicted wounding" that inhibits the development of the forms of subjectivity that psychoanalysis hopes to nurture (Layton 2008, 68–69). This would be a subjectivity characterised by the capacities for spontaneity, creativity, concern and autonomy, a subject that is capable of acknowledging dependence and their implication in the suffering of others (Layton 2009). Thomas Lemke describes neoliberalism as a "government of insecurity" (cited in Lorey 2015, 65). Contemporary society is governed through precarisation, a logic of insecurity characterised by anxiety (Butler 2009; Lorey 2015). As Dowling puts it, "not knowing where the next paycheck is going to come from, not knowing what may happen in the longer term, not having adequate sick pay or a pension – this produces feelings of insecurity" (2021, 2). Maurizio Lazzarato suggests that contemporary forms of government function through a logic of minimum provision, providing citizens with what is essential in order to mitigate disorder (2008, 58). Such states provide social safeguards, not social security. This evokes Nussbaum's distinction, mentioned in the previous Chapter, between the threshold level of capabilities and the level required for human flourishing (1995). Governments today are not interested in poverty as such, or its alleviation, but rather in absolute poverty, which would prevent citizens from "playing the game of competition" (Lazzarato 2008, 57). The welfare state is used to prevent citizens from reaching this level, but it is not concerned with providing the conditions necessary for them to live a flourishing life. In this context, the ideal subject is conceptualised as one capable of managing risk and coping with uncertainty, a "resilient" subject (Chandler and Reid 2016).

Anthony Giddens employs Winnicott's understanding of subjective development in order to theorise the environmental conditions required for such a subject to come into being (1990). Giddens uses Winnicott to emphasise the importance of the caregiver-child relationship in fostering the trust and ontological security needed to deal with the risk, uncertainty and contingency that characterise social life in "late modernity," a period that contains both threat and extensive opportunities for autonomy and self-realisation (1990, 1991). He writes that

> The confidence that most human beings have in the continuity of their self-identity and in the constancy of the surrounding and material environments of action. A sense of the reliability of persons and things, so central to the notion of trust, is basic to the feelings of ontological security; hence the two are psychologically related. Ontological security has to do with "being" or, in the terms of phenomenology, "being-in-the-world." But it is an emotional rather than a cognitive, phenomenon, and is rooted in the unconscious. (1990, 92)

Giddens suggests that the feeling of "ontological security" in adult life depends on a process of infantile development during which the child has learnt to have confidence in others. Basic trust evolves through our encounters with caregivers, whose *routine* attentions give us the faith to believe that others can be relied upon (Giddens 1991, 38–39). Giddens argues that late modern subjects can be inoculated against the existential anxieties of contemporary capitalism if they experience a consistent parental routine in their early lives. If they have this experience, they will be able to approach social life with agency, calculating potential risks and opportunities as they arise. Without this experience of routine, they are liable to self-pathologies, disturbed narcissism in particular (A. Elliott 2015, 72). On Giddens' analysis, parental holding is positioned as the necessary context for creating the modern productive worker, the entrepreneurial subject of neoliberal society who is "fit for labour" in a world of precarious employment and contingent opportunity (Hoggett 2000, 1).

Giddens is attentive to the relationship between experiences of care and the wider society in which they take place, and he provides an account of the emotional capacities best suited for negotiating modern life. However, his approach tends towards the normalisation of the subject in line with the imperatives of contemporary society, rather than cultivating capacities for resistance (A. Elliott 2015, 73). The characteristics possessed by the entrepreneurial subject his ideas conjure are closely related to the character of the care they receive. Giddens' focus on the significance of *routine* neglects the importance of the caregiver's attitude in care. As Winnicott puts it, "a baby can be *fed* without love, but loveless or impersonal *management* cannot succeed in producing a new autonomous human child" (1991a, 108, emphasis in the original). By focusing on routine alone, Giddens neglects important aspects of care, reducing it to a process of internalisation that neglects the significance of the quality of the care relationship. Whilst routine is important for the internalisation of behaviours that facilitate the ability to care for oneself and have agency, it does not account for the intersubjective dynamics of reverie, containment, holding and recognition. Steven Groarke suggests that Giddens' approach also reduces "potentials to competencies" (2014, 178). Rather than exploring how the potential for spontaneity and concern is realised through the experience of attuned care, Giddens' scheme is concerned with forms of self-regulation and discipline that develop through the experience of routine and "the reproduction of coordinating conventions" that serve to orientate the child "towards aspects of the object-world" (Giddens 1991, 39). The experience of routine in the early relationship with the caregiver allows a form of basic trust to develop that is equivalent to a form of risk management, a "screening off device" (39–40). What is not considered here is how the capacities for spontaneity, aliveness, care and autonomy actually depend on intersubjective dynamics that are in excess of routine management.

For Giddens, welfare provision should be imagined along the same lines as the routine parental care that produces the resilient and risk-taking subject. Groarke suggests that on his analysis, the role of welfare becomes to safeguard the conditions that will facilitate and support the development of specific competencies, namely the capacities for reflexivity and self-management (2014, 196). The function of welfare is conceived as the facilitation of psychic "well-being," rather than acknowledging dependency and meeting need through responsive care and the provision of economic support. Whilst accepting that people need support when things go wrong, Giddens suggests that they also need the material and moral capabilities to move through periods of transition (1999). Groarke suggests that, rather than responding to need, the welfare state is here reimagined as a form of government investment in human social capital, including "the acquisition of psychological skills and capacities over and above the provision of economic benefits" (2014, 196). Psychological counselling is conceived to be more helpful than direct economic support because it can help to foster a reflexive form of citizenship characterised by the capacity for self-management. Groarke also highlights that Giddens places emphasis on the cultivation of the capacity for self-control, a second-order virtue that can be employed to rescue the life of an individual whose habits of emotion and behaviour haven't been properly laid down (205). In failing to meet need and acknowledge dependence, this form of welfare does not provide the conditions for healthy emotional development to take place. Instead, it encourages the production of a false self, geared towards self-management rather than actual living. The neoliberal subject is "a subject that must permanently struggle to accommodate itself to the world" rather than seeking to transform it (Chandler and Reid 2016, 4).

Giddens' account of subjective development and welfare misses something fundamental: that a self that is capable of spontaneity is formed through an experience of reliability and intuitive management, an experience of care that holds and responds to need. Giddens' approach aims to facilitate knowledge of the self, which in turn forms the basis of a specific kind of self-managing subject. In recent years, this approach is reflected in the widespread endorsement and implementation of Cognitive Behavioural Therapy in treating the pandemic of depression and anxiety in global north societies. CBT aims to facilitate self-control and encourage reflexivity whilst responsibilising the subject, and their thought patterns, for their misery. Self-knowledge, however, is not the route to cure, which is achieved instead through specific forms of relational experience. In his clinical work, Freud soon came to realise that self-knowledge was not the core active element of the treatment, which lay rather in the transference relationship between analyst and patient (1910). Winnicott extended this insight through the concepts of holding and the facilitating environment: the provision of a setting in which psychic growth could take place. From one perspective, Giddens' approach is a sticking plaster designed to mitigate the effects of neoliberal attacks on holding. From another, it is an approach that actively undermines other forms of provision and the development of the capacities associated with the experience of holding.

Contemporary capitalism, Bernard Stiegler argues, involves the "destruction of proper care as attention and recognition" (2010, 16). Stiegler engages explicitly with psychoanalysis, and with Winnicott, in order to theorise the ways in which the social order thwarts capacities for thought, imagination and spontaneity. Following Winnicott, Stiegler is interested, amongst other things, in the question of what makes life worth living (2013). As Angie Voela and Louis Rothschild put it, "the question stems from the thesis that, apart from disenchantment, capitalism breeds stupidity, broadly defined as life without knowledge, and the atrophy of the *noetic*, that is, the mental faculty of critical, abstract and creative thinking" (2019, 55). The absence of the *noetic* capacity, a state that Stiegler calls *kenosis*, is a form of psychic breakdown in which one is incapable of relating to others in a mature or wise way (Stiegler 2013, 73; Voela and Rothschild 2019, 55). Moving out of kenosis involves tolerating "the pain and loneliness that come with the loss of imaginary omnipotence," a loss that "facilitates relational capacities" (Voela and Rothschild 2019, 56). However, the rigidity and lack of attention that characterise kenosis originate in "a failure of the holding environment" (57). A "nourishing holding environment" facilitates movement between states of rigidity and tolerance of difference, unintegration and integration, but an unsatisfactory holding environment fails to foster the attention necessary for noetic existence (57–8). For Stielger, the capacity to move out of a state of kenosis and into the noetic depend on relationships with "pharmakon," or (transitional) objects, which reach back to the quasi-original pharmakon of the holding relationship with the maternal other (2013, 4). Stiegler emphasises the significance of the relationships between adults and children in fostering attention and the development of the critical-creative capacity.

The adult's attention creates the child's attention, but in contemporary society, adults do not necessarily possess attention, and children are not guaranteed the attention of adults and the experience of play (14). To play with a child, Stiegler writes, is "to laugh and to 'forget about time' with them," it is "to take care of the child…from earliest childhood" by "opening the paths by which transitional spaces are created" (14). Transitional spaces are the locus of "imaginative living" (D. W. Winnicott 1991b, 14). When capitalism takes control of the development of attention, transitional space is destroyed, and "such spaces form the basis of all systems of care and nurturance: a transitional space is first and foremost a system of caring" (Stiegler 2013, 15).

Stiegler speaks of "systemic environmental disorders" and their relationship with "the destruction of caretaking systems" in richly suggestive ways (50). The attacks on holding that have long characterised neoliberal modes of governance, and are embodied in a welfare state that denies dependence and fails to meet need, erode the capacities for spontaneity, creativity, care and autonomy. The retrenchment of welfare states, justified by the logic of personal responsibility, and their reformulation as spaces of mechanised routine lacking care and attention, does not provide citizens with adequate holding. The kind of attention on offer here is not a mode of responsive looking that recognises the other as an independent subject with their own needs and wants. Rather, it is a form of interaction that oscillates between absence and a look that fixes and interpellates subjects into forms of false-self subjectivity. In either case, subjects are left alone, and being left alone is not good enough: in such situations, you have to take care of yourself, you can't simply be (Alford 2000, 245). The rigid self symptomatic of the state of kenosis has much in common with Winnicott's idea of the false self, which is produced as a result of failures of the holding environment to provide adequate care. The false self is a compliant self that fits in with the world, rather than challenging it. Mari Ruti notes that Winnicott's emphasis on the authenticity and spontaneity of the "true self" does not describe a fixed content, but rather a way of relating to the world, a flexibility that enables the fending off of psychic rigidity (2011, 361). The concept of the false self makes it possible to address instances when the ego is deeply wounded by environmental failures and oppressive conditions and its narcissistic abilities are destroyed (361). Focusing on the character of care provided by specific facilitating environments encourages thinking about the kind of environmental conditions that inhibit flourishing and necessitate a focus on survival, at the expense of other, more flexible or creative, forms of life (370–1).

As the authors of the *Care Manifesto* write, the violence of contemporary neoliberal markets leaves "most of us less able to *provide* care as well as less likely to *receive* it" (2020, 4). The ever-increasing demands of work and the erosion of welfare provision render people "less capable of caring for people even in our most intimate spheres" whilst we are concurrently encouraged "to restrict our care for strangers and distant others" (4). Stiegler sees kenosis as a general problem, the result of inadequate forms of care embedded in capitalism. For both adults and children, the absence of adequate holding leaves one incapable of caring about, and for, the world. Layton explores how the failure of adequate holding and containment leads to feelings of shame about dependency which manifest as a lack of empathy and an overly self-reliant way of being (Layton 2009; Peltz 2005). "The idealised self," Richard Sennett writes, "publicly eschews long-term dependency on others," which has consequences for politics (2006, 177). The neoliberal subject

> is ever more split from the citizen or social individual, which causes a crisis in empathy, responsibility, and accountability. Indeed, government and corporate abdication of responsibility for their citizens and workforce, and the privileged classes' colluding but understandable response—to disavow vulnerability and escape into manic activity—have together brought about a marked decline in social solidarity, the concern and empathy for the vulnerable and for the stranger that characterised the welfare state. (Layton 2009, 108)

In these circumstances, forms of authoritarian and right-wing populism have found increasing purchase, fuelled by "the profound difficulties and unbearable collective anxieties of living in an uncaring world" (The Care Collective 2020, 4). In recent decades, as Layton puts it, "fear has led to splitting and projective identification, and large segments of the population, traumatised in different ways depending on social location, have taken up polarised positions of 'us' vs 'them'" (2008, 71). Layton draws attention to how the insecurity endemic to neoliberal societies channels and reinforces psychological processes, in this instance splitting and projection, leading to the entrenchment of ideas of difference and separation rather than solidarity and connection. As Diane Reay puts it, "the hegemony of neoliberalism and the dominance of free market globalisation have created ever more pressure to construct independent, autonomous, entrepreneurial identities that repudiate the vulnerable and needy parts of the self" (2015, 15). The erosion of caring infrastructures is increasingly placing limits on "our caring capacities" for both near and distant others. The growth of neoliberal markets, then, has the capacity to shape subjectivities in uncaring ways, encouraging the adoption of rigidly individualised perspectives at odds with the capacities for intersubjectivity and identification necessary for a caring attitude. At the same time, the attacks on holding characteristic of neoliberalism produce a subject who has lost many of the capacities necessary for agency and resistance, including "fundamentally human capacities to think, imagine, know, create, and act purposely in the world" (Chandler and Reid 2016, 6).

Caring Relationships in an Uncaring World

The previous section focused on how the failures of holding characteristic of neoliberalism and its legacy affect capacities, shaping citizens who lack aliveness, concern and autonomy. This section considers in more detail how the organisation of care in contemporary society affects caring relationships. Evidently, failures of the social holding environment can impact the capacities of parents—the capacity for holding, attention and play—that form the basis for the development of children's capacities, as Stiegler suggests. Voela and Rothschild approach similar terrain, suggesting that a "brutalised (neoliberal) parent" may lack the capacity to provide the degree of otherness necessary to recognise the child's gesture. Neoliberalism produces repetitive (non)thinking and kenosis, leading to the inability to think and dream (2019, 66, 68). It has the potential to erode the relational exchanges through which the capacities to feel alive, to care and to be autonomous develop. Short on time and preoccupied by the manic productivity that characterises contemporary capitalism, parents may become mechanical, offering an inattentive and mechanised routine form of care, which may unwittingly reproduce compliant entrepreneurial subjects. For instance, the "primary maternal preoccupation" Winnicott theorises to characterise adequate care in the first weeks of life may be difficult if the primary caregiver lacks adequate support. In 2020, the USA, for instance, had no national provision for paid leave in the event of giving birth, the worst provision of any country in the OECD (Bryant 2020). Not only does this demonstrate an extreme failure to acknowledge the significance of care and dependence, but it is also likely to impact the development and practice of psychosocial caring capacities.

The failure of social forms of holding has similar effects in other care relationships within the care economy. Dowling describes the effect on care workers of the erosion and precarisation of their working conditions under neoliberalism. Carrying out care work "in both its emotional and physical dimensions requires time" (2021, 39). The increased marketisation of social care provision has led to insistent attempts to increase productivity and save money through processes of routinisation, standardisation and rationalisation, which "can lead to a sense of alienation" on the part of care workers, who are not allocated sufficient time "to really connect with a person and enable them to feel valued and cared for" (39). Dowling suggests that the conditions of care workers' employment have the potential to affect their "capacities to care adequately," and she describes the widespread practice of hospital volunteering as a related aspect of the "care fixes" characteristic of neoliberalism (39). She writes that

> The distinction between the duties of specialised staff and those expected of volunteers has a lot to do with what is considered to constitute expertise and skill. Indeed, the kinds of things volunteers do are the kinds of things we think anyone can do, in that they demand basic social competencies of care. Yet time is actually a key factor here, as is the propensity

of the assistive and affective dimensions of care to be externalised when time is scarce. (95)

Dowling is suggesting that when time is an issue, the emotional, intersubjective aspects of care are the first to be cut and outsourced. Under the pressures of contemporary care regimes, medical staff and care workers must focus on the mechanical aspects of care and forego the relational and attentional elements that are so central to development and positive change. Tellingly, it is the relational elements of care that are here devalued and redefined as unpaid work, an optional add-on rather than an integral part of the care process. When time is scarce, medical and care workers are unable to engage in the kind of thoughtful attention, the work of identification and imagination, that are central to Hollway's description of the capacity to care (2006). Dowling registers that the care contribution that volunteers make in this context is "the kind of thing *we think* anyone can do," which points to the fact that the capacity to care is not a natural given, but an achievement based on intersubjective experiences (2021, 95, emphasis added). Nonetheless, the experiences of care workers demonstrate one aspect of the ways in which the capacity to care, understood in psychosocial terms, exists in relation to social forms of power and environmental circumstance that can make it hard to exercise the capacity.

The "care fixes" that characterise the organisation of care and reproduction in contemporary capitalism have the potential to distort the development of capacities in a range of ways. Young argues that to some extent, all people who are oppressed "suffer some inhibition of their ability to develop and exercise their capacities and express their needs" (1990, 40). Neoliberal attacks on holding are likely to affect all subjects in some way, but they have particularly marked effects on care workers (and their families) who are required to meet the care deficits produced by the erosion of public provision and the increased entry of women into work taking place since the 1980s. Some parents and carers can afford to employ others to meet the care needs of their dependents, but this has implications for the care relationships of those engaged to perform the work of care and those cared for. Historically, the work of care has been unequally distributed along the axes of gender, 'race' and class, with the "universal subject"—straight, white, male, middle class—afforded a form of "privileged irresponsibility," whilst concurrently highly dependent on the "care services" of others (Tronto 2013, 102–3). In the decades since the Women's Liberation Movement, the psychic disposition towards defensive autonomy associated with masculinity has also become increasingly resonant for white middle-class women (Layton 2014, 169). Layton suggests that this can be explained by the fact that "the second wave socialist feminist agenda for an alteration of the social structure never achieved the same dominance that a more liberal feminist call for job equality achieved" (169). Given this reality, "what other way was there for women to be equal to men in the unchanged workplace besides taking on the psychic structure that fits the demands of the socio-economic system?" (169). Layton suggests that for her women students, born in the late 1970s and early 1980s, "their mothers had played a major role in making sure they did not become dependent on men" (169). These mothers, then, sought to instil in their daughters psychic dispositions that would help them to avoid a position of powerlessness characteristic of the traditional sexual division of labour in the middle-class heterosexual family. A disposition towards defensive autonomy, however, was also concordant with the liberal feminism that won out in the 1970s and 1980s, and the subsequent increased entry of middle-class women into the world of work. Bell hooks questions whether the desire for liberation from the middle-class home was an objective shared by all women. Betty Friedan's assertion that "I want something more than my husband and my children and my house" was not a universal desire, and hooks highlights the elisions within the appeal: Friedan "did not discuss who would be called to take care of the children and maintain the home if more like herself were free from their house labour and given equal access with white men to the professions" (1995, 270). In what she called for, and what she failed to question, Friedan "made her plight and the plight of white women like herself synonymous with a condition affecting all American women," when in reality her difficulties were different to those of "a babysitter, factory worker, clerk or prostitute" (270).

In a similar vein, S. Uma Devi, Arlie Hochschild and Lise Isaksen make explicit that there is a relationship between the enclosure of the commons that got underway in Europe in the sixteenth century and the unequal distribution of care and support in contemporary society (2013). "Just as public spaces can be placed off-limits to commoners," they write, "so too can access to social ties" (150). As discussed in Chapter 3, the enclosure of the common lands traditionally used by peasants for subsistence has been, and continues to be, a central element in the transition to capitalism. The erosion of relations of dependence—political and material—that this transition affected was mitigated by the transmogrification of women into a substitute-commons, now exclusively responsible for the care and material reproduction of the workforce in the home. This process took place in relation to a burgeoning colonialism that also sought to appropriate previously common lands and depended on the forced labour and reproduction of colonised and enslaved peoples. Capitalism, colonialism and empire have shaped contemporary care economies in which inequalities intersect.

Devi, Hochschild and Isaksen point out how the legacies of enclosure affect and shape emotional and social lives today in the context of global care chains. Writing on the phenomenon of "The Children Left Behind," the authors note that the costs of global care chains for the children of migrant workers are often not discussed, because many people have a vested interest in the smooth functioning of the process. However, they estimate the negative impact of these chains in terms of the breakdown of families and what Carmelita Erista et al. describe as the "deterioration and underdevelopment of the psychosocial growth of [migrant care workers'] children" (cited in Hochschild et al. 2013, 151). Cautious about providing fuel to anti-immigration discourses, or seeming to suggest that mothers should be at home, the authors nonetheless wish to provide an account of how the vicissitudes of the contemporary care economy are lived and experienced. They suggest that there is often a taboo on discussing how the children are doing, and list the effects on children as including loneliness, sadness, anger, confusion and apathy. In Mexico, the children of migrant care workers often "earn better grades in high school and can, courtesy of their parents' remittances, better afford to attend college than the children of non-migrants. But poignantly, they were less likely to want to" (152). Keralan workers in the Persian Gulf are reported to be permitted forty-five days postpartum leave for the birth of their children before they have to return to work, often for a year, before they can see the child again. As the authors insist, there is nothing to suggest that the children of migrant workers do not and cannot develop a wide range of other attachments that provide the care necessary for their development, but as Devi notes, older children of migrant workers stressed their sense of the human cost that resulted from the lack of contact with their parents. Often independent but distrustful of adults, the psychosocial development of these children can reveal "the hidden price tag of global inequality" (157). Some children of migrant workers wondered if the care they received from relatives was freely given out of love, or was rather undertaken out of a sense of duty or as a favour. Some felt like a guest in the environments where they stayed, rather than feeling they were at home.

These experiences evoke a distinction made by Lynch and Lyons between "love labour" and "secondary care labour," between "the work that could be done by others on a paid or support basis…and what could not" (2009, 67). The primary carers of young children that Lynch and Lyons interviewed perceived it possible for the "technical aspects" of care, such as feeding, washing, entertaining, fetching and collecting, to be commodified and done by others. However, the "quality of care that was contingent on a set of relationships where there was commitment, longstanding intimate knowledge and a strong sense of other-centredness" could not be commodified (67). This is because of "the intimate role that feelings play in primary relationships" (67). The carers felt that it is not possible to "contract out one's feelings for others and the character of a relationship" (67). Primary carers perceived themselves to have a "nurturing [and] developmental role in relation to their children at multiple relationship levels" (67). A substitute carer is likely to be highly able to perform secondary care labour, but is less likely to be able to provide the nurture that primary caregivers understand to be constitutive of love labour. Given that relations of love and care "help to establish a basic sense of importance, value and belonging, a sense of being appreciated, wanted and cared about," the prolonged attenuation of such relationships by the imperatives of the global care economy is likely to affect psychosocial development and experience (Lynch et al. 2009, 1).

Such discussions raise questions about the extent to which the care that primary caregivers, often but not necessarily the child's birth parents, feel for their child is a product of specific social relations that privatise care and make it the responsibility of parents, who "possess" their children and are responsible for their development. At the same time, they draw attention to what Stella Sandford describes as the specific emotional labour of mothering (or primary caregiving), in which the caregiver actually cares about the thing that is reproduced, a perspective that is often occluded in discussions of social reproduction (2011).

Sensitive to the nuances of care, Hollway also briefly considers "the case of women in the developing world who leave behind their own children to earn money by caring for children or dependent adults in the developed world" (2006, 137). She argues that the capacity of these care workers to care for, and respond to the dependence of, their employers "suggests the continuing tension of the power relations in recognition rather than their breakdown into monolithic domination" (137). Psychosocially, migrant care workers may well strive to provide good care, even in the exploitative environments of the care infrastructure under neoliberalism, but that does not mean there are no hidden costs. Hochschild writes that "often the care worker makes herself into what psychoanalyst Donald Winnicott has called a 'holding environment'—an ambience sealed against disturbing leakage of anxiety, anger, envy or sadness," emotions that might make the cared for "feel agitated, threatened, or unsafe" (2013, 27). The care worker may be required to bracket out their own emotional experience in order to perform this emotional labour, and the distribution of access to their capacity to care reflects global structures of social inequality and power. Devi, Hochschild and Isaksen note the widespread transfer of "care capital"—which describes "simply the capacity to care" (2013, 159)—from the global south to the north. However, they caution against a view that has the potential to eclipse what is really lost in the process: the opportunity to live as part of a family or a community, the simple experience of being together. The global market in care is eroding the emotional commons, acting as a care drain on the global south, that "disembeds" relations between primary carers and children.

Similarly to Threadcraft, whose work was discussed in the previous chapter, these authors identify the ways in which inequalities of power are shaped by and shape caring relationships (Threadcraft 2016). To restate Stone's definition of power relations: "members of group A have power over or relative to members of group B when those in A are more able than those in B (i) to steer the course of their own actions, desires, and lives; (ii) to affect how the other group's members act, desire, and live; and (iii) to shape arrangements that embody and prolong this state of affairs" (2019, 100). The absence of access to adequately compensated work leads citizens of the global south to migrate, steering "the course of their...actions, desires, and lives," and those of their children, in specific ways. Citizens of the global north have the capacity to "affect how [citizens of the global south] act, desire, and live" and they also have the capacity to "shape arrangements that embody and prolong this state of affairs." Global north citizens are able to harvest and hoard the capacities of global south citizens, in particular the capacity to care, even as the precarious conditions in which such workers often find themselves may have negative effects on their ability to put that capacity into practice.

This has the potential to affect the development of children in both contexts (global north and south). Though of course there are complex factors at work here, a "left behind" child's "basic sense of importance, value and belonging, a sense of being appreciated, wanted and cared about," may well be affected, as the research Devi, Hochschild and Isaksen draw on suggests (Lynch et al. 2009, 1). Would this, in turn, weaken these children's capacity for aliveness, autonomy and concern? At the same time, there are likely to be effects on global north children who benefit from the hoarding of care resources. As Barbara Ehrenreich puts it, "a servant economy breeds callousness and solipsism in the served" (cited in Tronto 2013, 112). It produces "a kind of blindness that affects everyone in the employing household. One of the effects of such a self-referential view on other people is surely the diminishment of a sense of equality," which is likely to inhibit care workers from feeling they have a right to speak in voices equal to those they serve (Tronto 2013, 113). At the same time, returning to the distinction between love labour and secondary care labour proposed by Lynch and Lyons, it is equally possible that cared for children may also fail to develop a sense of being wanted, cared about and important. Given the complex ways that these care arrangements are likely to affect the capacities of those involved, "unequal care produces greater inequality," including psychic inequality (113).

The care chains essential to the current (failing) organisation of care do not provide adequate holding environments for the reproduction of human capacities, including the capacities for aliveness, care and autonomy. Existing in intimate relation with the erosion of welfare states, these care chains result from neoliberal "attacks on holding," and they contain the potential to contribute to the reproduction of such attacks globally. Neoliberalism produces specific kinds of subjects, characterised by "resilience, adaptivity and vulnerability," because it undermines the intersubjective conditions required for human flourishing (Chandler and Reid 2016, 7). Fraser suggests that contemporary capitalism is destroying the conditions for its own reproduction, because it increasingly inhibits the ability of subjects to reproduce their own lives (2016). At the level of subjectivity, the destruction of the capacity for aliveness constitutes a primary mode of governance and a technology of the self, as neoliberalism reduces human capacities to a threshold level, just enough to keep subjects able to play the game of competition. The solution to this is not a return to the private family, or even the welfare states of the past, which have played their own role in the unequal reproduction of capacities, but lies in the pursuit of different ways of organising and collectivising care. This will be the subject of the final chapter.

References

Alford, C. Fred. 2000. 'Levinas and Winnicott: Motherhood and Responsibility'. *American Imago* 57 (3): 235–59. https://doi.org/10.1353/aim.2000.0015.

Benjamin, Jessica. 1990. *The Bonds of Love: Psychoanalysis, Feminism and the Problem of Domination.* London: Virago.

Boltanski, Luc, and Eve Chiapello. 2007. *The New Spirit of Capitalism.* Translated by Gregory Elliott. London; New York: Verso.

Bryant, Miranda. 2020. 'Maternity Leave: US Policy Is Worst on List of the World's Richest Countries'. *The Guardian*, 27 January 2020. https://www.theguardian.com/us-news/2020/jan/27/maternity-leave-us-policy-worst-worlds-richest-countries.

Butler, Judith. 2009. *Frames of War: When Is Life Grievable?* London; New York: Verso.

———. 2020. *The Force of Nonviolence: An Ethico-Political Bind*. London; New York: Verso.

Chandler, David, and Julian Reid. 2016. *The Neoliberal Subject: Resilience, Adaptation and Vulnerability*. London; New York: Rowman & Littlefield International.

Cooper, Andrew, and Julian Lousada. 2011. *Borderline Welfare: Feeling and Fear of Feeling in Modern Welfare*. London: Karnac.

Dowling, Emma. 2021. *The Care Crisis: What Caused It and How Can We End It?* London; New York: Verso.

Elliott, Anthony. 2015. *Psychoanalytic Theory: An Introduction*. London; New York: Palgrave Macmillan.

Folbre, Nancy. 1994. *Who Pays for the Kids? Gender and the Structures of Constraint*. London; New York: Routledge.

Fraser, Nancy. 2013. *Fortunes of Feminism: From Women's Liberation to Identity Politics to Anti-Capitalism*. Brooklyn, NY: Verso Books.

———. 2016. 'Contradictions of Capital and Care'. *New Left Review* 100 (August): 99–117.

Freud, Sigmund. 1910. '"Wild" Psycho-Analysis'. In *SE 11*, 219–27.

Gerson, Gal. 2004. 'Object Relations Psychoanalysis as Political Theory'. *Political Psychology* 25 (5): 769–94. https://doi.org/10.1111/j.1467-9221.2004.00397.

Giddens, Anthony. 1990. *The Consequences of Modernity*. Stanford: Stanford University Press.

———. 1991. *Modernity and Self-Identity: Self and Society in the Late Modern Age*. Stanford: Stanford University Press.

———. 1999. *The Third Way: The Renewal of Social Democracy*. Malden, MA: Polity Press.

Green, Maia, and Victoria Lawson. 2011. 'Recentring Care: Interrogating the Commodification of Care'. *Social & Cultural Geography* 12 (6): 639–54. https://doi.org/10.1080/14649365.2011.601262.

Groarke, Steven. 2014. *Managed Lives*. Hove; New York: Routledge.

Hall, Stuart. 1988. *The Hard Road to Renewal: Thatcherism and the Crisis of the Left*. London; New York: Verso.

———. 1990. *The Politics of Thatcherism*. London: Lawrence and Wishart.

———. 2003. 'New Labour Has Picked up Where Thatcherism Left Off'. *The Guardian*, 6 August 2003. https://www.theguardian.com/politics/2003/aug/06/society.labour.

———. 2011. 'The Neo-Liberal Revolution'. *Cultural Studies* 25 (6): 705–28. https://doi.org/10.1080/09502386.2011.619886.

Harvey, David. 2005. *A Brief History of Neoliberalism*. Oxford; New York: Oxford University Press.

Hobsbawm, Eric J. 1995. *The Age of Extremes: The Short Twentieth Century, 1914-1991*. London: Abacus.

Hochschild, Arlie Russell. 2003. *The Commercialization of Intimate Life: Notes from Home and Work*. Berkeley, CA: University of California Press.

———. 2013. *So How's the Family? And Other Essays*. Berkeley: University of California Press.

Hochschild, Arlie Russell, S. Uma Devi, and Lise Isaksen. 2013. 'Children Left Behind'. In *So How's the Family? And Other Essays*, by Arlie Russell Hochschild, 147–64. Berkeley, CA: University of California Press.

Hoggett, Paul. 2000. *Emotional Life and the Politics of Welfare*. Houndmills, Basingstoke, Hampshire; New York: Macmillan Press; St. Martin's Press.

Hollander, Nancy Caro, and Susan Gutwill. 2006. 'Despair and Hope in a Culture of Denial'. In *Psychoanalysis, Class and Politics: Encounters in the Clinical Setting*, edited by Lynne Layton, Nancy Caro Hollander, and Susan Gutwill, 81–91. London: Routledge.

Hollway, Wendy. 2006. *The Capacity to Care: Gender and Ethical Subjectivity*. London; New York: Routledge.

Honig, Bonnie. 2017. *Public Things: Democracy in Disrepair*. New York: Fordham University Press.

hooks, bell. 1995. 'Black Women Shaping Feminist Theory'. In *Words of Fire: An Anthology of African-American Feminist Thought*, edited by Beverly Guy-Sheftall, 170–82. New York: New Press.

Layton, Lynne. 2008. 'What Divides the Subject? Psychoanalytic Reflections on Subjectivity, Subjection and Resistance'. *Subjectivity* 22: 60–72. https://doi.org/10.1057/sub.2008.3.

———. 2009. 'Who's Responsible? Our Mutual Implication in Each Other's Suffering'. *Psychoanalytic Dialogues* 19 (2): 105–20. https://doi.org/10.1080/10481880902779695.

———. 2014. 'Maternally Speaking: Mother's Daughters and the Talking Cure'. In *Mothering and Psychoanalysis: Clinical, Sociological and Feminist Perspectives*, edited by Petra Bueskens, 161–76. Canada: Demeter Press.

Lazzarato, Maurizio. 2008. *Le gouvernement des inégalités: critique de l'insécurité néolibérale*. Démocritique. Paris: Éditions Amsterdam.

Lorey, Isabell. 2015. *State of Insecurity: Government of the Precarious*. Translated by Aileen Derieg. London; New York: Verso.

Lynch, Kathleen, and Maureen Lyons. 2009. 'Love Labouring: Nurturing Rationalities and Relational Identities'. In *Affective Equality: Love, Care, and Injustice*, edited by Kathleen Lynch, John Baker, and Maureen Lyons, 54–77. Houndmills, Basingstoke; New York: Palgrave Macmillan.

Lynch, Kathleen, Maureen Lyons, and John Baker. 2009. 'Introduction'. In *Affective Equality: Love, Care, and Injustice*, edited by Kathleen Lynch, John Baker, and Maureen Lyons, 1–11. Houndmills, Basingstoke; New York: Palgrave Macmillan.

Nussbaum, Martha C. 1995. *Women, Culture, and Development: A Study of Human Capabilities*. Edited by Jonathan Glover. Oxford; New York: Oxford University Press.

Peltz, Rachael. 2005. 'The Manic Society'. *Psychoanalytic Dialogues* 15 (3): 347–66. https://doi.org/10.1080/10481881509348834.

Philipson, Irene. 1994. *On the Shoulders of Women: The Feminization of Psychotherapy*. New York: Guilford Press.

Reay, Diane. 2015. 'Habitus and the Psychosocial: Bourdieu with Feelings'. *Cambridge Journal of Education* 45 (1): 9–23. https://doi.org/10.1080/0305764X.2014.990420.

Ruti, Mari. 2011. 'Winnicott with Lacan: Living Creatively in a Postmodern World'. *American Imago* 67 (3): 353–74. https://doi.org/10.1353/aim.2010.0016.

Sandford, Stella. 2011. 'What Is Maternal Labour?' *Studies in the Maternal* 3 (2): 1–11. https://doi.org/10.16995/sim.63.

Sennett, Richard. 2006. *The Culture of the New Capitalism*. New Haven, CT: Yale University Press.

Stiegler, Bernard. 2010. *Taking Care of Youth and the Generations*. Translated by Stephen J. Barker. Stanford, CA: Stanford University Press.

———. 2013. *What Makes Life Worth Living: On Pharmacology*. Translated by Daniel Ross. Cambridge; Malden, MA: Polity.

Stone, Alison. 2019. *Being Born: Birth and Philosophy*. Studies in Feminist Philosophy. Oxford: Oxford University Press.

Thatcher, Margaret. 1987. Interview for Woman's Own Interview by Douglas Keay. Margaret Thatcher Foundation. https://www.margaretthatcher.org/document/106689.

The Care Collective. 2020. *The Care Manifesto: The Politics of Interdependence*. London; New York: Verso Books.

Threadcraft, Shatema. 2016. *Intimate Justice: The Black Female Body and the Body Politic*. New York: Oxford University Press.

Tronto, Joan C. 2002. 'The "Nanny" Question in Feminism'. *Hypatia* 17 (2): 34–51.

———. 2013. *Caring Democracy: Markets, Equality, and Justice*. New York: New York University Press.

Voela, Angie, and Louis Rothschild. 2019. 'Creative Failure: Stiegler, Psychoanalysis and the Promise of a Life Worth Living'. *New Formations* 95 (95): 54–69. https://doi.org/10.3898/NEW F:95.04.2018.

Winnicott, Donald W. 1958. 'Clinical Varieties of Transference'. In *Collected Papers: Through Paediatrics to Psycho-Analysis*, 295–99. London: Tavistock.

———. 1987. 'Communication between Infant and Mother, and Mother and Infant, Compared and Contrasted'. In *Babies and Their Mothers*, 89–103. Reading, MA: Addison-Wesley.

———. 1990. 'Ego Integration in Child Development'. In *The Maturational Processes and the Facilitating Environment*, 56–63. London: Karnac and the Institute of Psycho-Analysis.

———. 1991a. 'The Place Where We Live'. In *Playing and Reality*, 104–10. London: Routledge.

———. 1991b. 'Transitional Objects and Transitional Phenomena'. In *Playing and Reality*, 1–25. London: Routledge.

Young, Iris Marion. 1990. *Justice and the Politics of Difference*. Princeton, NJ: Princeton University Press.

7

The Politics of Holding

> The healthiest society…in Winnicott's terms, is the one most capable of holding its vulnerable and troubled members…the question thus becomes: How can we support and facilitate the development of healthy subjects (in every sense of the term) in the context of a world that so often fails so many? (Bowker and Buzby 2017, 27)

How should we theorise the characteristics of a society most likely to foster the development of the capacities for spontaneity, authenticity, creativity, care and autonomy, and what is the relationship between this agenda and the erosion of (neoliberal) capitalism? Amy Buzby argues that Winnicott's work resonates with the Frankfurt School theorists, Horkheimer, Adorno and Marcuse, sharing their interest in understanding the psychic capacities necessary to bring about societal change (2017). Buzby suggests that fostering the true self and the capacity to be spontaneous is central to this process. We need, she writes, to "build models of praxis that open the subject's defences up for reflection" (244). On Buzby's analysis, critical theory itself can have a therapeutic function, contributing to repairing damaged experience by developing models of action that can produce psychic and societal change. Change can be facilitated by the production of work that is available "for use by those who would seek to work through personal and shared suffering" (244).

By identifying the supplement that Winnicott's thinking might offer to the critical theory of the first generation of the Frankfurt School, Buzby echoes the interventions of Benjamin and Honneth discussed in previous chapters. Benjamin critiques of the Frankfurt School's reliance on a Freudian model of subjective development, foregrounding the impasse produced when the development of agency is understood to be rooted in an identification with paternal authority (1978). Starting from this premise, in line with the dominant perspectives of the time, Horkheimer and Adorno were unable to give due weight to the significance of early relations, or to the integral role played by the holding environments of social life in supporting the development of capacities. Honneth's own work draws extensively on Benjamin, but neither thinker focuses overtly on what kind of environments would best support the development of capacities (Meehan 1995; Honneth 1996). Though Benjamin does give an account of how the nuclear family form splits capacities, and Honneth does acknowledge that experiences of oppression or neglect can affect the development of the capacity for recognition, for neither theorist is this the fulcrum around which their analysis pivots.

The last chapter explored how the distribution of care in contemporary capitalism affects and inflects the development and expression of capacities. Buzby highlights that the "monadism," or individualism, characteristic of contemporary society means that fewer families are likely to prove adequate at holding, as the concurrent pressures of hegemony encourage the creation of more and more rigid false selves (2017, 243). This chapter provides a psychosocial argument for a radical politics of care that attends to the dialectical relationship between subjective capacities and social change. Ultimately, I suggest that integrating and centralising the idea of holding in the politics of care represents a fruitful strategy for the therapeutic task of critical theory.

Holding and Growth

Steven Groarke identifies a tension in Winnicott's work between two competing tendencies: to lend support to "systems of security" or to advocate and strive for "acts of freedom" (2014, 6). On the one hand, he suggests, when the residential care of "difficult children" is used as a model for management, it becomes "a permanent task of social defence…linked to the theme of government" (6). However, Winnicott also approached childhood and the task of adult psychotherapy from "the developmental perspective of health and the ideal of active living" (6). The irreconcilability between these two perspectives demonstrates, for Groarke, an ambivalence in psychoanalysis, an oscillation between a commitment to the processes and progress of modern society and a "framework modelled on a form of maternal care adequate to innate potential and the creative process of maturation" (6). Groarke is critical of the first approach, which he aligns with the idea of reflexivity and a sociological tendency towards reductionism with regard to psychoanalysis that he traces in the work of Anthony Giddens (9). As a counterpoint, he endorses the Winnicottian ideal of spontaneity, a utopian capacity that depends on "the security of the framework" holding up, on the ontological security that might be experienced by a child who has known a "loving, responsive, and generative family environment. Life realises its potential as creativity in a reliable situation is the point Winnicott was making" (D. W. Winnicott 1986a, 98; Groarke 2014, 8).

Groarke stresses that, for Winnicott, the infant's sense that the world is reliable develops through the introjection of the "*experience of reliability*" (D. W. Winnicott 1987, 97, emphasis in the original). The infant relies on the caregiver for the enjoyment of being alive and is unable to make anything meaningful or worthwhile from an experience of unreliability. Groarke writes that:

> The primary situation of sensible beings one with another comprises a framing structure that Winnicott saw as the basis of psychological growth. In this case, the way to excel at being human is an altogether spontaneous matter and requires nothing in the way of training or the regulation of

appropriate aptitudes and competencies. Human life is understood as the impulse to dwell in its own nature, a pre-reflexive relation of immanence. (2014, 16)

The setting of care provided by the environment constitutes the necessary conditions for psychological growth, and human life unfolds in the context of an experience of reliability. Winnicott roots the development of inner security in the infants' bodily experience, taking place against an environmental background, in which the psyche comes to dwell in the soma. Through the process of personalisation, "the infant's sense of itself is securely located inside its body" and the infant "realises itself in this way by being loved" (16). The earliest period of development, prior to the experience of object relations, depends on "body management," understood as a form of love (D. W. Winnicott 1988, 123). Winnicott writes that "the beginning of that part of the baby's development, which I am calling personalisation, or which can be described as an in-dwelling of the psyche in the soma, is to be found in the mother or mother-figure's ability to join up her emotional involvement, which originally is physical and physiological" (D. W. Winnicott 1989, 264). In Groarke's words, "dwelling is the well-being that comes from the care of being," and this is an achievement that is never guaranteed (2014, 17).

What differentiates a good (facilitating) environment from a bad (impinging) one is "the mother's capacity (or not) to meet the infant's innate potential and developing needs" (18). Bollas writes that "in his work on the mother–child relation, Winnicott stresses what we might call its stillness: the mother provides a continuity of being, she 'holds' the infant in an environment of her making that facilitates his growth" (1987, 3). Groarke highlights that "the infant's dependence on the maternal frame for its development is the central premise of the argument, the idea that growth depends on 'the actual mother' being in a position to meet the absolute dependence of 'the actual infant' at the beginning; in which case a sense of inner security arises based on the reliability of 'holding'" (Groarke 2014, 18). The child's sense of the reliability of the environment develops through the experience of the first feed, the physical care of handling and the recognitive experience of mirroring (D. W. Winnicott 1988, 103, 122; 1991b). The facial recognition that the caregiver provides is paradigmatic of intuitive management, involving a response to what is encountered that is not identical but differentiated and feeds back into the infant's self. The experience of recognition facilitates the child's own creative looking. Having been seen, they can now afford to look and see. The experience of holding and handling, a form of care that meets needs and holds potentials, fosters a sense of reliability and inner security that makes it possible for the infant to live spontaneously and creatively.

A certain kind of management, namely intuitive, has the capacity to foster spontaneity. This insight is applicable to understanding infant development, the therapeutic action of psychoanalytic psychotherapy and the holding function of societal institutions. Working with patients exhibiting psychotic forms of disturbance led Winnicott to conceptualise psychoanalytic psychotherapy as a holding or facilitating environment analogous to maternal care. Such an environment would be characterised by an analyst who is "reliably there, on time, alive, breathing," who promises to "keep awake and become preoccupied with the patient" but who will remain relatively objective: ensuring not to make "moral judgements," "intrude" with details of her own life or "take sides in the persecutory systems" (D. W. Winnicott 1958, 285). The session will take place in a comfortable room, "not a passage," and the analyst will refrain from "temper tantrums" and "compulsive falling in love." Crucially, Winnicott writes in the last on this bullet-pointed list, "the analyst survives" (285–6). The particular form of psychotherapy that he describes aims to undo the effects of early environmental failure through the provision of previously unavailable forms of experience which replicate early care, providing the opportunity for the self to become unfrozen from the original failure situation and start up again. Yet for Winnicott, the inspiration for such transformation extends, potentially, far beyond the consulting room:

> It is from psychosis that a patient can make a spontaneous recovery, whereas psychoneurosis makes no spontaneous recovery and the psychoanalyst is truly needed. In other words, psychosis is closely related to health, in which innumerable environmental failure situations are frozen

but are reached and unfrozen by various healing phenomena of ordinary life, namely friendships, nursing during physical illness, poetry, etc., etc. (284)

It is worth noting that Winnicott's conception of "healing phenomena" extends over various aspects of collective life that are considered capable of holding the subject in such a way that damaged experience might be repaired.

In her memoir, *The Last Asylum*, Barbara Taylor offers an account of her experience of psychosis and the changing face of mental health care in the UK since the 1980s (2014). "Mental health care today," she writes, "is a fast-track system geared to getting people back on their feet, and back into work, as quickly as possible…Everywhere ongoing care and support are undermined and derogated" (251–2). Recovery and dependency have come to be conceived as antithetical propositions, resulting in the shutting of community centres where people could previously meet and talk, sharing their experiences (251–2). But "people need other people," and "true independence…is rooted in social connection" (252). Today, the need for connectedness is insufficiently acknowledged, and "the system has been stripped of the kind of ongoing care relationships necessary to build understanding and trust" (255). Taylor, an academic historian by trade, speaks from the position of service-user, but her comments are echoed by psychiatrists and psychotherapists. Anthony Bateman notes that "the relational, pastoral component of mental health care has been eliminated. All that is left now is a mechanistic, formulaic, depersonalised substitute for quality care" (cited in Taylor 2014, 257). Current treatment options are time-limited, so as to mitigate dependency. However, a "host of studies has shown that it is the quality of the relationship with the therapist that determines the outcome…[of] all therapeutic encounters" (260). What psychoanalyst Michael Balint considered the most powerful medication doctors prescribe—namely the therapeutic relationship—has largely been effaced, replaced by short-term solutions that ignore human dependence on others (Balint 2005).

Concluding her exploration, which mixes personal experience with a history of mental health provision, Taylor foregrounds the importance of the reliability of the setting. She writes that "the mental health system

I entered in the 1980s was deeply flawed, but at least it recognised needs – for ongoing care, for asylum, for someone to rely upon when self-reliance is no option – that the present system pretends do not exist, offering in their stead individualist pieties and self-help prescriptions that are a mockery of people's sufferings" (2014, 264). Taylor's memoir provides a vividly detailed and compelling account of her own long-term experience with psychoanalytic psychotherapy, and the ultimately transformative effects of open-ended care, a view that also characterises Victoria Sweet's account of "slow medicine" and the necessary conditions for healing in *God's Hotel* (2013). Current mental health provision, however, aligns with the critique of "dependency culture," which stresses "hand ups not handouts" (Hoggett 2000, 5). State investment focuses on building entrepreneurial competencies, rather than providing the kind of holding environment in which personal growth can take place.

Mental health care is one of the most obvious institutional holding environments of social life, directly tied to the clinical contexts in which Winnicott developed his ideas. Stiegler also provides an autobiographical account of psychic transformation with its own particular relationship with "time." In the short autobiographical text, *How I Became a Philosopher*, Stiegler locates his intellectual awakening during a five-year term in prison in his twenties, which he served for armed robbery (2009). Stiegler describes how, whilst doing time, he was able to break free of a state of kenosis (stupidity) and begin to achieve a noetic (creative, critical) form of subjectivity through the study of philosophy, in particular the "old masters" (Aristotle, Marx, Saussure, Wittgenstein). Voela and Rothschild gloss the process of change that took place: "as an intellectual pursuit, philosophy allows him to redefine the relationship between self (inside) and space (outside)" (2019, 64). Stiegler writes that philosophy "consisted of considering the milieu while being able to extract oneself from it, in the same way as a flying fish can leave the water: intermittently" (2009, 14). Taking his distance from the world, the proto-philosopher "no longer lived in the world, but rather in the absence of the world" (2009, 17). In this state, a transformation took place. Stielger writes that "I found first an absence of world, this 'learnèd lack,' which, as such (a lack) is rather a fault [*défaut*] and a necessity [*il faut*], that which gives and gives place, rather than what 'lacks place.' The lack, in this case, is the inability to know how to live this absence and in this absence; it does not know how to find the learning necessitated by default, *that is, to invent it*" (23, emphasis in the original). Drawing on Winnicott in order to interpret Stiegler's account, Voela and Rothschild write that:

> To be alone with someone allows another to concentrate on a task. Such capacities are consistent with the idea that one begins in an unselfconscious manner. Aligning Stiegler to Winnicott we could argue that relationality is fostered in solitude. It chimes with attention and being able to focus (give attention to) and think, developing the noetic qua abstract thinking. This is directly related to dealing with the inevitability of suffering and the capacity to imagine solutions to expectations created. (2019, 64)

Stiegler is able to develop a new way of relating because of the experience of solitude provided by prison. As Voela and Rothschild put it, "the space of thought and loneliness (prison) creates a generating matrix of the psychic formations which are able to evolve" (64). What bears emphasising is how the space and time of prison, the reality of Stiegler "doing time," create the necessary context for this psychic change. The time of Stiegler's sentence is not the open-ended time of psychoanalysis encountered by Taylor, but rather a form of holding, of "being alone with someone," that cultivates the capacity for attention and thinking. This analysis is not intended to romanticise the experience of prison, but rather to highlight how Stiegler is able to make use of a setting that facilitated rather than impinging, in order to develop the creative capacity for thinking that is at the heart of his conception of the noetic.

If there is a tendency inherent in psychoanalysis generally and in Winnicott's thinking, as Groarke demonstrates, towards normalisation and governance, there is also an inherently radical counter-tendency that is not reducible in this way, a tendency that emphasises the role of holding, or a non-intrusive form of care and intuitive management, in facilitating the development of subjective capacities capable of producing psychic change. Such care makes growth possible, it fosters the faith that life is worth living, facilitating the creation of potential space and the realisation of creativity and spontaneity. Groarke does not develop an alternative account of welfare, but the emphasis he places on the provision of a reliable setting, on spontaneity and creativity, represents an important contribution to thinking and theorising a form of transformative politics.

The Radical Politics of Holding-Care

Voela and Rothschild recognise the political significance of holding (2019). Writing of how the "traumatised relational ground between citizens" can be transformed by "socio-political action" and "civic responsibility," they name that action as a "holding" capable of reactivating "long circuits of desire," a "relational gesture which synthesises care (*besorgen*) and attention" (69). Informed here by Heidegger's account of care as "concern" (*besorgen*), Voela and Rothschild suggest that psycho-socio-political healing will involve the work of care, a holding in mind of citizens capable of reactivating the processes constitutive of noetic (creative, critical) subjectivity. Linking the absence of "holding-relationality" to modern capitalism, they suggest that holding can "bring about not just another shift but structural change," including change "on all levels" and "care between generations and in all fields" (69). They conclude that "care and living an affected life may not precipitate a revolution but certainly make life worth living" (69).

As Voela and Rothschild's evaluation suggests, shifting the focus to holding-care is likely to be incompatible with established ideas of social revolution, however this does not mean that the change such a shift can facilitate is any less radical. Such change would involve a reorientation of society and its institutions in ways resonant with the political demands of feminists dating back to the 1970s. Writing of the second wave, Fraser notes that "unlike some of their countercultural comrades, most feminists did not reject state institutions simpliciter" (2013, 216). Instead, they sought "to infuse the latter with feminist values, they envisioned a participatory democratic state that empowered its citizens" (216). They imagined, in short, state institutions capable of holding, caring and facilitating the development and expression of subjective capacities. "The development of human potentialities and capabilities," Michael

Rustin writes, "depends essentially on the quality of relationships within which they are nurtured. This is a proposition to which…a redesign of our economy and social system needs to give deep attention" (2015, 11). In accord with longstanding feminist approaches, Rustin advocates reformed modes of governance, ones informed by an understanding of the importance of care and relationality for life. Prioritising holding and care in political thinking has the capacity to bring about widespread transformation.

The politics of holding-care is inherently radical because it demands that the means to reproduce life and facilitate psychic growth, which are privatised and distorted within capitalism, are socialised in the name of justice. If holding is understood to refer to the conditions necessary for health, and to involve the provision of a setting in which dependence is acknowledged and needs are met, then the social relations of pre-modern/pre-capitalist society functioned as more effective holding environments than the privatised and commodified environments that have become the norm in capitalist society. Again, I do not wish to romanticise pre-modern societies, which were characterised by complex and multifaceted forms of exploitation, domination and oppression. However, access to land did give peasants the means to reproduce themselves and provided some basis for resistance to the demands of the feudal lords. Pre-capitalist societies are generally considered to have been characterised by forms of community and commoning that were lost in the transition to capitalism, through which they were privatised in the modern family and became associated almost exclusively with the relationship between mother and child, which remained a locus of connection, relation and nostalgia (see Chapters 3 and 4). The postwar welfare state represents an imperfect and short-lived attempt to de-privatise, or re-socialise at least, the idea of holding as a collective endeavour and responsibility (see Chapter 4). Providing the conditions, the forms of holding, necessary for the development of the capacities associated with human flourishing represents an important way of conceptualising social justice (see Chapter 5) and offers a means for critiquing the contemporary organisation of capitalism, in which access to holding is unequally and inadequately distributed (see Chapter 6). A politics of holding-care would enact the socialisation of what has been privatised, facilitating the commoning of the resources needed to reproduce life, both materially and psychically.

Given that holding encompasses both the psychic and the material resources needed to reproduce a life worth living, and capitalism does not adequately acknowledge or value these resources, ensuring access to them for all would challenge the structure of both the social relations and the political economy that characterises capitalism. As Joan Tronto points out, those who wish to maintain the status quo have a vested interest in eliding care: "to call attention to care is to raise questions about the adequacy of care in our society. Such an inquiry will lead to a profound rethinking of moral and political life" (1993, 111). Tronto goes as far as to suggest that a politics of care may be inherently anti-capitalist, because it views human needs, as opposed to profit, as the highest human goal. Ensuring access to the holding structures needed to reproduce a life worth living, a life characterised by creativity, spontaneity, care and autonomy, is not compatible with neoliberal modes of political economy and social policy. With regard to social provision, markets, financialisation and austerity do not constitute or facilitate environments of holding. The privatisation of care also produces care chains that undermine the provision of holding on a global scale. Providing the conditions necessary for the development of healthy subjectivities, those capable of developing and exercising their capacities, will involve a range of measures. Downing suggests that, in addition to recognising the importance of care in everyone's lives, and valuing it, various shifts are central to overcoming the current care crisis, including removing financialisation; improving recompense and support for carers; the provision of the time to care, in the form of a Universal Basic Income or a four-day week; encouraging and building communities of care; and the democratisation of care (2021).

Certainly, the desire to prioritise needs over profit would necessitate the definancialisation of care and public services. The widespread practice of privatising and outsourcing services to companies or hedge funds that seek to extract profit from their investments has a negative effect on the abilities of staff to provide care that is good enough. Despite working in difficult circumstances, the fact that carers often care deeply about those they care for means they are likely to self-exploit in order to provide a service they deem adequate. However, this does not change the fact that there is a fundamental contradiction between a service run exclusively on a principle of efficiency and the conditions necessary for good-enough care, time in particular. Taking care seriously would necessitate investment in caring infrastructures, financed by progressive taxation, where the time and space of care are adequately recognised, and the work of carers sufficiently remunerated (Tronto 2003).

In addition to reorganisation and redistribution in the field of social care and public services, in order to carve out the time on which care depends, taking care seriously would require recognition of the unpaid caregiving responsibilities of citizens, and the pursuit of policies that would support carers in finding the time for caregiving. There have been long-running debates about whether the time given over to unpaid forms of care work should be compensated. Some feminists have argued for the work of reproduction to be recast as productive in order to make plain the contribution it makes to the economy; the demand that the cost of care and social reproduction be met through investment in caring infrastructures, for instance child care, education, health care, elder care and community services; and demands for support for those who undertake unpaid care work in the form of direct payments, paid leave, care allowances, pensions, or more radical proposals for a Universal Basic Income (Dowling 2021). The Wages for Housework campaign that began in the early 1970s in a range of countries including the UK, Italy, the USA and Germany was active in this capacity, demanding wages for the unpaid work of care that fell heavily on women (Dalla Costa and James 1975). As Dowling notes, the movement aimed to show that the unpaid work of social reproduction and care undertaken in the home was "not remunerated by capital because it was a key source of its surplus" (200). The campaign was designed to show that capitalism cannot in fact pay for this work and still maintain a profit motive.

When compensating citizens for care work is mooted, it is vital that the emphasis falls not on simply maintaining the status quo. As Fraser notes, many welfare states favour a "caregiver parity" model which ostensibly recognises the importance of care and supports this work through the provision of benefits and infrastructure, but does not fundamentally challenge the distribution of caring responsibilities (2013). In place of this model, Fraser advocates a "universal caregiver model" which would involve degendering the work of care and shifting perceptions in such a way that everyone is assumed to have caring responsibilities. On this approach, all jobs would be designed for workers who are also presumed to be caregivers. Other care work would be located outside of the household. "In state-funded but locally organised institutions, childless adults, older people and others without kin-based responsibilities would join parents and others in democratic, self-managed carework activities," she writes (134). The universal caregiver model would force a confrontation between capitalism and the unacknowledged and underpaid work of care on which it depends.

In her recent work, Tronto has called for caring to be placed at the centre of contemporary democratic thinking, defining a "caring democracy" as one that takes care seriously and places it above the imperative of economic production (2013, 156). A caring democracy would address how responsibility for care is assigned, focusing on facilitating citizens' involvement in assigning caring responsibilities (7). The state and civil society, she suggests, should guarantee that the caring needs of citizens and of their loved ones are met (44). Concurrently, "citizens must become more committed to producing the kinds of values, practices, and institutions that will allow democratic society to more coherently provide for its democratic caring citizens" (44). Challenging the idea that we are "creatures of the market," Tronto insists instead that we are "creatures of care" (45). Democratic societies need to reorientate their values "to support for the means for people to live human lives," focusing on how interdependence can be organised through caring institutions that take "everyone's equal capacity both for care and for freedom" seriously (45).

Tronto rightly identifies the importance of taking care seriously, and the significance of the relationship between the organisation of institutions and caring capacities. However, as previous chapters have explored, the realisation of the inherent potential for capacities like caring and freedom depends on the specific qualities of the environment, and on the relationship between that environment and the subject. As previously discussed, Hollway critiques Tronto and other care theorists for the rationalism of their approach, which does not explore the unconscious and intersubjective dynamics of caring, nor the early intersubjective experiences through which the capacity to care develops. The next section explores the psychosocial dimensions and implications of pursuing a radical politics of care, using the concept of holding in order to foreground the advantages of such an approach.

A Psychosocial Argument

Holding describes a form of care or management that finds purchase in multiple contexts ranging from infant care to public institutions. It describes a mode of care that is non-intrusive, one that "holds" the infant/patient/citizen in a kind of stillness that facilitates the continuity of being and psychic growth. To prioritise holding in thinking about care provision would necessitate an awareness of the importance of time in creating a space for unfolding. As such, recognising holding as the condition of possibility for spontaneity, and the ground of the faith that life is worth living, makes it imperative to pursue radical policy proposals, such as a Universal Basic Income, that acknowledge the time needed for care.

The idea at the heart of proposals for a Universal Basic Income is that the state provides all citizens, regardless of their financial situation, with a guaranteed income on an ongoing basis that they may spend as they wish. The idea of a UBI, or something approximating it, is not new. John Lanchester points towards Thomas More's *Utopia*, published in 1516, as offering an early instance, and something like the idea was "very much alive in the early second half of the twentieth century," in the work of figures as disparate as Martin Luther King Jr. and the Chicago School neoliberal Friedrich Hayek (Lanchester 2019; Bidadanure 2019, 482). It was considered by the Black Panther Party as a way to address racial discrimination in the USA (challenging the power of the "malfare" states Threadcraft describes) and by feminists involved in the Wages for Housework movement who discussed an income separate from labour as a way of challenging the hegemony of the male breadwinner model (Threadcraft 2016, 156; Dalla Costa and James 1975). Normative discussions of

UBI took shape in the early 1990s, and in recent years, the concept has been of interest to post-Marxist scholars concerned with the futures of work and care (Parijs 1992; Weeks 2011). In recent years, there have been trials of UBI around the world, including recent plans for a pilot scheme in Wales focusing on care leavers (Goodman et al. 2021; Morris 2021). Whilst there are many different arguments for UBI, and debates about the relationship between the provision of UBI and public services (Parijs 1992; Lanchester 2019; Stronge 2020), I want to focus on developing a perspective that centralises the psychosocial meanings and theorises the potential psychic effects of this kind of provision, whilst at the same time keeping the relationship between these factors and political economy, anti-capitalism and social change in view.

The idea of a UBI, that all citizens should receive a specific sum of money from the state regardless of their means, may in fact constitute a "holding" form of care very different from contemporary welfare regimes. As was discussed in Chapter 4, the post-war welfare state was designed to offer protection against the "five great evils" of society, namely want, disease, ignorance, squalor and idleness. It recognised the effects of insecurity, acknowledging and meeting needs for dependence and support. As discussed in Chapter 6, in more recent decades, however, under the auspices of neoliberal thinking, the welfare state has been reconceived through the lens of an ideology of personal responsibility, eschewing public responsibility for care and exhibiting a hatred for dependency (Hoggett 2000). There have been hand ups not hand outs, and the production of subjects fit for work. Welfare has been conceived in terms of an exchange; support is given on the expectation that something will be received in return, namely productivity. Help is not provided simply because need exists, and dependence implies the need for care. Contrastingly, Hoggett points to the fact that UBI "is non-conditional." He continues:

> There is no means-testing nor any set of obligations attached to it. Van Parijs argues that as such it maximises the possibilities for 'real freedom,' a society in which each individual has the greatest opportunity to do whatever she might want to do including, in his by now famous example, the opportunity to spend every day surfing if this is what she wished. In

other words a citizen's income assumes the form of a gift that seeks no return. (2000, 206)

Conceptualising UBI in this way, as a gift that seeks no return, evokes the psychosocial meanings of the post-war welfare state described by Steedman, a form of public and collective concern capable of producing confidence in one's right to exist (1986, 121–22). UBI, like the post-war welfare state, involves the recognition and meeting of need. Richard Norman defines need in terms of "deficiencies in respect to well-being" (1992, 141). UBI provides the means to satisfy the basic needs that most impede well-being, the five great evils identified by the welfare state. Recently, Guy Standing has cast UBI in similar but updated terms, positioning it as a response to *Battling Eight Giants* of contemporary society: inequality, insecurity, debt, stress, precarity, automation, populism and extinction (2020). As a response to need that seeks nothing in return, UBI constitutes a form of holding-care that evokes, whilst also transcending, the ethos of the post-war welfare state.

UBI eschews the responsibilising demands of an insurance or asset-based welfare system, which make care conditional, restricting it to those who have contributed "enough" (an implicitly anti-immigrant position) or dependent on forms of self-management and economic advantage not available to all. It also departs from the punitive and invasive approaches to assessing claims for support that have become the norm since the imposition of austerity policies (Gentleman 2011). Lanchester points to the fact that for Van Parijs, one of the key figures in debates about the normative basis for introducing a UBI, the initiative offers "freedom from anxiety, from the often humiliating and chaotic process of applying for means-tested benefits in a welfare state, from the need to take demeaning or exhausting or damagingly precarious work" (2019). The freedom from anxiety that UBI could offer evokes its capacity to function as a means of holding-care. By providing a form of holding, UBI mitigates the experience of anxiety and facilitates going-on-being. This, in turn, has the capacity to support psychic growth. To restate Groarke's articulation on this, "growth depends on 'the actual mother' being in a position to meet the absolute dependence of 'the actual infant' at the beginning; in which case a sense of inner security arises based on the reliability of 'holding'" (2014, 18). Though citizens are not babies, UBI would involve the state in meeting needs for dependence both in adult citizens and in the children and others they may care for. Offering a form of non-intrusive support that meets needs for dependence and enables the continuity of being, UBI could well provide a context more amenable to psychological growth than existing forms of provision. As Groarke highlights, spontaneity flourishes when the framework holds up.

Lisa Baraitser notes that UBI occupies an important place within a post-work politics that appreciates the disciplinary function of waged work and its historical role in the privatisation of caring and reproductive labour (Baraitser 2016; Weeks 2011). "Postwork," Baraitser glosses, "undoes the relation between wage and labour through an analysis of social reproduction in neoliberal conditions, calling not just for the common production of value but for a basic income for the common reproduction of 'life'" (2016, 395). Emphasising that the idea of a UBI "allows care to circulate as everybody's business," Baraitser also highlights the psychic dimension of the reproduction of life that such a strategy would foreground (396). "A postwork notion of care requires not just the reorganisation of the social reproduction of 'life,'" she writes, "but the time it takes to live out the complexities of caring relations, and the development of capacities that may enable the reparation of psychic life" (396). This is a formulation that evokes the holding character of UBI as capable of bringing about psychic change, potentially repairing damaged experience. In a slightly different formulation, Baraitser reiterates the time it takes "for the emergence of the capacity for reparation in psychic life" (406). Here, the emphasis falls on the need to acknowledge the time of unfolding, the time of relationships and intersubjective exchange through which the capacity for what Klein calls reparation, and Winnicott concern, characterised by the spontaneous reparative gesture, develops. This is also the capacity that Hollway describes as central to being able to care, and as key to the cultivation of a form of relational autonomy. Both of these formulations represent avenues for thinking through the psychosocial justification for, and implications of, the kind of holding that provisions like UBI might offer.

Certainly, the implementation of UBI would loosen the imperatives of waged work and provide increased opportunities to devote more time to caring. It also has the capacity to shift the balance of power in favour of employees, who would no longer be completely beholden to their employers for the means to sustain their own lives. However, I want to explore the capacity for what could be conceptualised as the holding environment of post-work care, or UBI, to produce psychic change in citizens. The previous chapter explored how the inequalities characteristic of neoliberal capitalism affect the development of capacities, and I emphasised how contemporary social formations erode and distort capacities that are central to psychic resistance and the fending off of compliance—namely the capacities for spontaneity, creativity, care and autonomy. Such an approach is vulnerable to the criticism that it offers no way out because the capacity for resistance is conceived to be so fundamentally eroded by the environments of late capitalism.

Winnicott himself draws attention to the potentially catastrophic effects of deprivation and oppression. Thinking freedom in relation to the concepts of health and creativity, he writes that "no one is independent of the environment, and there are environmental conditions which destroy the feeling of freedom even in those who have enjoyed it" (1986b, 232). Though he asserts that "it is probably wrong to think of creativity as something that can be destroyed utterly," he goes on to discuss the situation of those who are "dominated at home, or spending their lives in concentration camps or under lifelong persecution because of a cruel political régime." In these situations, he contends, "one feels that it is only a few of the victims who remain creative." The rest "have lost the characteristic that makes them human, so that they no longer see the world creatively" (1991a, 68). Being able to see the world creatively, a capacity that develops through the experience of intuitive management, means being able to create and recreate the world, to exercise the powers of imagination in order to think up, that is to invent, the phenomena that meet a need. Winnicott suggests that this capacity probably cannot be completely destroyed, but it can be seriously impeded by environmental conditions. This is an idea that evokes Nussbaum's distinction between the basic capabilities of human existence and the level of capability characteristic of human flourishing, discussed in Chapter 5 (1995). Capitalism does not (necessarily) destroy the human as such, but rather reduces it to a base level of existence that does not constitute flourishing.

Writing of the relationship between childhood and social reproduction, Susan Ferguson sets out how "the fundamental demands of capital for a renewable supply of labour power exert strong pressures for certain (privatised) forms, (disciplining) practices, and (alienated) states of being to emerge. At the same time, they generate forces that obstruct the likelihood that other (communal, open-ended, integrated) childhoods will develop" (2017, 113). The focus falls here on the reproduction of the worker, rather than the facilitation of healthy, caring forms of subjectivity. However, there are many ways in which the creative capacity might be awoken or maintained: through the experience of holding associated with psychoanalytic psychotherapy, aesthetic experience, or progressive forms of social provision.

How might reformed kinds of social provision, UBI for instance, contribute to psychic transformation for citizens brutalised by the neoliberal agendas of late capitalism? Recent psychoanalytic accounts of the transference supply tools to think about the character of this process. Stone discusses the capacity for the transference relationship to bring about changes in the patient's sense of their past (2012). The transference is an intersubjective process to which the analyst brings their own relational history and experience to the encounter and to their responses to how the patient positions them. "At best," Stone writes, "the analyst does not simply fall in with the position attributed to [them] by the patient, but holds onto [their] own relational history and therefore reacts to the patient's attributions in ways that the patient finds novel, unexpected, and surprising" (2012, 143). As a result of the analyst's unexpected behaviour, the patient is able to access "fresh memories," prompting them to "re-evaluate [their] past so that new elements and strands surface within it. Ultimately, over time, this process can change the whole content of the patient's past" (143). The patient may come to narrate their past differently, because they are able to draw on memory residues that were previously unavailable. The process of remembering differently contributes to the production of psychic change. The patient is no longer constituted by the memories that had previously shaped their psychic structure, but is reformulated on the basis of new experiences, newly accessible memories made available by the analyst's care.

However, as Stone points out, "this only highlights a general feature of all social encounters...The other's responses will always exceed my expectations, however minimally or imperceptibly. Confronted with someone who exceeds my expectations in this way, I shift my expectations and the memories that organise them so that I can continue to relate to the other on the basis of a changed internal horizon" (144). Therefore, our sense of the past is in a state of constant revision, modified by the events that I encounter and their capacity to make me reassess my experience. Stone suggests that "the past organises each individual's openness to the future, but the future as it unfolds reciprocally shapes and re-shapes each individual's past" (144). It is possible to imagine that the experience of different forms of collective holding, such as the recognition of dependency needs represented by UBI, could function like the analytic experience Stone describes, which is, in fact, "a general feature of all social encounters" (144). Confronted by a state capable of acknowledging and holding dependence, previously inaccessible memories could be triggered that would allow citizens to re-evaluate their pasts. This process could in turn facilitate the reactivation of the spontaneity and creativity that Winnicott suggests are probably never completely destroyed but can be damaged by forms of deprivation and impingement that work counter to human flourishing. As Winnicott put it, it is from psychotic illness that patients can make a spontaneous recovery through an experience of "healing phenomena." UBI could function as a setting that might play a role in repairing damaged experience.

Tronto suggests that in order for citizens to revalue care and become motivated to pursue the ends of a caring democracy capable of taking on capitalism, all members of society must come to realise that they are care receivers (2013, 146). She suggests that until this happens, there will be no change in how care is valued (150). Many people, those with medical conditions or disabilities, or those receiving social or elder care, may well be aware of themselves as care receivers, however there are many people who may not recognise their own vulnerability or inherent dependence on others, a situation that is only intensified by the erosion and inhibition of relationships and caring capacities under neoliberal conditions. There are, however, many ways in which this awareness can be cultivated, and engaging in the care of others can be an important source of awareness of our own vulnerability. Whilst Tronto acknowledges that developing an awareness of dependence can come about through practices of caring, she eschews a focus on the caregiver-child relation as a model for care, in fact suggesting that the dyad is an inherently illusory idea (2013, 152). Tronto points out that there is always reciprocity happening in the relationship between caregiver and infant, and there are always others helping with care in ways that challenge the idea of a closed dyad. Additionally, she suggests that the dyadic model precludes the idea that the caregiver is also a needy being.

However, in the light of the arguments developed throughout this book, Tronto's arguments can be disputed. To emphasise the importance of the caregiver-child dyad as both a model and locus of care does not necessitate a rejection of the idea that the relationship involves reciprocity. As Tronto says, infants often seek to reciprocate the care they receive. However, caregivers are not dependent on infants for care in the way that infants are dependent on caregivers. Though the child may try to reciprocate the care they receive, they are not, at least during early life, caring for their caregiver, or if they are, development is likely to go awry (forming a false self). Care is asymmetric, this does not mean that it is not intersubjective or relational. The goal of care is to facilitate reciprocal relations, but this is a capacity that has to be developed. As Hollway puts it, "reciprocal care never obliterates the original mother–child positions" (2006, 77). Additionally, the perspective I have set out in no way denies that the caregiver is highly unlikely to be caring without the involvement or support of others, or that caregivers are needy. In fact, the perspectives explored so far insist that the need for caregivers to be cared for in chains of nested dependency is of paramount importance. It may also be the case that caring for young children involves caregivers in a confrontation with their own neediness, as it calls up memories of their own experiences of infantile care (A. Stone 2012), in ways that are directly relevant to Tronto's claim that the revaluation of care will depend on all citizens coming to recognise themselves as care receivers.

Stone uses the psychoanalytic understanding of the transference to theorise the intersubjective experiences of primary caregivers of young children, mothers in particular. "If our relations with other persons always modify our pasts," she writes, "a relation with a child can induce particularly dramatic shifts in a person's internal past" (146). Stone suggests that a new mother's encounter with her infant confronts her with "something new and unexpected," in the same way that the encounter with the analyst "prompts the patient to unearth neglected strata of [their] history" (145). Viewing this interaction from the mother's perspective, she is no longer positioned as the proto-analyst of the emergent child-subject, but as the patient in the analytic relationship. This formulation evokes the fact that the mother's relationship with the child triggers recollections, quite possibly unthought knowns laid down before the development of an integrated sense of self, of the mother's experiences with her own maternal caregiver, the proto-analyst. Stone explores how the mother's experience with her infant reforms her sense of her own past relationship with her mother along the lines set out earlier. Whilst the mother should not be reduced to the position of daughter here, she is "no longer *only* a daughter," the awakening of memory material relating to being a daughter puts the mother in touch with themselves as a care receiver as well as a caregiver (147). "The mother's position," Stone writes, "is that of being a daughter once again, with a difference."

Stone's argument raises the question of whether it is only female birth parents who are able to experience this transferential relationship with an infant, or what the consequences for maternal subjectivity might be if a mother or other primary caregiver did not have a relationship with a mother of their own. Stone is committed to the idea that "to mother is to re-enter the field of maternal body relations," and she does articulate a form of what Stella Sandford describes as "biological sex essentialism," suggesting that newborn infants are likely to gravitate towards female carers because they are "of woman born" and are thus perceived by the infant as "beings whose bodies continue the prenatal, uterine environment, which was a female and maternal one" (A. Stone 2012, 1, 81; Sandford 2012, 4). Without wanting to enter into debates about the status of the category of "woman," suffice to say that the reality of transfathers giving birth, the practice of surrogacy and the fact of maternal mortality all complicate any straightforward association between gestation and (maternal?) care. This is not to deny, however, that the familiarity of the heartbeat, smell and voice of the person who gestates a baby may well offer a source of comfort after birth. Given that, as Laplanche identifies, the condition of possibility for human development is to be cared for by those who are older than us, it is likely that anyone who has made it to adulthood and takes on the primary care of an infant would experience something of the transferential relationship Stone describes, which triggers—for better or worse—experiences of one's own intersubjective experience as a care receiver (Laplanche 1989). Again, this is not to deny that sex, gender and the presence or absence of a biological relationship with one's own caregivers, and with the child one cares for, are likely to inflect this process in complex ways. In Stone's defence, her project is concerned with theorising the experience of becoming a mother, understood as the gestator and primary caregiver of a child, but her theory is also useful for thinking through how caring for an infant might contribute to developing awareness of oneself as a care receiver.

From a slightly different perspective, but also in the context of exploring maternal subjectivity, Hollway discusses the effects of caring for a child on subjectivity. Charting the development in mothers of the capacity to care, she suggests that a child's "ruthless demands place great pressure on mothers to develop out of their own childlike narcissism" (2006, 77). If one of the psychic results of women's liberation has been the development in women of the kind of mind best suited to a historically male-dominated work environment, based in defensive autonomy, Hollway suggests that an encounter with the absolute dependence of a newborn would likely put a mother with a differentiated subjectivity "under considerable strain" (2006, 78). However, Hollway proposes that a mother whose subjectivity is structured in this way is likely to be "conscious of her own wishes" and "her own subjectivity will be more or less available [to be modified] in the unique third intersubjective space created with her baby" (78). The mother's capacity to differentiate between her own mind and her baby's introjections is central to the development of the capacity to care, which involves thinking about what the baby needs, modifying and containing projections and surviving "its ruthlessness" in order to gradually provide access to "a reality that alters its omnipotence and curbs its narcissism" (78). The mother's "previous access to independent subjectivity" will facilitate the development of her own capacity to care, and that of the infant, if she can "resist being under the infant's control" (78). In becoming a mother, a woman's subjectivity is "changed in the intersubjective space of the third" created between her and the infant (78). Similarly, Roszkia Parker suggests the need to recognise a specifically maternal depressive position, characterised by the capacity to hold love and hate for the child together, which emerges particularly in the experience of mothering (2005).

The capacities to care that are developed in the changing relationship between the mother and the child, as the child moves out of a state of dependence and towards the interdependence of adulthood are valuable in a range of contexts. They can "enhance our capacities as friends, lovers, team-members, managers neighbours, as siblings, sons and daughters," enhancing the capacities of others in turn (Hollway 2006, 80). Significantly, Hollway does not think that only mothers are able to develop these capacities, nor that they can only be developed in relationships with children. "Equivalent capacities to care," she writes, "could be precipitated by other caring relationships and responsibilities," though in adult relationships it is important that caring capacities are reciprocated in subject-subject relations (80). For this reason, there may be something specific if not unique about the encounter with a very young child, whether "yours" or not. As Baraitser glosses, maternal subjectivity "is thought about as arising through a relationship to a child that is characterised by a oneway, non-negotiable dependency" (2009, 17).

Musing on the abilities of fathers to develop the capacity to care, Hollway suggests that being faced with the "uncompromising dependency and vulnerability" of an infant may act to precipitate a man "out of his remaining narcissism" (2006, 84). However, the likelihood of this happening will be affected by both "past and present conditions" (84). These include the extent to which a man has been able to maintain his own ability to identify with the mother's experience, and therefore to care about her, and has managed to avoid repudiating the mother and the femininity culturally associated with women, as well as the contemporary social relations in which caring takes place (93–4). The persistence of a gendered division of labour in societies often organised in terms of a caregiver parity model for distributing care has meant that fathers have often been "semi-detached," from children due to their association with the world of employment and/or gendered norms of care, and they have therefore not had to negotiate the transformational experience of being responsible for an infant (84).

Benjamin acknowledges that equal parenting in heterosexual families will not solve the problem of the reproduction of gender norms as long as they continue to suffuse the wider culture, and Hollway insists that the association of women with caring is rooted in the physical relationship between an infant and a female body during gestation (Benjamin 1990, 217; Hollway 2006, 90). However, a male child's capacity to avoid repudiation of the relationship with the mother at the oedipal stage can be supported if his experience with his pre-oedipal father has taken a specific form. Benjamin emphasises the difference between the renunciation of the mother and her repudiation on the boy's part (1995). Repudiation involves a form of paranoid-schizoid functioning in which the masculine and feminine become split and the latter is rejected. Renunciation, on the other hand, is characterised by a depressive mode of relating, in which the boy can hold onto the good and bad parts of both the feminine and masculine in himself and retain an identification with maternal caring. Hollway writes that "if boys come to terms with oedipal loss more gradually, and in a context where the father does not only represent harsh authority and the threat of (symbolic) castration, but also love, then his coming to terms with the loss associated with being a boy and not like his mother will be bearable and is less likely to result in paranoid–schizoid defences and depletion of the self" (2006, 95). Therefore, a male child's retention of the capacity to care is likely to be influenced by the kind of caregiving he received and, if he has at least one male parent, the role played by this parent in relation to caring. A father who has had this experience is more likely to be able to develop a form of "maternal" subjectivity when confronted with the "non-negotiable dependency" of a young infant.

However, the development of these capacities in infancy and adulthood exists in complex dialogue with the specific organisation of the social relations in which relationships take place. If the significance of care is not acknowledged, and the provision of care remains largely privatised and disproportionately gendered, then the conditions under which adults and infants develop and exercise their capacities are likely to be unfavourable. UBI, however, aligns with Fraser's idea of the "universal caregiver" model for distributing care (2013). Not only does it acknowledge human dependence, but it also contributes to undoing the hierarchical relationship between productive and reproductive work. Additionally, on this model, the distribution of support for care is not gendered, or tied to gestation and biological reproduction. The proposal, then, does not presume that care will be organised within the heterosexual nuclear family so central to the reproduction of capitalism and its distortive distribution of capacities. A policy like UBI would provide more opportunities for caring, increasing the time available for care and the likelihood that care might be "commoned." Dowling suggests that commoning care "means recognising – giving space and time to – the affective and emotional labour that is needed to maintain relationships" (2021, 202). However, it also involves recognising and giving space to the intersubjective processes through which caring subjectivities develop, for citizens of all genders and at all ages. A UBI has the capacity to pluralise the opportunities available for care, challenging the private family as the locus of care and the norms of caring that are so often reproduced there. It could support more opportunities for forms of collective and community care to develop, because it would redistribute time away from work. Such networks of care could begin to undo the entrenched association of women with caregiving, fostering in children of all genders continued identifications with care in adult life.

A UBI has the capacity to recognise the needs of caregivers, which could have positive implications for those giving and receiving care. In particular, supporting caregivers would increase the possibility of children developing their own caring capacities. In many ways, these ideas echo and develop proposals put forward by Margaret and Michael Rustin many years ago (1984). The Rustins turned to Winnicott to understand "the preconditions for the formation of altruistic capacities so important in socialist ideas of humanity" (210). How might institutions, they asked, instil in individuals the kinds of altruistic capacities that would make them tend towards socialist politics? For the Rustins, the primary caregiver must have "security and emotional space" and provision must be made for "caregivers themselves to be cared for" if infants are to "grow beyond a self-centred and narcissistic attitude to their human environment" (213, 210). Caring for children involves having both mental space and time to care. By encouraging the commoning of care and pluralising opportunities to care, a UBI could provide a holding environment for carers, and increase the number of people who identify as caregivers. This would ameliorate the chances of children of all genders developing and maintaining their own subjective capacities for spontaneity, creativity, care and autonomy, because it would raise the likelihood of men being primary caregivers, supporting boys' association of male caregivers with love and facilitating a wider variety of identifications during the over-inclusive stage of child development.

In addition to increasing the likelihood that children will have access to adequate and diverse forms of care, which in turn can help to foster their capacities for spontaneity, creativity, care and autonomy, work on maternal subjectivity emphasises the transformative effect of the intersubjective experience of caring for infants on caregivers' subjectivities too. In pluralising the sites and relationships of care, a UBI would increase opportunities for citizen-subjects, whether they care for their 'own' children or not, to develop a form of maternal subjectivity with broad benefits, and become aware of themselves as both caregivers and care receivers, which Tronto sees as necessary for the establishment of caring democracy. As Orlie puts it, "all great wisdom traditions concur, our children are not our children, they belong to themselves and all of life" (2017, 108). Social policies geared towards holding would create opportunities for more communal forms of care, encouraging the widespread development of more caring kinds of subjectivity among citizens. Modes of holding-care could facilitate the development of caring subjectivities in subjects of all genders who may have been brutalised by the holding failures of neoliberal capitalism.

This proposal does not imply that giving people time to care will simply result in the development of caring capacities, or that exercising such capacities is easy. Rather, there is a need for specific kinds of provision, forms of holding-care, that create the space and time for a range of intersubjective relationships capable of developing capacities to flourish. Good enough care involves, to quote Alford again, "a subtle combination of otherness and identification" that fosters the continuity of being (2000, 246). Harm involves "intruding on the otherness of the other," subordinating "the other's self to oneself" (247). Benjamin, however, warns against forgetting that caring is a difficult operation, reminding us of "the necessary process wherein recognition breaks down and must be restored" (1998, xviii). Caring is not easy, it requires skill and is likely to fail even in the best circumstances, but the capacity to make reparation and re-establish relation is a significant achievement, and an ability fostered though experiences of care and holding. A UBI would not, of course, guarantee that individuals would develop or even exercise caring capacities, but it would provide favourable conditions for those capacities to grow and be put to work.

Fostering caring capacities in subjects, and developing everyone's sense that they are care receivers, may in turn encourage sensibilities that make a positive contribution to fostering caring institutions. Returning to the view expressed by Virginia Held, which was discussed in Chapter 4, Ruddick's conception of "maternal thinking" is once again relevant in this context. Held writes that

> What can we learn from being engaged in practices of care that might be relevant if we cared about others in a way that was less encompassing than parental care but not so different as to approach the emotional indifference assumed by liberal theories? Sara Ruddick emphasises how the experience of mothering, or "fathering" (if we understand it not in its traditional sense but as similar to mothering), is highly relevant to fostering peace in the world....those *thoughtfully involved in the work of bringing up children or caring for the dependent may design better public institutions for child care, education, health care, welfare, and the like— not just better in terms of efficiency but in embodying the relevant values.* (2006, 77–78 emphasis added)

Social holding environments that meet dependence and support the going-on-being of citizens, whilst pluralising the opportunities available to engage in practices of care, have the potential to facilitate the capacities of all citizens to be spontaneous, creative, caring and autonomous. In turn, these capacities can help us to care about, and for, the world, cultivating attentiveness towards the needs of human and non-human others and their existence as beings separate from, yet intimately related to, ourselves. This capacity could then inform political deliberations about the kinds of social provision we want to see, the kind of institutions that would best hold citizens, as Winnicott advocated, best meeting the needs and supporting the flourishing of all.

In a way that evokes the foregoing discussion, Honig writes that "holding environments are part of the infrastructure of human development and of the active human life" (2017, 85). They shape our capacities, and they therefore demand our concern and deliberation. Using Winnicott, Honig offers an account of how a sense of institutions and infrastructures as *public*, and engagement in the contestation of the form they take, represents the "necessary conditions" of democracy (13). She is conscious that public things have received little attention from political theorists, and, as she stresses, public things constitute "site[s] of care, holding and handling" that make up a democratic holding environment (54). Whilst Honig's focus is on the conditions of possibility and character of the political as such, my attention in this chapter has fallen on the forms of social provision and policy intervention that are most likely to facilitate the creative-critical-caring capacities of citizens of all ages and genders. As I have tried to suggest, the principle of holding should be central to reimagining the form and character of public things. Providing holding environments for citizens allows them to develop capacities that can then feed back into political deliberation in positive ways; enabling them to recognise needs, acknowledge differences and design more caring institutions and infrastructures that put need above profit. This also constitutes an acknowledgement of the work of care and social reproduction, in particular a recognition of the space, time and forms of relationship they require and produce. Recognising and providing remuneration for the work of care and reproduction is also an important aspect of the process of eroding and taming capitalism, because it places the conditions of possibility for a life worth living above the imperatives of profit (Brenner 2014; Wright 2015).

In this chapter, and throughout this book, I have tried to provide an account, imperfect no doubt, of the significance of Winnicott's ideas for understanding and reimagining the place of care in contemporary life. My stance is unapologetically utopian and cleaves to a radical form of hope. It shares its utopian spirit with Winnicott. Carlo Strenger notes that Winnicott's utopia "is called the good enough mother (a modest title for a utopia…). The good enough mother need not be perfect; she must be capable of protecting the child from impingement which breaks the child's capability of maintaining its own, natural rhythm, its true self" (1997, 232). Utopia, then, can be understood as the provision of the conditions of possibility—the forms of holding-care—that are required for a life worth living. Winnicott identifies a fundamental relationship between care and human flourishing, a connection effaced in and by dominant conceptions of subjectivity that take shape in modernity and the transition to capitalism. Winnicott's articulation of the fact of human dependence, and the vital importance of meeting dependence if life is to flourish, constitutes an ethic of care that justifies social provision and suggests what a 'good enough' form of welfare, to borrow a phrase from Fiona Williams, might look like (Williams 1999). Given the centrality of relations with others in the development of our capacities, the recognition and redistribution of care are central to achieving justice. The contemporary organisation of care, and the attitudes that inform it, represent attacks on holding and are fundamentally unjust and oppressive. My approach has been to stress the importance of holding in supporting the interrelated capacities for spontaneity, creativity, care and autonomy, and to emphasise both the material and psychic ways in which their cultivation can contribute to the anti-capitalist project of socialising care and the means of reproduction. The psychic and the social are inherently interdependent, and changing one necessarily and unavoidably requires and affects change in the other. Holding-care is central to both, offering the possibility for forms of experience and being that have transformative potential and foster the hope that life might be worth living, after all.

References

Alford, C. Fred. 2000. 'Levinas and Winnicott: Motherhood and Responsibility'. *American Imago* 57 (3): 235–59. https://doi.org/10.1353/aim.2000.0015.

Balint, Michael. 2005. *The Doctor, His Patient and the Illness*. Edinburgh: Churchill Livingstone.
Baraitser, Lisa. 2009. *Maternal Encounters: The Ethics of Interruption*. Hove, East Sussex; New York: Routledge.
———. 2016. 'Postmaternal, Postwork and the Maternal Death Drive'. *Australian Feminist Studies* 31 (90): 393–409. https://doi.org/10.1080/08164649.2016.1278156.
Benjamin, Jessica. 1978. 'Authority and the Family Revisited: Or, a World without Fathers?' *New German Critique*, no. 13: 35–57.
———. 1990. *The Bonds of Love: Psychoanalysis, Feminism and the Problem of Domination*. London: Virago.
———. 1995. *Like Subjects, Love Objects: Essays on Recognition and Sexual Difference*. New Haven; London: Yale University Press.
———. 1998. *Shadow of the Other: Intersubjectivity and Gender in Psychoanalysis*. New York: Routledge.
Bidadanure, Juliana Uhuru. 2019. 'The Political Theory of Universal Basic Income'. *Annual Review of Political Science* 22: 481–501.
Bollas, Christopher. 1987. *The Shadow of the Object: Psychoanalysis of the Unthought Known*. New York: Columbia University Press.
Brenner, Johanna. 2014. '21st Century Socialist-Feminism'. *Socialist Studies/Études Socialistes* 10 (1). http://www.socialiststudies.com/sss/index.php/sss/article/viewArticle/355.
Buzby, Amy. 2017. 'Vanquishing the False Self: Winnicott, Critical Theory, and the Restoration of the Spontaneous Gesture'. In *D.W. Winnicott and Political Theory: Recentering the Subject*, edited by Matthew H. Bowker and Amy Buzby, 229–46. New York: Palgrave Macmillan.
Dalla Costa, Mariarosa, and Selma James. 1975. *The Power of Women and the Subversion of the Community*. Bristol: Falling Wall Press.
Dowling, Emma. 2021. *The Care Crisis: What Caused It and How Can We End It?* London; New York: Verso.
Ferguson, Susan. 2017. 'Children, Childhood and Capitalism: A Social Reproduction Perspective'. In *Social Reproduction Theory: Remapping Class, Recentering Oppression*, edited by Tithi Bhattacharya, 112–30. London: Pluto Press.
Fraser, Nancy. 2013. *Fortunes of Feminism: From Women's Liberation to Identity Politics to Anti-Capitalism*. Brooklyn, NY: Verso Books.
Gentleman, Amelia. 2011. 'Benefits Assessment Firm Causing "Fear and Loathing" among Claimants, Says MP'. *The Guardian*, 24 July 2011,

sec. Politics. https://www.theguardian.com/politics/2011/jul/24/atos-faces-critical-report-by-mps.

Goodman, Cleo, James Muldoon, Guy Standing, David Frayne, and Jack Kellam. 2021. 'Piloting a Basic Income in Wales: A Briefing'. *Autonomy* (blog). https://autonomy.work/portfolio/ubi-in-wales/.

Groarke, Steven. 2014. *Managed Lives*. Hove; New York: Routledge.

Held, Virginia. 2006. *The Ethics of Care: Personal, Political, and Global*. Oxford: Oxford University Press.

Hoggett, Paul. 2000. *Emotional Life and the Politics of Welfare*. Houndmills, Basingstoke, Hampshire; New York: Macmillan Press; St. Martin's Press.

Hollway, Wendy. 2006. *The Capacity to Care: Gender and Ethical Subjectivity*. London; New York: Routledge.

Honig, Bonnie. 2017. *Public Things: Democracy in Disrepair*. New York: Fordham University Press.

Honneth, Axel. 1996. *The Struggle for Recognition: The Moral Grammar of Social Conflicts*. Translated by Joel Anderson. Cambridge, MA: MIT Press.

Lanchester, John. 2019. 'Good New Idea'. *London Review of Books*, 18 July 2019. https://www.lrb.co.uk/the-paper/v41/n14/john-lanchester/good-new-idea.

Laplanche, Jean. 1989. *New Foundations for Psychoanalysis*. Translated by David Macey. Oxford; New York: Basil Blackwell.

Meehan, Johanna. 1995. 'Autonomy, Recognition, and Respect: Habermas, Benjamin, and Honneth'. In *Feminists Read Habermas: Gendering the Subject of Discourse*, edited by Johanna Meehan, 231–46. New York: Routledge.

Morris, Steven. 2021. 'Wales to Launch Pilot Universal Basic Income Scheme'. *The Guardian*, 14 May 2021. https://www.theguardian.com/society/2021/may/14/wales-to-launch-universal-basic-income-pilot-scheme.

Norman, Richard. 1992. 'Equality, Needs, and Basic Income'. In *Arguing for Basic Income: Ethical Foundations for a Radical Reform*, edited by Philippe van Parijs, 141–52. London; New York: Verso.

Nussbaum, Martha C. 1995. *Women, Culture, and Development: A Study of Human Capabilities*. Edited by Jonathan Glover. Oxford; New York: Oxford University Press.

Orlie, Melissa A. 2017. 'The Psychoanalytic Winnicott We Need Now: On the Way to a Real Ecological Thought'. In *D.W. Winnicott and Political Theory: Recentering the Subject*, edited by Matthew H. Bowker and Amy Buzby, First edition, 87–109. New York, NY: Palgrave Macmillan.

Parijs, Philippe van, ed. 1992. *Arguing for Basic Income: Ethical Foundations for a Radical Reform*. London; New York: Verso.

Parker, Rozsika. 2005. *Torn in Two: The Experience of Maternal Ambivalence*. London: Virago.
Rustin, Margaret, and Michael Rustin. 1984. 'Relational Preconditions of Socialism'. In *Capitalism and Infancy: Essays on Psychoanalysis and Politics*, edited by Barry Richards, 207–25. London: Free Associations Books.
Rustin, Michael. 2015. 'A Relational Society'. Edited by Stuart Hall, Doreen Massey, and Michael Rustin. *Afterneoliberalism? The Kilburn Manifesto*. https://www.lwbooks.co.uk/soundings/kilburn-manifesto.
Sandford, Stella. 2012. 'Alison Stone, Feminism, Psychoanalysis, and Maternal Subjectivity'. *Studies in the Maternal* 4 (2). https://doi.org/10.16995/sim.44.
Standing, Guy. 2020. *Battling Eight Giants: Basic Income Now*. London; New York; Oxford; New Delhi; Sydney: I.B. Tauris.
Steedman, Carolyn. 1986. *Landscape for a Good Woman: A Story of Two Lives*. London: Virago.
Stiegler, Bernard. 2009. *Acting Out*. Translated by David Barison, Daniel Ross, and Patrick Crogan. Stanford, Calif: Stanford University Press.
Stone, Alison. 2012. *Feminism, Psychoanalysis, and Maternal Subjectivity*. New York; Abingdon: Routledge.
Strenger, Carlo. 1997. 'Further Remarks on the Classic and Romantic Visions in Psychoanalysis: Klein, Winnicott, and Ethics'. *Psychoanalysis and Contemporary Thought* 20 (2): 207–44.
Stronge, Will. 2020. 'What Counts as Basic? A New Angle on the Services / Cash Transfer Debate'. *Autonomy* (blog). 2020. https://autonomy.work/portfolio/incomenotservices/.
Sweet, Victoria. 2013. *God's Hotel: A Doctor, a Hospital, and a Pilgrimage to the Heart of Medicine*. New York: Riverhead Books.
Taylor, Barbara. 2014. *The Last Asylum: A Memoir of Madness in Our Times*. London: Hamish Hamilton.
Threadcraft, Shatema. 2016. *Intimate Justice: The Black Female Body and the Body Politic*. New York: Oxford University Press.
Tronto, Joan C. 1993. *Moral Boundaries: A Political Argument for an Ethic of Care*. New York: Routledge.
———. 2003. 'Time's Place'. *Feminist Theory* 4 (2): 119–38. https://doi.org/10.1177/14647001030042002.
———. 2013. *Caring Democracy: Markets, Equality, and Justice*. New York: New York University Press.

Voela, Angie, and Louis Rothschild. 2019. 'Creative Failure: Stiegler, Psychoanalysis and the Promise of a Life Worth Living'. *New Formations* 95 (95): 54–69. https://doi.org/10.3898/NEW F:95.04.2018.

Weeks, Kathi. 2011. *The Problem with Work: Feminism, Marxism, Antiwork Politics, and Postwork Imaginaries*. Durham, NC: Duke University Press.

Williams, Fiona. 1999. 'Good-Enough Principles for Welfare'. *Journal of Social Policy* 28 (4): 667–87. https://doi.org/10.1017/S0047279499005760.

Winnicott, Donald W. 1958. 'Metapsychological and Clinical Aspects of Regression within the Psycho-Analytical Set-Up'. In *Collected Papers: Through Paediatrics to Psycho-Analysis*, 278–94. London: Tavistock.

———. 1986a. 'Delinquency as a Sign of Hope'. In *Home Is Where We Start from: Essays by a Psychoanalyst*, 90–11. Harmondsworth: Penguin.

———. 1986b. 'Freedom'. In *Home Is Where We Start From: Essays by a Psychoanalyst*, 228–38. Harmondsworth: Penguin.

———. 1987. 'Communication between Infant and Mother, and Mother and Infant, Compared and Contrasted'. In *Babies and Their Mothers*, 89–103. Reading, MA: Addison-Wesley.

———. 1988. *Human Nature*. New York: Routledge.

———. 1989. 'On the Basis for Self in Body'. In *Psycho-Analytic Explorations*, 261–83. London: Karnac.

———. 1991a. 'Creativity and Its Origins'. In *Playing and Reality*, 65–85. London: Routledge.

———. 1991b. 'Mirror-Role of Mother and Family in Child Development'. In *Playing and Reality*, 111–18. London: Routledge.

Wright, Erik Olin. 2015. 'Why Class Matters'. *Jacobin*, 23 December 2015. https://www.jacobinmag.com/2015/12/socialism-marxism-democracy-inequality-erik-olin-wright/.

References

Abou-Rihan, Fadi. 2008. *Deleuze and Guatarri: A Psychoanalytic Itinerary*. London; New York: Continuum.

Abram, Jan. 2007. *The Language of Winnicott a Dictionary of Winnicott's Use of Words*. London: Karnac.

———. 2012. 'The Evolution of Winnicott's Theoretical Matrix: A Brief Outline'. In *Donald Winnicott Today*, edited by Jan Abram, 73–112. The New Library of Psychoanalysis. London; New York: Routledge.

Agamben, Giorgio. 1998. *Homo Sacer*. Meridian. Stanford, CA: Stanford University Press.

Alexander, Meena. 1989. *Women in Romanticism: Mary Wollstonecraft, Dorothy Wordsworth, and Mary Shelley*. Women Writers. Savage, MD: Barnes and Noble.

Alexander, Sally. 2013. 'Primary Maternal Preoccupation: D. W. Winnicott and Social Democracy in Mid-Twentieth-Century Britain'. In *History and Psyche: Culture, Psychoanalysis, and the Past*, edited by Barbara Taylor and Sally Alexander, 149–72. Basingstoke; New York: Palgrave Macmillan.

———. 2016. 'D. W. Winnicott and the Social Democratic Vision'. In *Psychoanalysis in the Age of Totalitarianism*, edited by Matt Ffytche and Daniel Pick, 114–30. London; New York: Routledge.

Alford, C. Fred. 1989. *Melanie Klein and Critical Social Theory: An Account of Politics, Art, and Reason Based on Her Psychoanalytic Theory*. New Haven: Yale University Press.
———. 2000. 'Levinas and Winnicott: Motherhood and Responsibility'. *American Imago* 57 (3): 235–59. https://doi.org/10.1353/aim.2000.0015.
———. 2002. *Levinas, the Frankfurt School and Psychoanalysis*. London: Continuum.
Allen, Amy and Brian O'Connor, eds. 2019. *Transitional Subjects: Critical Theory and Object Relations*. New York; Chichester: Columbia University Press.
Althusser, Louis. 1969. *Lenin and Philosophy and Other Essays*. London: Verso.
Apollodorus, and C. Julius Hyginus. 2007. *Apollodorus' Library and Hyginus' Fabulae: Two Handbooks of Greek Mythology*. Translated by R. Scott Smith and Stephen Trzaskoma. Indianapolis, IN: Hackett Publishing.
Aristotle. 2000. *Nicomachean Ethics*. Edited and translated by Roger Crisp. Cambridge; New York: Cambridge University Press.
Balint, Michael. 2005. *The Doctor, His Patient and the Illness*. Edinburgh: Churchill Livingstone.
Baraitser, Lisa. 2009. *Maternal Encounters: The Ethics of Interruption*. Hove, East Sussex; New York: Routledge.
———. 2016. 'Postmaternal, Postwork and the Maternal Death Drive'. *Australian Feminist Studies* 31 (90): 393–409. https://doi.org/10.1080/08164649.2016.1278156.
Bar-Haim, Shaul. 2021. *The Maternalists: Psychoanalysis, Motherhood, and the British Welfare State*. Philadelphia: University of Pennsylvania Press.
Barnes, Marian. 2012. *Care in Everyday Life: An Ethic of Care in Practice*. Bristol: Policy.
Barrett, Michèle. 2014. *Women's Oppression Today: The Marxist/Feminist Encounter*. London; New York: Verso.
Barrett, Michèle, and Mary McIntosh. 2015. *The Anti-Social Family*. Brooklyn, NY: Verso.
Beauvoir, Simone de. 2011. *The Second Sex*. Translated by Constance Borde and Sheila Malovany-Chevallier. New York: Vintage Books.
Benjamin, Jessica. 1977. 'The End of Internalization: Adorno's Social Psychology'. *Telos* 32: 42–64. https://doi.org/10.3817/0677032042.
———. 1978. 'Authority and the Family Revisited: Or, a World without Fathers?' *New German Critique*, no. 13: 35–57.
———. 1990. *The Bonds of Love: Psychoanalysis, Feminism and the Problem of Domination*. London: Virago.

———. 1994. 'The Omnipotent Mother: A Psychoanalytic Study of Fantasy and Reality'. In *Representations of Motherhood*, 129–46.
———. 1995. *Like Subjects, Love Objects: Essays on Recognition and Sexual Difference*. New Haven; London: Yale University Press.
———. 1998. *Shadow of the Other: Intersubjectivity and Gender in Psychoanalysis*. New York: Routledge.
Beveridge, William. 1942. 'Social Insurance and Allied Services'. https://archive.org/stream/in.ernet.dli.2015.275849/2015.275849.The-Beveridge_djvu.txt.
Bhambra, Gurminder K., and John Holmwood. 2018. 'Colonialism, Postcolonialism and the Liberal Welfare State'. *New Political Economy* 23 (5): 574–87. https://doi.org/10.1080/13563467.2017.1417369.
Bhattacharya, Tithi, ed. 2017. *Social Reproduction Theory: Remapping Class, Recentering Oppression*. London: Pluto Press.
Bidadanure, Juliana Uhuru. 2019. 'The Political Theory of Universal Basic Income'. *Annual Review of Political Science* 22: 481–501.
Bion, Wilfred. 1988. 'A Theory of Thinking'. In *Melanie Klein Today: Developments in Theory and Practice*, edited by Elizabeth Bott Spillius, 1: 174–82. London: Routledge.
Bollas, Christopher. 1987. *The Shadow of the Object: Psychoanalysis of the Unthought Known*. New York: Columbia University Press.
Boltanski, Luc, and Eve Chiapello. 2007. *The New Spirit of Capitalism*. Translated by Gregory Elliott. London; New York: Verso.
Booth, Robert, and Maya Wolfe-Robinson. 2021. 'Homecare Services Crisis in England at Worst Point yet, Say Operators'. *The Guardian*, 12 December 2021, sec. Society. https://www.theguardian.com/society/2021/dec/12/homecare-services-crisis-uk-at-worst-point-yet-say-operators.
Bowker, Matthew H., and Amy Buzby, eds. 2017a. *D.W. Winnicott and Political Theory: Recentering the Subject*. 1st ed. New York: Palgrave Macmillan.
———. 2017b. 'Introduction'. In *D.W. Winnicott and Political Theory: Recentering the Subject*, edited by Matthew H. Bowker and Amy Buzby. 1st ed., 1–34. New York: Palgrave Macmillan.
Brennan, Teresa. 1993. *History after Lacan*. London; New York: Routledge.
Brenner, Johanna. 2014. '21st Century Socialist-Feminism'. *Socialist Studies/Études Socialistes* 10 (1). http://www.socialiststudies.com/sss/index.php/sss/article/viewArticle/355.
Britton Winnicott, Clare. 2012. 'Introduction'. In *Deprivation and Delinquency*, by Donald W. Winnicott, edited by Clare Winnicott, Ray Shepherd, and Madeleine Davis. London; New York: Routledge.

Bryant, Miranda. 2020. 'Maternity Leave: US Policy Is Worst on List of the World's Richest Countries'. *The Guardian*, 27 January 2020. https://www.theguardian.com/us-news/2020/jan/27/maternity-leave-us-policy-worst-worlds-richest-countries.

Burston, Daniel. 1996. 'Conflict and Sociability in Hegel, Freud, and Their Followers: Tzvetan Todorov's "Living Alone Together"'. *New Literary History* 27 (1): 73–82.

Butler, Judith. 2004. *Precarious Life: The Powers of Mourning and Violence*. London; New York: Verso.

———. 2009. *Frames of War: When Is Life Grievable?* London; New York: Verso.

———. 2020. *The Force of Nonviolence: An Ethico-Political Bind*. London; New York: Verso.

Buzby, Amy. 2017. 'Vanquishing the False Self: Winnicott, Critical Theory, and the Restoration of the Spontaneous Gesture'. In *D.W. Winnicott and Political Theory: Recentering the Subject*, edited by Matthew H. Bowker and Amy Buzby, 229–46. New York: Palgrave Macmillan.

Caldwell, Lesley. 2013. 'Foreword'. In *Little Madnesses: Winnicott, Transitional Phenomena and Cultural Experience*, edited by Annette Kuhn, xv–xx. London; New York: I.B. Tauris.

Calhoon, Kenneth Scott. 1992. *Fatherland: Novalis, Freud, and the Discipline of Romance*. Detroit: Wayne State University Press.

Campbell, Kirsten. 2004. *Jacques Lacan and Feminist Epistemology*. London; New York: Routledge.

Cavarero, Adriana. 2011. *Horrorism: Naming Contemporary Violence*. New York: Columbia University Press.

———. 2016. *Inclinations: A Critique of Rectitude*. Translated by Amanda Minervini and Adam Sitze. Stanford, CA: Stanford University Press.

Chandler, David, and Julian Reid. 2016. *The Neoliberal Subject: Resilience, Adaptation and Vulnerability*. London; New York: Rowman & Littlefield International.

Chang, Clio. 2020. 'Once Social Isolation Is Over, We Can't Return to a World That Doesn't Value Care'. Vice. 2020. https://www.vice.com/en/article/jge39g/taking-care-of-each-other-is-essential-work.

Chodorow, Nancy. 1978. *The Reproduction of Mothering: Psychoanalysis and the Sociology of Gender*. Berkeley, CA: University of California Press.

———. 1989. *Feminism and Psychoanalytic Theory*. New Haven; London: Yale University Press.

Chodorow, Nancy, and Susan Contratto. 1989. 'The Fantasy of the Perfect Mother'. In *Feminism and Psychoanalytic Theory*, by Nancy Chodorow, 79–96. New Haven; London: Yale University Press.

Clarke, Simon, Herbert Hahn, and Paul Hoggett, eds. 2008. *Object Relations and Social Relations: The Implications of the Relational Turn in Psychoanalysis*. London: Karnac.

Cooper, Andrew, and Julian Lousada. 2011. *Borderline Welfare: Feeling and Fear of Feeling in Modern Welfare*. London: Karnac.

Dalla Costa, Mariarosa, and Selma James. 1975. *The Power of Women and the Subversion of the Community*. Bristol: Falling Wall Press.

Darwall, Stephen L. 2002. *Welfare and Rational Care*. Princeton, NJ: Princeton University Press.

Davin, Anna. 1978. 'Imperialism and Motherhood'. *History Workshop Journal* 5: 9–65.

Day, Chris. 2017. 'The National Archives - The Beveridge Report and the Foundations of the Welfare State'. The National Archives Blog. The National Archives. 7 December 2017. https://blog.nationalarchives.gov.uk/beveridge-report-foundations-welfare-state/.

De Angelis, Massimo. 2017. *Omnia Sunt Communia: On the Commons and the Transformation to Postcapitalism*. London: Zed Books.

De Boever, Arne. 2013. *Narrative Care: Biopolitics and the Novel*. London; New York: Bloomsbury Academic.

Descartes, René. 2006. *A Discourse on the Method of Correctly Conducting One's Reason and Seeking Truth in the Sciences*. Translated by Ian Maclean. Oxford; New York: Oxford University Press.

Dever, Carolyn. 1998. *Death and the Mother from Dickens to Freud: Victorian Fiction and the Anxiety of Origins*. Cambridge; New York: Cambridge University Press.

Dews, Peter. 1995. 'The Crisis of Oedipal Identity: The Early Lacan and the Frankfurt School'. In *Psychoanalysis in Contexts: Paths between Theory and Modern Culture*, edited by Anthony Elliott and Stephen Frosh, 53–71. London; New York: Routledge.

Dinnerstein, Dorothy. 1999. *The Mermaid and the Minotaur: Sexual Arrangements and Human Malaise*. New York: Other Press.

DiQuinzio, Patrice. 1993. 'Exclusion and Essentialism in Feminist Theory: The Problem of Mothering'. *Hypatia* 8 (3): 1–20.

Doane, Janice, and Devon Hodges. 1993. *From Klein to Kristeva: Psychoanalytic Feminism and the Search for the 'Good Enough' Mother*. Ann Arbor: University of Michigan Press.

Dolar, Mladen. 1998. 'Cogito as the Subject of the Unconscious'. In *Cogito and the Unconscious*, edited by Slavoj Žižek, 11–40. Durham, NC: Duke University Press.

Dowling, Emma. 2021. *The Care Crisis: What Caused It and How Can We End It?* London; New York: Verso.

Eagleton, Terry. 1990. *The Ideology of the Aesthetic*. Oxford; Cambridge, MA: Blackwell.

Ehrenreich, Barbara, and Arlie Russell Hochschild, eds. 2003. *Global Woman: Nannies, Maids, and Sex Workers in the New Economy*. London: Granta Books.

Eigen, Michael. 2005. *Psychic Deadness*. Repr. London: Karnac.

Elliott, Anthony. 2015. *Psychoanalytic Theory: An Introduction*. London; New York: Palgrave Macmillan.

Elliott, Larry. 2021. 'During the Pandemic, a New Variant of Capitalism Has Emerged'. *The Guardian*, 30 July 2021. https://www.theguardian.com/commentisfree/2021/jul/30/pandemic-new-variant-of-capitalism-spending-covid-state.

Engels, Friedrich. 2010. *The Origin of the Family, Private Property, and the State*. London; New York: Penguin Classics.

Erikson, Erik Homburger, and Joan Mowat Erikson. 1998. *The Life Cycle Completed*. Extended version. New York: W.W. Norton.

Fairbairn, W. Ronald D. 1994. *Psychoanalytic Studies of the Personality*. London; New York: Routledge.

Farley, Lisa. 2012. 'Analysis On Air: A Sound History of Winnicott in Wartime'. *American Imago* 69 (4): 449–71.

Federici, Silvia. 2014. *Caliban and the Witch: Women, the Body and Primitive Accumulation*. New York: Autonomedia.

———. 2019. *Re-Enchanting the World: Feminism and the Politics of the Commons*. Oakland, CA: PM Press.

Ferguson, S. Alease, and Toni C. King. 2014. 'Dark Animus: A Psychodynamic Interpretation of the Consequences of Diverted Mothering Among African-American Daughters'. In *Mothering and Psychoanalysis: Clinical, Sociological and Feminist Perspectives*, edited by Petra Bueskens, 177–96. Canada: Demeter Press.

Ferguson, Susan. 2017. 'Children, Childhood and Capitalism: A Social Reproduction Perspective'. In *Social Reproduction Theory: Remapping Class, Recentering Oppression*, edited by Tithi Bhattacharya, 112–30. London: Pluto Press.

Flax, Jane. 1985. 'Mother-Daughter Relationships: Psychodynamics, Politics, and Philosophy'. In *The Future of Difference*, edited by Hester Eisenstein and Alice Jardine, 20–40. New Brunswick, NJ: Rutgers University Press.

———. 1991. *Thinking Fragments: Psychoanalysis, Feminism, and Postmodernism in the Contemporary West*. Berkeley, CA: University of California Press.

Flynn, Thomas. 1980. 'Angst and Care in the Early Heidegger: The Ontic/Ontologic Aporia'. *International Studies in Philosophy* 12 (1): 61–76.

Folbre, Nancy. 1994. *Who Pays for the Kids? Gender and the Structures of Constraint*. London; New York: Routledge.

Fraser, Derek. 2017. *The Evolution of the British Welfare State: A History of Social Policy since the Industrial Revolution*, 1st ed. London: Palgrave Macmillan Education.

Fraser, Nancy. 2013. *Fortunes of Feminism: From Women's Liberation to Identity Politics to Anti-Capitalism*. Brooklyn, NY: Verso Books.

———. 2016. 'Contradictions of Capital and Care'. *New Left Review* 100 (August): 99–117.

Fraser, Nancy, and Linda Gordon. 2013. 'A Geneaology of "Dependency": Tracing a Keyword of the US Welfare State'. In *Fortunes of Feminism: From Women's Liberation to Identity Politics to Anti-Capitalism*, 1st ed., 83–110. Brooklyn, NY: Verso Books.

Freud, Sigmund. 1895. 'The Psychotherapy of Hysteria'. In *SE 2*, 253–305.

———. 1907. 'Delusions and Dreams in Jensen's "Gradiva"'. In *SE 9*, 7–95.

———. 1910. '"Wild" Psycho-Analysis'. In *SE 11*, 219–27.

———. 1923a. 'The Ego and the Id'. In *SE 19*, 3–66.

———. 1923b. 'Two Encyclopaedia Articles'. In *SE 18*, 235.

———. 1927. 'The Future of an Illusion'. In *SE 21*, 1–56.

———. 1930. 'Civilization and Its Discontents'. In *SE 21*, 59–145.

———. 1931. 'Female Sexuality'. In *SE 21*, 223–43.

Friedan, Betty. 2010. *The Feminine Mystique*. London: Penguin.

Frosh, Stephen. 1999. *The Politics of Psychoanalysis: An Introduction to Freudian and Post-Freudian Theory*. Basingstoke: Macmillan.

Gentleman, Amelia. 2011. 'Benefits Assessment Firm Causing "Fear and Loathing" among Claimants, Says MP'. *The Guardian*, 24 July 2011, sec. Politics. https://www.theguardian.com/politics/2011/jul/24/atos-faces-critical-report-by-mps.

George, Margaret. 1973. 'From "Goodwife" to "Mistress": The Transformation of the Female in Bourgeois Culture'. *Science & Society* 37 (2): 152–77.

Gerson, Gal. 2004a. 'Object Relations Psychoanalysis as Political Theory'. *Political Psychology* 25 (5): 769–94. https://doi.org/10.1111/j.1467-9221.2004.00397.
———. 2004b. 'Winnicott, Participation and Gender'. *Feminism & Psychology* 14 (4): 561–81. https://doi.org/10.1177%2F0959353504046872.
———. 2005a. 'Liberalism, Sociability, and Object Relations Theory'. *The European Legacy* 10 (5): 421–37. https://doi.org/10.1080/10848770500173623.
———. 2005b. 'Individuality, Deliberation and Welfare in Donald Winnicott'. *History of the Human Sciences* 18 (1): 107–26.
———. 2017. 'Winnicott and the History of Welfare State Thought in Britain'. In *D.W. Winnicott and Political Theory: Recentering the Subject*, edited by Matthew H. Bowker and Amy Buzby, 311–32. New York: Palgrave Macmillan.
Giddens, Anthony. 1990. *The Consequences of Modernity*. Stanford: Stanford University Press.
———. 1991. *Modernity and Self-Identity: Self and Society in the Late Modern Age*. Stanford: Stanford University Press.
———. 1999. *The Third Way: The Renewal of Social Democracy*. Malden, MA: Polity Press.
Gilligan, Carol. 1990. *In a Different Voice: Psychological Theory and Women's Development*. Cambridge, MA: Harvard University Press.
Gilson, Erinn C. 2014. *The Ethics of Vulnerability: A Feminist Analysis of Social Life and Practice*. New York: Routledge.
Goethe, Johann Wolfgang von. 2009. *Faust: The Second Part of the Tragedy*. Edited and translated by David Constantine. London: Penguin.
Goodman, Cleo, James Muldoon, Guy Standing, David Frayne, and Jack Kellam. 2021. 'Piloting a Basic Income in Wales: A Briefing'. *Autonomy* (blog). https://autonomy.work/portfolio/ubi-in-wales/.
Goux, Jean-Joseph. 1993. *Oedipus, Philosopher*. Stanford, CA: Stanford University Press.
Green, André. 2005. *On Private Madness*. London: Hogarth.
Green, Maia, and Victoria Lawson. 2011. 'Recentring Care: Interrogating the Commodification of Care'. *Social & Cultural Geography* 12 (6): 639–54. https://doi.org/10.1080/14649365.2011.601262.
Greenberg, Jay, and Stephen A. Mitchell. 1983. *Object Relations in Psychoanalytic Theory*. Cambridge, MA: Harvard University Press.
Groarke, Steven. 2014. *Managed Lives*. Hove; New York: Routledge.

Guntrip, Henry James Samuel. 1973. *Psychoanalytic Theory, Therapy, and the Self*. New York: Basic Books.
Hall, Stuart. 1988. *The Hard Road to Renewal: Thatcherism and the Crisis of the Left*. London; New York: Verso.
———. 1990. *The Politics of Thatcherism*. London: Lawrence and Wishart.
———. 2003. 'New Labour Has Picked up Where Thatcherism Left Off'. *The Guardian*, 6 August 2003. https://www.theguardian.com/politics/2003/aug/06/society.labour.
———. 2011. 'The Neo-Liberal Revolution'. *Cultural Studies* 25 (6): 705–28. https://doi.org/10.1080/09502386.2011.619886.
Harcourt, Edward. 2015. 'The Place of Psychoanalysis in the History of Ethics'. *Journal of Moral Philosophy* 12 (5): 598–618. https://doi.org/10.1163/17455243-4681030.
Harvey, David. 2005. *A Brief History of Neoliberalism*. Oxford; New York: Oxford University Press.
Held, David. 2004. *Introduction to Critical Theory: Horkheimer to Habermas*. Cambridge: Polity Press.
Held, Virginia. 2006. *The Ethics of Care: Personal, Political, and Global*. Oxford: Oxford University Press.
Hobart, Hiʻilei Julia Kawehipuaakahaopulani, and Tamara Kneese. 2020. 'Radical Care: Survival Strategies for Uncertain Times'. *Social Text* 38 (1 (142)): 1–16. https://doi.org/10.1215/01642472-7971067.
Hobsbawm, Eric J. 1995. *The Age of Extremes: The Short Twentieth Century, 1914-1991*. London: Abacus.
Hochschild, Arlie Russell. 2001. *The Time Bind: When Work Becomes Home and Home Becomes Work*. New York: Owl Books Holt.
———. 2003. *The Commercialization of Intimate Life: Notes from Home and Work*. Berkeley, CA: University of California Press.
———. 2013. *So How's the Family? And Other Essays*. Berkeley: University of California Press.
Hochschild, Arlie Russell, S. Uma Devi, and Lise Isaksen. 2013. 'Children Left Behind'. In *So How's the Family? And Other Essays*, by Arlie Russell Hochschild, 147–64. Berkeley, CA: University of California Press.
Hoggett, Paul. 1992. *Partisans in an Uncertain World: The Psychoanalysis of Engagement*. London: Free Association Books.
———. 2000. *Emotional Life and the Politics of Welfare*. Houndmills, Basingstoke, Hampshire; New York: Macmillan Press; St. Martin's Press.
Hollander, Nancy Caro, and Susan Gutwill. 2006. 'Despair and Hope in a Culture of Denial'. In *Psychoanalysis, Class and Politics: Encounters in the*

Clinical Setting, edited by Lynne Layton, Nancy Caro Hollander, and Susan Gutwill, 81–91. London: Routledge.

Hollway, Wendy. 2006a. 'Family Figures in 20th-Century British "Psy" Discourses'. *Theory & Psychology* 16 (4): 443–64. https://doi.org/10.1177/0959354306066200.

———. 2006b. 'Paradox in the Pursuit of a Critical Theorization of the Development of Self in Family Relationships'. *Theory & Psychology* 16 (4): 465–82. https://doi.org/10.1177/0959354306066201.

———. 2006c. *The Capacity to Care: Gender and Ethical Subjectivity*. London; New York: Routledge.

Honderich, Ted, ed. 2005. *The Oxford Companion to Philosophy*. Oxford; New York: Oxford University Press.

Honig, Bonnie. 2012. 'The Politics of Public Things: Neoliberalism and the Routine of Privatization'. *No Foundations 10*, 59–76.

———. 2017. *Public Things: Democracy in Disrepair*. New York: Fordham University Press.

Honneth, Axel. 1996. *The Struggle for Recognition: The Moral Grammar of Social Conflicts*. Translated by Joel Anderson. Cambridge, MA: MIT Press.

———. 1999. 'Postmodern Identity and Object-Relations Theory: On the Seeming Obsolescence of Psychoanalysis'. *Philosophical Explorations* 2 (3): 225–42. https://doi.org/10.1080/10001999098538708.

———. 2007. *Disrespect: The Normative Foundations of Critical Theory*. Cambridge: Polity Press.

hooks, bell. 1995. 'Black Women Shaping Feminist Theory'. In *Words of Fire: An Anthology of African-American Feminist Thought*, edited by Beverly Guy-Sheftall, 170–82. New York: New Press.

Horkheimer, Max. 1949. 'Authoritarianism and the Family Today'. In *The Family: Its Function and Destiny*, edited by Ruth Nanda Ashen, 359–74. New York: Harper & Brothers.

———. 2002. 'Authority and the Family'. In *Critical Theory: Selected Essays*, translated by Matthew J. O'Connell, 47–128. New York: Continuum.

Irigaray, Luce. 1985. *Speculum of the Other Woman*. Translated by Gillian C. Gill. Ithaca, NY: Cornell University Press.

———. 1991. 'The Bodily Encounter with the Mother'. In *The Irigaray Reader*, edited by Margaret Whitford, translated by David Macey, 34–46. Cambridge, MA: Basil Blackwell.

Jacobs, Amber. 2007. *On Matricide: Myth, Psychoanalysis, and the Law of the Mother*. New York: Columbia University Press.

Jones, Owen. 2012. *Chavs: The Demonization of the Working Class*. London; New York: Verso.

Kanter, Joel. 2000. 'The Untold Story of Clare and Donald Winnicott: How Social Work Influenced Modern Psychoanalysis'. *Clinical Social Work Journal* 28 (3): 245–61.

Kaplan, E. Ann. 1992. *Motherhood and Representation: The Mother in Popular Culture and Melodrama*. London; New York: Routledge.

Keller, Evelyn Fox. 1995. *Reflections on Gender and Science*. New Haven, MA: Yale University Press.

Kierkegaard, Søren. 2001. *Johannes Climacus: Or: A Life of Doubt*. Translated by T. H. Croxall. London: Serpent's Tail.

King, Pearl, and Riccardo Steiner. 1991. *The Freud-Klein Controversies 1941-1945*. London: Tavistock/Routledge.

Kittay, Eva Feder. 1999. *Love's Labor: Essays on Women, Equality, and Dependency*. Thinking Gender. New York: Routledge.

Klein, Melanie. 1975. 'A Contribution to the Psychogenesis of Manic Depressive States'. In *Love, Guilt and Reparation*, 262–89. London: Virago.

Koven, Seth, and Sonya Michel. 1993. 'Introduction: "Mother Worlds"'. In *Mothers of a New World: Maternalist Politics and the Origins of Welfare States*, edited by Seth Koven and Sonya Michel, 1–42. New York: Routledge.

Lacan, Jacques. 1988. *The Seminar of Jacques Lacan. Book II, The Ego in Freud's Theory and in the Technique of Psychoanalysis 1954–1955*. Translated by Sylvana Tomaselli. New York: Norton.

———. 1995. 'The Oedipus Complex'. In *Polysexuality*, edited by François Peraldi, translated by Andrea Kahn, 190–200. New York: Semiotext(e).

———. 2001. 'Les Complexes Familiaux Dans La Formation de l'individu'. In *Autres Écrits*, edited by Jacques-Alain Miller, 23–84. Paris: Editions du Seuil.

———. 2006. 'Aggressiveness in Psychoanalysis'. In *Écrits: The First Complete Edition in English*, translated by Héloïse Fink and Bruce Fink, 82–101. New York: W.W. Norton & Co.

———. 2008. *The Seminar of Jacques Lacan: Book XVII: The Other Side of Psychoanalysis, 1969–70*. Edited by Jacques-Alain Miller. Translated by Russell Grigg. New York; London: Norton.

Lanchester, John. 2019. 'Good New Idea'. *London Review of Books*, 18 July 2019. https://www.lrb.co.uk/the-paper/v41/n14/john-lanchester/good-new-idea.

Laplanche, Jean. 1989. *New Foundations for Psychoanalysis*. Translated by David Macey. Oxford; New York: Basil Blackwell.

Laplanche, Jean, and J. B. Pontalis. 1988. *The Language of Psychoanalysis*. Translated by Donald Nicholson-Smith. London: Karnac.

Layton, Lynne. 2008a. 'Relational Thinking: From Culture to Couch and Couch to Culture'. In *Object Relations and Social Relations: The Implications of the Relational Turn in Psychoanalysis*, edited by Simon Clarke, Herb Hahn, and Paul Hoggett, 1–24. London: Karnac.

———. 2008b. 'What Divides the Subject? Psychoanalytic Reflections on Subjectivity, Subjection and Resistance'. *Subjectivity* 22: 60–72. https://doi.org/10.1057/sub.2008.3.

———. 2009. 'Who's Responsible? Our Mutual Implication in Each Other's Suffering'. *Psychoanalytic Dialogues* 19 (2): 105–20. https://doi.org/10.1080/10481880902779695.

———. 2013. 'Psychoanalysis and Politics: Historicising Subjectivity'. *Mens Sana Monographs* 11 (1): 68–81. https://doi.org/10.4103/0973-1229.104493.

———. 2014. 'Maternally Speaking: Mother's Daughters and the Talking Cure'. In *Mothering and Psychoanalysis: Clinical, Sociological and Feminist Perspectives*, edited by Petra Bueskens, 161–76. Canada: Demeter Press.

———. 2020. *Toward a Social Psychoanalysis: Culture, Character, and Normative Unconscious Processes*. Edited by Marianna Leavy-Sperounis. Abingdon, Oxon; New York, NY: Routledge.

Lazzarato, Maurizio. 2008. *Le gouvernement des inégalités: critique de l'insécurité néolibérale*. Démocritique. Paris: Éditions Amsterdam.

Lear, Jonathan. 1991. *Love and Its Place in Nature*. New York: Noonday Press.

———. 1998. *Open Minded: Working out the Logic of the Soul*. Cambridge, MA; London: Harvard University Press.

———. 2001. *Happiness, Death, and the Remainder of Life*. Cambridge, MA: Harvard University Press.

Lebeau, Vicky. 2019. 'Feeling Poor: D.W. Winnicott and Daniel Blake'. *New Formations* 96 (96): 160–76. https://doi.org/10.3898/NEWF:96/97.07.2019.

Linebaugh, Peter. 2014. *Stop, Thief! The Commons, Enclosures and Resistance*. Oakland, CA: PM.

Linebaugh, Peter, and Marcus Rediker. 2012. *The Many-Headed Hydra: Sailors, Slaves, Commoners, and the Hidden History of the Revolutionary Atlantic*. London: Verso.

Lomas, Peter. 1999. *Doing Good?: Psychotherapy Out of Its Depth*. Cambridge; New York: Oxford University Press.

Lorey, Isabell. 2015. *State of Insecurity: Government of the Precarious*. by Aileen Derieg. London; New York: Verso.
Lynch, Kathleen, and Maureen Lyons. 2009. 'Love Labouring: Nurturing Rationalities and Relational Identities'. In *Affective Equality: Love, Care, and Injustice*, edited by Kathleen Lynch, John Baker, and Maureen Lyons, 54–77. Houndmills, Basingstoke; New York: Palgrave Macmillan.
Lynch, Kathleen, Maureen Lyons, and John Baker. 2009. 'Introduction'. In *Affective Equality: Love, Care, and Injustice*, edited by Kathleen Lynch, John Baker, and Maureen Lyons, 1–11. Houndmills, Basingstoke; New York: Palgrave Macmillan.
MacCannell, Juliet Flower. 1991. *The Regime of the Brother: After the Patriarchy*. London; New York: Routledge.
MacIntyre, Alasdair C. 2006. *Dependent Rational Animals: Why Human Beings Need the Virtues*. Chicago: Open Court.
———. 2011. *After Virtue: A Study in Moral Theory*. London: Bloomsbury.
Mackenzie, Catriona, and Natalie Stoljar. 2000. 'Introduction: Autonomy Refigured'. In *Relational Autonomy: Feminist Perspectives on Autonomy, Agency, and the Social Self*, edited by Catriona Mackenzie and Natalie Stoljar, 3–31. New York: Oxford University Press.
Marcuse, Herbert. 2009. 'Philosophy and Critical Theory'. In *Negations: Essays in Critical Theory*, translated by Jeremy J. Shapiro, 99–118. http://mayfly books.org/wp-content/uploads/2010/07/9781906948054Negations.pdf.
Martel, James. 2019. '"True-Enough Self": Winnicott, Object Relations Theory and the Bases of Identity'. In *Transitional Subjects: Critical Theory and Object Relations*, edited by Amy Allen and Brian O'Connor, 159–83. New York; Chichester: Columbia University Press.
May, Rollo. 2007. *Love and Will*. New York: W.W. Norton.
Maynes, Mary Jo, and Ann Beth Waltner. 2012. *The Family: A World History*. Oxford; New York: Oxford University Press.
McNay, Lois. 2008a. *Against Recognition*. Cambridge: Polity.
———. 2008b. 'The Trouble with Recognition: Subjectivity, Suffering, and Agency'. *Sociological Theory* 26 (3): 271–96.
McNeill, John Thomas. 1977. *A History of the Cure of Souls*. New York: Harper and Row.
Meehan, Johanna. 1995. 'Autonomy, Recognition, and Respect: Habermas, Benjamin, and Honneth'. In *Feminists Read Habermas: Gendering the Subject of Discourse*, edited by Johanna Meehan, 231–46. New York: Routledge.
———. 2019. 'Intersubjectivity on the Couch: Destruction and Recognition in the Work of Jessica Benjamin'. In *Transitional Subjects: Critical Theory*

and Object Relations, edited by Amy Allen and Brian O'Connor, 185–208. New York; Chichester: Columbia University Press.

Mellor, Anne K. 1993. *Romanticism and Gender*. New York: Routledge.

Mies, Maria. 2014. *Patriarchy and Accumulation on a World Scale: Women in the International Division of Labour*. London: Zed Books.

Mignolo, Walter. 2011. *The Darker Side of Western Modernity: Global Futures, Decolonial Options*. Durham, NC: Duke University Press.

Mitchell, Juliet. 1974. *Psychoanalysis and Feminism: A Radical Reassessment of Freudian Psychoanalysis*. London: Allen Lane.

———. 1978. 'Erosion of the Family'. *New Society*, 2 July 1978.

———. 2009. 'Using Winnicott'. In *Emotion: New Psychosocial Perspectives*, edited by Shelley Day-Sclater, David W. Jones, Heather Price, and Candida Yates, 46–56. New York; Basingstoke: Palgrave Macmillan.

———. 2015. *Woman's Estate*. London: Verso.

Morris, Steven. 2021. 'Wales to Launch Pilot Universal Basic Income Scheme'. *The Guardian*, 14 May 2021. https://www.theguardian.com/society/2021/may/14/wales-to-launch-universal-basic-income-pilot-scheme.

Nelson, Maggie. 2016. *The Argonauts*. Minneapolis, MN: Graywolf Press.

Nicholson, Linda J. 1986. *Gender and History: The Limits of Social Theory in the Age of the Family*. New York: Columbia University Press.

Norman, Richard. 1992. 'Equality, Needs, and Basic Income'. In *Arguing for Basic Income: Ethical Foundations for a Radical Reform*, edited by Philippe van Parijs, 141–52. London; New York: Verso.

Nussbaum, Martha C. 1994. *The Therapy of Desire: Theory and Practice in Hellenistic Ethics*. Princeton, NJ: Princeton University Press.

———. 1995a. *Poetic Justice: The Literary Imagination and Public Life*. Boston, MA: Beacon Press.

———. 1995b. *Women, Culture, and Development: A Study of Human Capabilities*. Edited by Jonathan Glover. Oxford; New York: Oxford University Press.

———. 2001. *Upheavals of Thought: The Intelligence of Emotions*. Cambridge; New York: Cambridge University Press.

———. 2004. *Hiding from Humanity: Disgust, Shame, and the Law*. Princeton, NJ: Princeton University Press.

Ogden, Thomas. 1989. *The Primitive Edge of Experience*. London; Northvale, NJ: J. Aronson.

———. 1992. 'The Dialectically Constituted/Decentred Subject of Psychoanalysis: II. The Contributions of Klein and Winnicott.' *The International Journal of Psychoanalysis* 73 (4): 613–26.

———. 2004. 'On Holding and Containing, Being and Dreaming'. *International Journal of Psycho-Analysis* 85: 1349–64. https://doi.org/10.1516/T41H-DGUX-9JY4-GQC7.

Okin, Susan Moller. 1989. *Justice, Gender, and the Family*. New York: Basic Books.

Orlie, Melissa A. 2017. 'The Psychoanalytic Winnicott We Need Now: On the Way to a Real Ecological Thought'. In *D.W. Winnicott and Political Theory: Recentering the Subject*, edited by Matthew H. Bowker and Amy Buzby, First edition, 87–109. New York, NY: Palgrave Macmillan.

Parijs, Philippe van, ed. 1992. *Arguing for Basic Income: Ethical Foundations for a Radical Reform*. London; New York: Verso.

Parker, Rozsika. 2005. *Torn in Two: The Experience of Maternal Ambivalence*. London: Virago.

Pateman, Carole. 1988. *The Sexual Contract*. Stanford, CA: Stanford University Press.

Patterson, Orlando. 2018. 'Authority, Alienation, and Social Death'. In *Critical Readings on Global Slavery*, edited by Damian Alan Pargas and Felicia Roşu, 90–146. Leiden; Boston: Brill.

Peltz, Rachael. 2005. 'The Manic Society'. *Psychoanalytic Dialogues* 15 (3): 347–66. https://doi.org/10.1080/10481881509348834.

Petherbridge, Danielle. 2013. *The Critical Theory of Axel Honneth*. Lanham: Lexington Books.

Philipson, Irene. 1994. *On the Shoulders of Women: The Feminization of Psychotherapy*. New York: Guilford Press.

Phillips, Adam. 1994. *On Kissing, Tickling, and Being Bored: Psychoanalytic Essays on the Unexamined Life*. Harvard University Press.

———. 2007. *Winnicott*. London: Penguin.

Phillips, Judith. 2007. *Care*. Cambridge; Malden, MA: Polity.

Pitcher, Ben. 2016. 'Race, Debt and the Welfare State'. *New Formations* 87 (87): 47–63. https://doi.org/10.3898/NEWF.87.3.2016.

Poster, Mark. 1982. *Critical Theory of the Family*. London: Pluto Press.

Rayner, Eric. 1991. *The Independent Mind in British Psychoanalysis*. New Jersey, NY: J. Aronson.

Reay, Diane. 2015. 'Habitus and the Psychosocial: Bourdieu with Feelings'. *Cambridge Journal of Education* 45 (1): 9–23. https://doi.org/10.1080/0305764X.2014.990420.

Reich, Warren Thomas. 2004. 'Care'. In *Encyclopedia of Bioethics*, edited by Stephen Garrard Post, 348–59. New York: Macmillan Reference USA.

Richards, Barry. 1984. 'Introduction'. In *Capitalism and Infancy: Essays on Psychoanalysis and Politics*, edited by Barry Richards, 7–21. London; Atlantic Highlands, NJ: Free Association Books; Humanities Press.

Richardson, Alan. 1988. 'Romanticism and the Colonization of the Feminine'. In *Romanticism and Feminism*, edited by Anne K. Mellor, 13–25. Bloomington: Indiana University Press.

Rieff, Philip. 1966. *The Triumph of the Therapeutic: Uses of Faith After Freud*. London: Chatto and Windus.

Riley, Denise. 1983. *War in the Nursery: Theories of the Child and Mother*. London: Virago.

Rodman, F. Robert. 2003. *Winnicott: Life and Work*. Cambridge, MA: Perseus.

Rorty, Richard. 1980. *Philosophy and the Mirror of Nature*. Princeton, NJ: Princeton University Press.

Rose, Jacqueline. 2004. *On Not Being Able to Sleep Psychoanalysis and the Modern World*. London: Vintage. http://www.vlebooks.com/vleweb/product/openreader?id=none&isbn=9781446418413.

Rose, Nikolas S. 2005. *Governing the Soul: The Shaping of the Private Self*. London: Free Association Books.

Roudinesco, Elisabeth. 2003. *Why Psychoanalysis?* Translated by Rachel Bowlby. New York; Chichester: Columbia University Press.

Rousseau, Jean-Jacques. 1979. *Emile: Or, On Education*. Edited and translated by Allan Bloom. New York: Basic Books.

———. 1984. *A Discourse on Inequality*. Translated by Maurice Cranston. London: Penguin.

Rowbotham, Sheila. 2010. *Dreamers of a New Day: Women Who Invented the Twentieth Century*. London; New York: Verso.

Rubin, Gayle. 1975. 'The Traffic in Women: Notes on the "Political Economy" of Sex'. In *Toward an Anthropology of Women*, edited by Rayna R. Reiter, 157–210. London; New York: Monthly Review Press.

Ruddick, Sara. 1995. *Maternal Thinking: Toward a Politics of Peace*. Boston, MA: Beacon Press.

Rudnytsky, Peter L. 1991. *The Psychoanalytic Vocation: Rank, Winnicott, and the Legacy of Freud*. New Haven, CT: Yale University Press.

Rustin, Margaret, and Michael Rustin. 1984. 'Relational Preconditions of Socialism'. In *Capitalism and Infancy: Essays on Psychoanalysis and Politics*, edited by Barry Richards, 207–25. London: Free Associations Books.

Rustin, Michael. 1991. *The Good Society and the Inner World: Psychoanalysis, Politics, and Culture*. London; New York: Verso.

———. 2001. *Reason and Unreason: Psychoanalysis, Science, and Politics*. London; New York: Continuum.

———. 2014. 'Belonging to Oneself Alone: The Spirit of Neoliberalism'. *Psychoanalysis, Culture & Society* 19 (2): 145–60. https://doi.org/10.1057/pcs.2014.7.

———. 2015. 'A Relational Society'. Edited by Stuart Hall, Doreen Massey, and Michael Rustin. *Afterneoliberalism? The Kilburn Manifesto.* https://www.lwbooks.co.uk/soundings/kilburn-manifesto.

Ruti, Mari. 2011. 'Winnicott with Lacan: Living Creatively in a Postmodern World'. *American Imago* 67 (3): 353–74. https://doi.org/10.1353/aim.2010.0016.

Sandford, Stella. 2011. 'What Is Maternal Labour?' *Studies in the Maternal* 3 (2): 1–11. https://doi.org/10.16995/sim.63.

———. 2012. 'Alison Stone, Feminism, Psychoanalysis, and Maternal Subjectivity'. *Studies in the Maternal* 4 (2). https://doi.org/10.16995/sim.44.

Santner, Eric L. 1990. *Stranded Objects: Mourning, Memory, and Film in Postwar Germany*. Ithaca, NY: Cornell University Press.

———. 2006. *On Creaturely Life: Rilke, Benjamin, Sebald*. Chicago: University of Chicago Press.

Sayers, Janet. 1991. *Mothering Psychoanalysis*. London: Penguin.

Sennett, Richard. 2006. *The Culture of the New Capitalism*. New Haven, CT: Yale University Press.

Sevenhuijsen, Selma. 1998. *Citizenship and the Ethics of Care: Feminist Considerations on Justice, Morality, and Politics*. London; New York: Routledge.

Shapira, Michal. 2015. *The War inside: Psychoanalysis, Total War, and the Making of the Democratic Self in Postwar Britain*. Cambridge: University of Cambridge Press.

Shklar, Judith N. 1972. 'Subversive Genealogies'. *Daedalus* 101 (1): 129–54.

Silverstone, Roger. 1994. *Television and Everyday Life*. London; New York: Routledge.

———. 2007. *Media and Morality: On the Rise of the Mediapolis*. Cambridge; Malden, MA: Polity Press.

Sprengnether, Madelon. 1990. *The Spectral Mother: Freud, Feminism, and Psychoanalysis*. Ithaca: Cornell University Press.

Standing, Guy. 2020. *Battling Eight Giants: Basic Income Now*. London; New York; Oxford; New Delhi; Sydney: I.B. Tauris.

Steedman, Carolyn. 1986. *Landscape for a Good Woman: A Story of Two Lives*. London: Virago.

Stephens, Julie. 2011. *Confronting Postmaternal Thinking: Feminism, Memory, and Care*. New York: Columbia University Press.
Stiegler, Bernard. 2009. *Acting Out*. Translated by David Barison, Daniel Ross, and Patrick Crogan. Stanford, Calif: Stanford University Press.
———. 2010. *Taking Care of Youth and the Generations*. Translated by Stephen J. Barker. Stanford, CA: Stanford University Press.
———. 2013. *What Makes Life Worth Living: On Pharmacology*. Translated by Daniel Ross. Cambridge; Malden, MA: Polity.
Stoller, Sarah. 2018. 'Forging a Politics of Care: Theorizing Household Work in the British Women's Liberation Movement'. *History Workshop Journal* 85 (April): 95–119. https://doi.org/10.1093/hwj/dbx063.
Stone, Alison. 2012. *Feminism, Psychoanalysis, and Maternal Subjectivity*. New York; Abingdon: Routledge.
———. 2014. 'Psychoanalysis and Maternal Subjectivity'. In *Mothering and Psychoanalysis: Clinical, Sociological and Feminist Perspectives*, edited by Petra Bueskens, 325–42.
———. 2019. *Being Born: Birth and Philosophy*. Studies in Feminist Philosophy. Oxford: Oxford University Press.
Stone, Lawrence. 1990. *The Family, Sex and Marriage in England 1500-1800*. London: Penguin.
Strenger, Carlo. 1997. 'Further Remarks on the Classic and Romantic Visions in Psychoanalysis: Klein, Winnicott, and Ethics'. *Psychoanalysis and Contemporary Thought* 20 (2): 207–44.
Stronge, Will. 2020. 'What Counts as Basic? A New Angle on the Services / Cash Transfer Debate'. *Autonomy* (blog). 2020. https://autonomy.work/portfolio/incomenotservices/.
Suttie, Ian D. 1999. *The Origins of Love and Hate*. London: Routledge.
Swartz, Sally. 2019. *Ruthless Winnicott: The Role of Ruthlessness in Psychoanalysis and Political Protest*. London; New York: Routledge.
Sweet, Victoria. 2013. *God's Hotel: A Doctor, a Hospital, and a Pilgrimage to the Heart of Medicine*. New York: Riverhead Books.
Taveleski, Toni. 2014. 'Mothers at the Margins: Psychodynamic Therapy with Mothers in the Welfare System'. In *Mothering and Psychoanalysis: Clinical, Sociological and Feminist Perspectives*, edited by Petra Bueskens, 197–212. Canada: Demeter Press.
Taylor, Barbara. 2014. *The Last Asylum: A Memoir of Madness in Our Times*. London: Hamish Hamilton.

Thatcher, Margaret. 1987. Interview for Woman's Own Interview by Douglas Keay. Margaret Thatcher Foundation. https://www.margaretthatcher.org/document/106689.
The Care Collective. 2020. *The Care Manifesto: The Politics of Interdependence*. London; New York: Verso Books.
Thompson, Simon. 2009. 'Against Recognition'. *Contemporary Political Theory* 8 (2): 248–50. https://doi.org/10.1057/cpt.2008.55.
Threadcraft, Shatema. 2016. *Intimate Justice: The Black Female Body and the Body Politic*. New York: Oxford University Press.
Tilly, Louise A., and Joan Wallach Scott. 2016. *Women, Work and Family*. London; New York: Routledge.
Tronto, Joan C. 1993. *Moral Boundaries: A Political Argument for an Ethic of Care*. New York: Routledge.
———. 2002. 'The "Nanny" Question in Feminism'. *Hypatia* 17 (2): 34–51.
———. 2003. 'Time's Place'. *Feminist Theory* 4 (2): 119–38. https://doi.org/10.1177/14647001030042002.
———. 2013. *Caring Democracy: Markets, Equality, and Justice*. New York: New York University Press.
Varga, Somogy, and Shaun Gallagher. 2012. 'Critical Social Philosophy, Honneth and the Role of Primary Intersubjectivity'. *European Journal of Social Theory* 15 (2): 243–60. https://doi.org/10.1177/1368431011423606.
Voela, Angie, and Louis Rothschild. 2019. 'Creative Failure: Stiegler, Psychoanalysis and the Promise of a Life Worth Living'. *New Formations* 95 (95): 54–69. https://doi.org/10.3898/NEW F:95.04.2018.
Vogel, Lise. 2013. *Marxism and the Oppression of Women: Toward a Unitary Theory*. Leiden: Brill.
Waddell, Margot. 2002. *Inside Lives: Psychoanalysis and the Growth of the Personality*. London: Karnac.
Weeks, Kathi. 2011. *The Problem with Work: Feminism, Marxism, Antiwork Politics, and Postwork Imaginaries*. Durham, NC: Duke University Press.
Whitford, Margaret. 1991. *Luce Irigaray: Philosophy in the Feminine*. London; New York: Routledge.
Widlöcher, Daniel. 2012. 'Winnicott and the Acquisition of Freedom of Thought'. In *Donald Winnicott Today*, edited by Jan Abram. The New Library of Psychoanalysis. London; New York: Routledge.
Williams, Fiona. 1999. 'Good-Enough Principles for Welfare'. *Journal of Social Policy* 28 (4): 667–87. https://doi.org/10.1017/S0047279499005760.

———. 2001. 'In and Beyond New Labour: Towards a New Political Ethics of Care'. *Critical Social Policy* 4: 467–93.

Wilson, Elizabeth. 1980. *Only Halfway to Paradise: Women in Postwar Britain, 1945–1968*. London; New York: Tavistock Publications.

Winnicott, Donald W. 1958a. 'A Note on Normality and Anxiety'. In *Collected Papers: Through Paediatrics to Psycho-Analysis*, 3–21. London: Tavistock.

———. 1958b. 'Aggression in Relation to Emotional Development'. In *Collected Papers: Through Paediatrics to Psycho-Analysis*, 204–18. London: Tavistock.

———. 1958c. 'Anxiety Associated with Insecurity'. In *Collected Papers: Through Paediatrics to Psycho-Analysis*, 97–100. London: Tavistock.

———. 1958d. 'Appetite and Emotional Disorder'. In *Collected Papers: Through Paediatrics to Psycho-Analysis*, 33–51. London: Tavistock.

———. 1958e. 'Clinical Varieties of Transference'. In *Collected Papers: Through Paediatrics to Psycho-Analysis*, 295–99. London: Tavistock.

———. 1958f. *Collected Papers: Through Paediatrics to Psycho-Analysis*. London: Tavistock.

———. 1958g. 'Hate in the Countertransference'. In *Collected Papers: Through Paediatrics to Psycho-Analysis*, 194–203. London: Tavistock.

———. 1958h. 'Metapsychological and Clinical Aspects of Regression within the Psycho-Analytical Set-Up'. In *Collected Papers: Through Paediatrics to Psycho-Analysis*, 278–94. London: Tavistock.

———. 1958i. 'Paediatrics and Psychiatry'. In *Collected Papers: Through Paediatrics to Psycho-Analysis*, 157–73. London: Tavistock.

———. 1958j. 'Primary Maternal Preoccupation'. In *Collected Papers: Through Paediatrics to Psycho-Analysis*, 300–305. London: Tavistock.

———. 1958k. 'The Manic Defence'. In *Collected Papers: Through Paediatrics to Psycho-Analysis*, 129–44. London: Tavistock.

———. 1986a. 'Cure'. In *Home Is Where We Start From: Essays by a Psychoanalyst*, 112–20. Harmondsworth: Penguin.

———. 1986b. 'Delinquency as a Sign of Hope'. In *Home Is Where We Start from: Essays by a Psychoanalyst*, 90–11. Harmondsworth: Penguin.

———. 1986c. 'Freedom'. In *Home Is Where We Start From: Essays by a Psychoanalyst*, 228–38. Harmondsworth: Penguin.

———. 1986d. 'Some Thoughts on the Meaning of the Word "Democracy"'. In *Home Is Where We Start From: Essays by a Psychoanalyst*, 239–59. Harmondsworth: Penguin.

———. 1986e. 'The Concept of a Healthy Individual'. In *Home Is Where We Start From: Essays by a Psychoanalyst*, 21–38. Harmondsworth: Penguin.

———. 1986f. 'The Mother's Contribution to Society'. In *Home Is Where We Start from: Essays by a Psychoanalyst*, 123–27. Harmondsworth: Penguin.

———. 1987. 'Communication between Infant and Mother, and Mother and Infant, Compared and Contrasted'. In *Babies and Their Mothers*, 89–103. Reading, MA: Addison-Wesley.

———. 1988. *Human Nature*. New York: Routledge.

———. 1989. 'On the Basis for Self in Body'. In *Psycho-Analytic Explorations*, 261–83. London: Karnac.

———. 1990a. 'A Personal View of the Kleinian Contribution'. In *The Maturational Processes and the Facilitating Environment: Studies in the Theory of Emotional Development*, 166–70. London: Karnac and the Institute of Psycho-Analysis.

———. 1990b. 'Ego Distortion in Terms of True and False Self'. In *The Maturational Processes and the Facilitating Environment*, 140–52. London: Karnac and the Institute of Psycho-Analysis.

———. 1990c. 'Ego Integration in Child Development'. In *The Maturational Processes and the Facilitating Environment*, 56–63. London: Karnac and the Institute of Psycho-Analysis.

———. 1990d. 'From Dependence Towards Independence in the Development of the Individual'. In *The Maturational Processes and the Facilitating Environment*, 83–92. London: Karnac and the Institute of Psycho-Analysis.

———. 1990e. 'Psycho-Analysis and the Sense of Guilt'. In *The Maturational Processes and the Facilitating Environment: Studies in the Theory of Emotional Development*, 15–28. London: Karnac and the Institute of Psycho-Analysis.

———. 1990f. 'The Development of the Capacity for Concern'. In *The Maturational Processes and the Facilitating Environment*, 73–82. London: Karnac and the Institute of Psycho-Analysis.

———. 1990g. 'The Theory of the Parent-Infant Relationship'. In *The Maturational Processes and the Facilitating Environment: Studies in the Theory of Emotional Development*, 37–55. London: Karnac and the Institute of Psycho-Analysis.

———. 1991a. 'Creativity and Its Origins'. In *Playing and Reality*, 65–85. London: Routledge.

———. 1991b. 'Interrelating Apart from Instrinctual Drive and in Terms of Cross-Identifications'. In *Playing and Reality*, 119–37. London: Routledge.

———. 1991c. 'Mirror-Role of Mother and Family in Child Development'. In *Playing and Reality*, 111–18. London: Routledge.

———. 1991d. *Playing and Reality*. London: Routledge.

———. 1991e. 'Tailpiece'. In *Playing and Reality*, 151. London: Routledge.

———. 1991f. *The Child, the Family and the Outside World*. London: Penguin.

———. 1991g. 'The Location of Cultural Experience'. In *Playing and Reality*, 95–103. London: Routledge.

———. 1991h. 'The Place Where We Live'. In *Playing and Reality*, 104–10. London: Routledge.

———. 1991i. 'The Use of an Object and Relating Through Identifications'. In *Playing and Reality*, 86–94. London: Routledge.

———. 1991j. 'Transitional Objects and Transitional Phenomena'. In *Playing and Reality*, 1–25. London: Routledge.

———. 2006. 'The Family and Emotional Maturity'. In *The Family and Individual Development*, 128–38. London: Routledge.

———. 2012a. 'Evacuation of Small Children'. In *Deprivation and Delinquency*, 11–19. London; New York: Routledge.

———. 2012b. 'Residential Management as Treatment for Difficult Children'. In *Deprivation and Delinquency*, 49–64. London; New York: Routledge.

———. 2017. *The Collected Works of D. W. Winnicott*. Edited by Lesley Caldwell and Helen Taylor Robinson. Oxford; New York: Oxford University Press.

Wollstonecraft, Mary. 1985. *Vindication of the Rights of Women*. London: Penguin.

Wood, Ellen Meiksins. 2002. *The Origin of Capitalism: A Longer View*. London: Verso.

Wordsworth, William. 1959. *The Prelude*. Edited by H. Darbishire. Oxford: Clarendon Press.

Wright, Erik Olin. 2015. 'Why Class Matters'. *Jacobin*, 23 December 2015. https://www.jacobinmag.com/2015/12/socialism-marxism-democracy-inequality-erik-olin-wright/.

Young, Iris Marion. 1990. *Justice and the Politics of Difference*. Princeton, NJ: Princeton University Press.

———. 2007. 'Recognition of Love's Labor: Considering Axel Honneth's Feminism'. In *Recognition and Power: Axel Honneth and the Tradition of Critical Social Theory*, edited by Bert van den Brink and David Owen, 189–212. Cambridge; New York: Cambridge University Press.

Young-Bruehl, Elisabeth. 2011. 'Psychoanalysis and Social Democracy: A Tale of Two Developments'. *Contemporary Psychoanalysis* 47 (2): 179–203. https://doi.org/10.1080/00107530.2011.10746450.

Zaretsky, Eli. 2005. *Secrets of the Soul: A Social and Cultural History of Psychoanalysis*. New York: Vintage.

Zournazi, Mary, and Julia Kristeva. 2002. 'Joyful Revolt: A Conversation with Julia Kristeva'. In *Hope: New Philosophies for Change*, 64–77. Annandale, NSW: Pluto Press Australia.

Index

A
Abram, Jan 3, 38, 40, 43, 45, 46, 110, 111
Affective inequality 151
Agamben, Georgio 16
Aggression 17, 45–48, 52, 115, 172
Alexander, Sally 109, 115, 116, 118
Alford, Fred 5, 124, 219
Aliveness 7, 34, 41, 45, 46, 48, 175, 180, 187, 188
  and aggression 45–47
  and creativity 45–47
  and the experience of reliability 195, 196
  destruction of 188
  relationship with care 45
Antisocial tendency 111, 116
Anxiety 19, 34, 51, 77, 116, 152, 172, 173, 176
  UBI and freedom from 208, 209
  unthinkable 172, 173
Aristotle 35, 37, 38, 54
Attention 177, 178
Autonomy 7, 12, 33, 56, 64, 138, 142, 150, 153, 166, 167, 173–175, 178, 183, 187, 188, 203, 215, 222
  and independence 72
  and intersubjectivity 149, 180
  and maternal care 92, 150
  and nurturance 100, 101
  and paternal identification 80
  and personal responsibility 167, 168
  and reason 87
  and recognition 156
  as freedom from others 73
  as masculine value 81
  defensive 11, 158, 183, 215
  relational 148, 156, 209

Index

B

Baraitser, Lisa 85, 209–211, 216
Bar-Haim, Shaul 105, 108, 122
Bechdel, Alison 5
Benjamin, Jessica 5, 12, 74, 79, 84, 90, 91, 139, 141, 149–151, 194, 220
   critique of theory of recognition 154
   on the Oedipus complex and the repudiation of femininity 80–82
   philosophical and political significance of ideas 100–102
   renunciation vs repudiation of femininity 217–218
   role of maternal subjectivity in development 99–103
Beveridge Report 117
Bion, Wilfred 140, 141
Biopolitics 16
Boever, Arne de 16
Bollas, Christopher 140, 196
Boltanski, Luc 168
Bowker, Matthew 15–18
Brennan, Theresa 65, 82
Brenner, Johanna 160
Britton Winnicott, Clare 111, 114–117
Butler, Judith 16, 125, 133
Buzby, Amy 15–18, 193, 194

C

Campbell, Kristen 78, 79, 80–84, 87
Capacities 49
   and adult life 142–144
   and justice 136–137, 143–144
   and social provision 152, 166–168, 172–175
   capitalism and the unequal distribution of 151–155, 157
   development in early childhood 38–57, 146–150
   effect of care chains on development of 184–198
   political implications 143–145
Capitalism
   and enclosure 68–70
   and social reproduction 69–71
   origins of 69–71
Care
   and aliveness 41
   and anti-capitalist politics 203–206
   and autonomy 90, 142
   and caregiver's subjectivity 44–47
   and concern 51–57
   and cure 1–3
   and democracy 212–213
   and domestic labour 9
   and existentialism 36
   and hate 44
   and inequality 124
   and justice 133–145
   and omnipotence 47
   and politics 13, 14
   and psychology 33
   and redistribution 160
   and second wave feminism 8
   and social reproduction 8
   and the depressive position 51
   and the foucauldian tradition 16
   and the good life 34
   as practice 13, 134–136
   awareness of self as receiver of 212–214

capacity to 54, 55
capital 186
chains 6, 23, 171, 184, 188, 203
challenge of 44
commodification of 171
commoning of 218
crisis of 5–8, 165
deficit 171
definition of 13
drain 186
economy 180–182
ethic of 12, 134
fixes 182
good enough 49
in feminist theory 16
in nineteenth century psychology 104–107
motherhood paradigm 14, 148
of Souls tradition 33–35
politics of 134
unequal distribution of 151–154
Winnicott as theorist of 2–5
Winnicott's understanding of 43, 44
Care Collective, the 6, 127, 165, 179
Caregiver parity 159
Caring democracy 212–213, 220
Cavarero, Adriana 73, 86, 125
Chiapello, Eve 168
Chodorow, Nancy 5, 10–13, 91, 150, 151
Cognitive behavioural therapy 176
Commons, the 15
  and contemporary global care economy 184
  and holding 201, 202
  and women 71
  emotional 186

Concern 7, 32–34, 39, 63, 119, 122, 123, 138, 147, 153, 159, 166, 169, 172, 173, 175, 179, 180, 187, 201, 207–209, 221
  absence of in early life 49
  and ethical subjectivity 50
  and social change 67
  caregiver's capacity for 44
  development of the capacity for 49–53, 57
  role in shaping social environments 54
  welfare state as a public form of 207, 208
Containment 140
Creativity 45–48, 75, 166, 173, 178, 203, 210, 212, 219, 222
  and freedom 208–209, 212
  and health 46
  and omnipotence 46
  borne out of meeting of need 47
Critical Theory 18, 22, 193, 194
Cura, myth of 33, 34

D

Deleuze, Gilles 5
Delinquency. *See* Antisocial tendency
Democratic tendency 116, 118
Dependence 3, 7, 10, 22, 43, 49, 52, 64, 66, 68, 71, 72
  denial of 72–84
  ethical response to 125
Depressive position 49, 50
  and care 51
Descartes, Rene 65, 66
Devi, S. Uma 183–186
Dinnerstein, Dorothy 11, 89

Discourse of the Master, the 82–84
Dowling, Emma 9, 15, 167, 168, 170, 171, 173, 181, 182, 204, 218

E

Eigen, Michael 45
Enclosure. *See* Capitalism
Environment
   and emotional well-being 108–112
   and hostel provision 116
   as setting for psychological growth 195, 196
   facilitating 126, 154
   good vs bad 196
   holding 111, 177, 186, 199
   pathogenic 152
   psychotherapy as provision of 197
   traumatogenic 172–180
Eudaimonia. *See* Flourishing; Good life, the
Evacuation 112, 113

F

Fairbairn, Roger 108–109
Family, the
   and primitive accumulation 67
   and the oppression of women 9
   forms of subjectivity associated with 78
   role in the transition to capitalism 67–69
Federici, Silvia 69–71, 80
Ferguson, Alease 152–154
Flax, Jane 5, 12

Flourishing 22, 35, 40–42, 100, 119, 137, 166, 173, 179, 188, 202, 210, 212, 221, 222
   and creativity 48
   and emotional development 40
   and good enough care 49
   and health 40
   and object relations theory 39
   and practical reason 40
   and recognition 48
   and socialisation 54
   and society 54
   Freud and 37
Fraser, Nancy 8, 72, 158–160, 168–170
Freud, Anna 107, 112
Freud, Sigmund 35–37, 47, 64, 65, 74, 79, 87, 90, 106, 107, 176

G

Gerson, Gal 5, 105–107, 118–121
Giddens, Anthony 5, 174–177, 195
Gilligan, Carol 12, 134
Good life, the 35, 36
   and psychoanalysis 36
Goux, Jean-Joseph 63–66
Governmentality 122
Green, Andre 42, 110
Groarke, Steven 175, 176, 195–198
Guattari, Felix 5

H

Harcourt, Edward 38, 39
Health 7, 14, 15, 17, 35, 36, 120, 137, 138, 152, 156, 165, 176, 198, 199, 202–204, 210, 211, 220

and emotional development 39
Winnicott as psychoanalyst of 38
Held, Virginia 126, 127, 220
Hobsbawm, Eric 170
Hochschild, Arlie 183–185
Hoggett, Paul 107, 122, 125, 168, 207
Holding 2, 4, 5, 7, 11, 23, 24, 41, 44, 45, 48, 65, 116, 140, 141, 149, 152–154, 157, 166, 171, 172, 177
   and anti-capitalist politics 203–204
   and antisocial tendency 111
   and continuity of being 47
   and handling 7
   and psychic growth 202–204
   and public things 221
   and radical politics 201–205
   and second wave feminism 201
   and social provision 115
   and the welfare state 108–121
   as an ethic of care 124
   as model for ethos and character of social provision 121
   environment 111
   failures of and effect in care economy 181–183
   failures of and effect on capacities 181–183
   failures of and effect on careworkers 181–186
Hollway, Wendy 5, 13, 14, 19–21, 147–151, 154–156, 182–183, 205
Honig, Bonnie 5, 172, 221
Honneth, Axel 5, 141–143, 146, 147, 194
hooks, bell 183

Horkheimer, Max 18, 22, 71, 72, 74, 75
   Oedipus complex and historical dialectic 79
   on the family and modern capitalism 74
   positive aspects of oedipal identification 75

Identification
   and care 43–46
   and the gendered division of labour 10, 11
   and the social tie 79
   Maternal caregiver's capacity for 100
   with the father 78
Illusion 46–48
Independent group, the 108–110
Internalisation 89
Intersubjectivity 49, 52, 89, 91, 92, 140
   and power 146–148
Irigaray, Luce 5, 84, 85
Isaksen, Lise 183–186

Jacobs, Amber 85
Justice 134–160
   and capacities 136–138
   and care 136–138
   and holding-care 202
   capability theory of 137–139
   distributive paradigm 136

K

Keller, Evelyn Fox 12
Kenosis 177
King, Toni 153–156
Klein, Melanie 49, 50, 106, 107

L

Labour
  domestic 8
  emotional labour of mothering 186
  love 196
  secondary care 185
Lacan, Jacques 17, 65, 74, 75
  critique of the philosophical subject 65
  Oedipus complex and historical dialectic 75, 75
  on the Oedipus complex and the modern family 74
  positive aspects of oedipal identification 75
  the ego's era and narcissism 78
  the family and modern subjectivity 82
Laplanche, Jean 148
Layton, Lynne 90–91, 122, 179, 183
Lazzarato, Maurizio 173
Lebeau, Vicky 122
Liberal reformism 105–107
Life
  and creativity 48
  and health 41, 42
  positive conception of 41

M

MacIntyre, Alisdair 39

Mackenzie, Catriona 149
Marx, Karl 67
Maternalism 104–105, 108
  and origins of welfare state 100
  and post-war public sphere 124
  and the welfare state 105
Maternal subjectivity 214–216, 219
  men's capacity to develop 215–217
  relevance in other contexts 215
Maternal thinking 99–107
McNay, Lois 145–147
Meiksins Wood, Ellen 68, 69
Mies, Maria 71
Mitchell, Juliet 9–11
Mother, the
  and progressive politics 104–113
  as subject 83–85
  in British culture and society of 1930s 106
  in psychoanalysis 106–107
  law of the 85

N

Nelson, Maggie 5
Neo-Aristotelianism 38
Neoliberalism 166
  and hatred of dependency 125
  and insecurity 173
  and personal responsibility 169–171
  and retrenchment of welfare state 167–169
  and second wave feminism 169–171
  and the privatisation of care 170–171

as theory and practice of subjectivity 166
as theory of political economy 166
Noetic 177, 199, 200
Nussbaum, Martha C. 5, 38, 126, 137–139, 144, 173

O

Oedipus complex 74–85
   and effacement of care/social reproduction 92, 123–126
   and ego's era 77–79
   and repudiation of dependence 82
   and repudiation of femininity 81
   and submission to authority 76, 79–80
   and the development of individual subjectivity 75
   and the Discourse of the Master 82–84
Oedipus Rex 66–68
   and the effacement of care 64–66
   and the philosophical subject 65
Ogden, Thomas H. 141
Omnipotence 47
Orlie, Melissa 219

P

Paranoid-schizoid position 49, 50
Pateman, Carol 79–81
Phillips, Adam 36, 45, 46, 140, 141
Power 145–156, 186, 187
Primary maternal preoccupation 43–46
Primitive accumulation 10

and the privatisation of care/reproduction 10

R

Reay, Diane 180
Recognition 139–142, 144
   and power 145–156
   and the development of subjectivity 100–102
   critique of 146–148
   of maternal caregiver's subjectivity 80–82
Reich, Warren Thomas 32–34
Relationality 144
Reverie 140, 140
Riley, Denise 103, 104, 112, 118, 120
Robertson, James 143
Romanticism
   and care 40
   and the revaluation of the feminine 101–103
Rothschild, Louis 180–183, 199–203
Rousseau, Jean-Jacques 55, 56, 101
Ruddick, Sara 11, 12, 124, 220
Rustin, Margaret 219
Rustin, Michael 53, 54, 122, 202, 218
Ruthlessness 45–48

S

Sandford, Stella 186, 214
Santner, Eric 16, 102
Second World War, the 112
Self
   as potential 48

false 48, 178, 213
true 47, 48, 178, 222
Sevenhuijsen, Selma 13, 14, 135, 136
Sexual contract 68, 71, 80
Silverstone, Roger 5
Social contract 80
Social reproduction 8, 9
  and biological reproduction 9
  and maternal care 10–12
  and psychic reproduction 9–13
Spontaneity 7, 48, 53, 173, 175–178, 197, 200, 201, 203, 206, 209, 210, 212, 219, 222
  and freedom 210–212
  and intuitive management 200
Steedman, Carolyn 123, 146–148
Stephens, Julie 124
Stiegler, Bernard 5, 41, 42, 177–180, 199, 200
Stoljar, Natalie 149
Stone, Alison 148, 149, 153, 211–213
Subjectivity
  and health 43
  and maturity 53
  and power 145–156
  and separation from the mother 73
  and the Oedipus complex 74, 75
  ethical 50
  object relations account of 138, 139
  of maternal caregiver 44–46, 87–89, 147
  poststructural critique of 16–18
  psychosocial conception of 18–20
  Winnicott's normative view of 18
Suttie, Ian 108–109

T
Taylor, Barbara 198–200
Thatcher, Margaret 169
Threadcraft, Shatema 152–155
Transference 213–215
  and experience of primary caregivers 213–215
Tronto, Joan 12, 13, 134, 135, 212–214

U
Universal Basic Income 204–206
  and post-work politics 209
  and recognition of dependence 212–213
  and universal caregiver 218
  psychosocial implications 208–218
Universal breadwinner 158
Universal caregiver 159, 160
  and UBI 218

V
Virtue ethics. *See* Neo-Aristotelianism
Voela, Angie 177–179, 199–203
Vulnerability 133

W
Waddell, Margot 138
Welfare state, the 99, 105, 108, 109, 116, 118–120, 122–124, 126, 152, 159, 171, 178, 179, 188, 208
  and caregiver parity 204
  and dissemination of caring function 121

and human capital 180
and neoliberalism 169–171
and recognition of dependence 133, 134
and the family 121, 122–126
and the oppression of women 119–121
and UBI 207, 208
as a public form of concern 135
as holding environment 124
maternal model 124
post-war 99, 100
Williams, Fiona 13, 134, 135
Winnicott
    Clare. *See* Britton Winnicott, Clare
Winnicott, D.W. *See* Aggression; Aliveness; Antisocial tendency; Capacities; Care; Concern; Creativity; Dependence; Depressive position; Environment; Evacuation; Flourishing; Health; Holding; Intersubjectivity; Life; Maternalism; Mother, the; Primary maternal preoccupation; Self; Spontaneity; Subjectivity; Welfare state, the
    and care-cure 2, 3
    and freedom 205, 210–212
    and Neo-Aristotelianism 38–40
    and philosophical interest in care 39
    and systems of security 195
    and the myth of Cura 33, 34
    and the welfare state 139
    conception of health 41
    contribution to the critique of the philosophical subject 91
    feminist critiques of 85–87
    history-taking 110
    in feminist debates about care 15
    Influence of ideas 5
    interwar work 113
    positive conception of subjectivity 17
    recognition of caring labour 91
    theory of emotional development 53
    theory of the caring subject 6–8
    theory of the development of subjectivity 54
    the place of care and concern in the development of subjectivity 54
    the relationship between care and subjectivity 43
    the role of social environments in development 67
    valuing of care 3

Y

Young-Bruehl, Elisabeth 37, 117
Young, Iris Marion 136, 182

Z

Zaretsky, Eli 106, 107

CPSIA information can be obtained
at www.ICGtesting.com
Printed in the USA
LVHW082141230322
714261LV00004B/52